IMAGINING WHAT WE DON'T KNOW

Before you start to read this book, take this moment to think about making a donation to punctum books, an independent non-profit press,

@ https://punctumbooks.com/support/

If you're reading the e-book, you can click on the image below to go directly to our donations site. Any amount, no matter the size, is appreciated and will help us to keep our ship of fools afloat. Contributions from dedicated readers will also help us to keep our commons open and to cultivate new work that can't find a welcoming port elsewhere. Our adventure is not possible without your support.

Vive la Open Access.

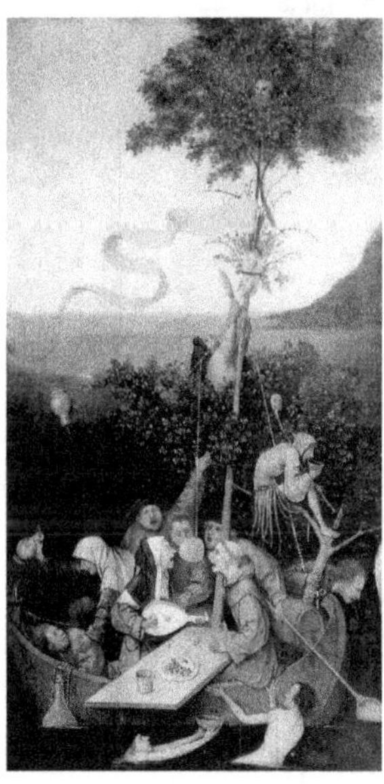

Fig. 1. Detail from Hieronymus Bosch, *Ship of Fools* (1490–1500)

Published in 2026 by punctum books, Earth, Milky Way
https://punctumbooks.com

ISBN-13: 978-1-68571-204-4 (paperbound)
ISBN-13: 978-1-68571-205-1 (PDF)
ISBN-13: 978-1-68571-308-9 (EPUB)

DOI: 10.53288/0483.1.00

LCCN: 2026932501
Library of Congress Cataloging Data is available from the Library of Congress

Editing: SAJ and Eileen A. Fradenburg Joy
Book design: Hatim Eujayl
Cover image: Lisa Samuels, *Magnetism*
Cover design: Vincent W.J. van Gerven Oei

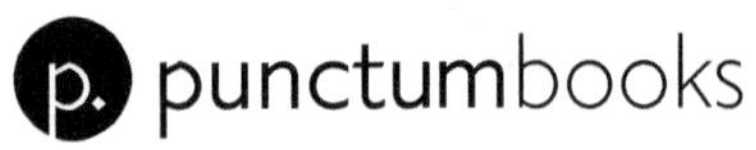

spontaneous acts of scholarly combustion

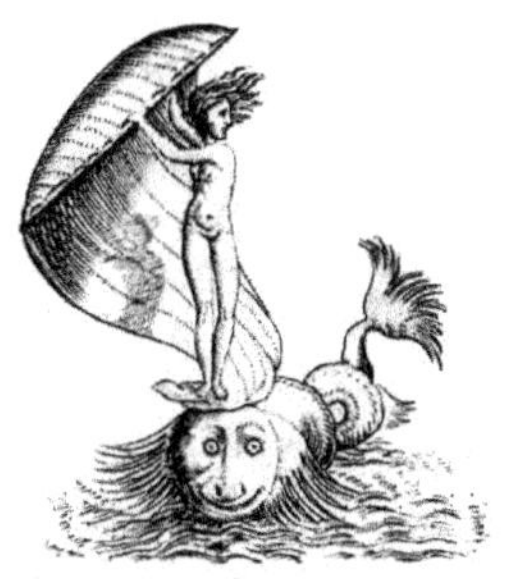

HIC SVNT MONSTRA

Imagining What
Imagining What
Imagining What
Imagining What
Imagining What

Imagining What We Don't Know

Creative Theory and Critical Bodies

Lisa Samuels

p.

Contents

Acknowledgments

A number of pieces in this book appeared in earlier versions: All are re-written, some with new titles. Entries marked with & indicate topically linked work reconfigured here as joined essays. My thanks to the editors, technicians, and publishers who launched these earlier pieces:

— "Umbral Poetics." *Poetry Salzburg Review* 38 (2022).
— "Withness in Kind." *Performance Paradigm* 16 (2021): 60–73. https://www.performanceparadigm.net/index.php/journal/article/view/240.
— "Distributed Centrality Again." *Ka Mate Ka Ora* 18 (2020): 86–89. https://www.nzepc.auckland.ac.nz/kmko/18/kmko18_08_samuels2.pdf.
  — & "Distributed Centrality." In *Counter-Desecration: A Glossary for Writing within the Anthropocene,* edited by Marthe Reed and Linda Russo. Wesleyan University Press, 2018.
  — & "Everything Speaks — How Do We Listen?" *Qui Parle* 26, no. 2 (2017): 318–19.
— "Luminol Historiography." *Ka Mate Ka Ora* 18 (2020): 11–13. https://www.nzepc.auckland.ac.nz/kmko/18/kmko18_02_samuels1.pdf.
— "Soft Text and the Open Line." *Axon: Creative Explorations* 8, no. 1 (2018). https://axonjournal.com.au/issues/8-1/soft-text-and-open-line/.

— "The Right to Be Transplace." In *Wretched Strangers,* edited by Ágnes Lehóczky and JT Welsch. Boiler House Press, 2018.
— "Bioautography and VULVA'S MORPHIA." *Chicago Review* 60, no. 4 (2017): 154–74.
— "Thought Point." *New Theory* 2 (2016). https://new-theory.net/article/thought-point/.
— "Contemporanullity in the Digitas." *Journal of Poetics Research* 2 (2015).
— "Rapacity Culture and the Body." *Chicago Review* 59, nos. 1–2 (2015): 204–5.
  — & "The Body Rights Movement." *Hotel Amerika,* December 9, 2014. https://www.hotelamerika.net/the-body-rights-movement/.
— "Syllabus." *Brief* 50 (2014): 101–4.
— "Membranism, Wet Gaps, Archipelago Poetics." *Reading Room: A Journal of Art and Culture* 4 (2010): 157–67.
— "Why I Hate Realism." *Aufgabe* 7 (2008): 253–55.
— "Relinquish Intellectual Property." *New Literary History* 33, no. 2 (2002): 357–74.
— "The T-function in Laura Riding's *Though Gently.*" *Delmar* 8 (2002): 81–86.
— "If Meaning, Shaped Reading, and Leslie Scalapino's *way.*" *Qui Parle* 12, no. 2 (2001): 179–200.
— "Introduction to Poetry and the Problem of Beauty." *Modern Language Studies* 27, no. 2 (1997): 1–7.

I send waves of life energy and thanks to punctum books for being the idealist flourishing publisher of this selected gathering, with gratitude to SAJ for astute copyediting queries. I thank Toyah Webb for early assistance in wrangling the manuscript and Joan Retallack for ringing in the book with her words. For artistic solidarity and collaborations across the last decade I thank Charles Alexander, Elle Loui August, Elisabeth Bekers, Charles Bernstein, Amaranth Borsuk, Colin Browne, Don Mee Choi, Jen Crawford, Jennifer K. Dick, Bill Direen, Murray Edmond, Tony Frazer, Nathan Hamilton, Duriel E. Harris, Lyn

Hejinian, Hannah van Hove, Michele Leggott, Ágnes Lehóczky, Alys Longley, Sean Martin-Buss, Lila Matsumoto, Janaína Moraes, Judd Morrissey, Erín Moure, Laura Mullen, Sawako Nakayasu, Alice Notley, Tru Paraha, Frédéric Pattar, Milan Pupezin, Elizabeth Robinson, Wes Tank, Carol Watts, and John Wilkinson. Many conversations with students, across years and countries, have contributed to my sense of the pleasure and ethical necessity of encouraging each other to think and feel and create works like those in this book. And for the two who've made this century a home with me, love's portion of infinity: Mark Amsler and Rowan Samuels.

:

I dream my jaw is missing and in its place a bolt
Of red cloth weighted to the loom, silk skeins
And trembling tucked deep into my pockets
As I dive into clear water.

—Duriel E. Harris, *No Dictionary of a Living Tongue*

The fact that all approved traditional philosophy from Plato down to the semanticists has been allergic to expression, this fact accords with a propensity of all Enlightenment: to punish undisciplined gestures. It is a trait extending all the way to logic, a defense mechanism of the materialized consciousness.

—Theodor W. Adorno, *Negative Dialectics*

Through all the stammerings of strange tongues and murmurings of obscure invocations she still upholds her cause; the cause of the unseen against the seen, of the weak against the strong, of that which is not, and yet is, against that which is, and yet is not.

—John Cowper Powys, *A Glastonbury Romance*

Foyer

Imagining What We Don't Know: Creative Theory and Critical Bodies presents essays and theory poems engaged with experimental arts, critical practices, and relational ethics. The book's neologisms are part of its methods for reorienting our positions as embodied interpreters. Visionary philosophers join the book's calls for thought, and there are readings of UK, Caribbean, US, Australasian, Oceanian, and Algerian writing and art. This book performs in argument many facets of what I've also been making in creative works — in books of poetry and other writing experiments, and in visual art, soundwork, and performance — as a writer and artist shaped in transnational living in North America, Europe, the Middle East, Asia, and Oceania. *Imagining What We Don't Know* is a first gathering of some of my essays and critical-performance texts as a joined book.

By way of a foyer, a welcoming entryway to this built work, what follows are summaries of the book's twenty-four pieces. This foyer is a pointing, as a loving and respecting host might do, to the rooms of the interior parts as they are placed in the book. If you wish, you can compare it to the Contents page: it posits four sections, with six pieces in each, a numerology that echoes a poetic attraction toward ideas of (provisional) order. The orders index an arrangement of variegations, a sweet-smelling quantum bouquet, in an amassing complex of arguments and visions. This complex is built with theories of embodied mind—elemental, entangled, electrified with the political—that are positioned toward the kinds of art and interpretation that hold open our attentions, that encourage a hovering with relational alterity, with making room for imagining what we don't know.

1

"Wild Dialectics" is a theory of knowing as ongoing alterity focused on the nature of the start, the multiplicity of the hinges, the equality of the elements, and apical holes in think-feeling. This essay thinks in relation with sources such as Theodor Adorno's *Negative Dialectics*, Charles Sanders Peirce's "continuity," and the writings of Édouard Glissant. Alongside "Peirce's Cave," it resembles an orienting for the book. **"Peirce's Cave"** is an image for sensory knowing's transformational non-conclusions; an extrapolation of Charles S. Peirce's "continuity" and his explanations that signs always include the signers; and a shift from Plato's cave of perceptual delusions and from Avicenna's cave of the focally enlightened soloist. **"Distributed Centrality"** is an ethical value term for the equal centrality of every planetary being, place, and event, recognizing the co-constitutive fluidity of those three forces. On the surface of our planet, there are no margins and there is no center: distributed centrality posits a center at every point. **"Umbral Poetics"** considers temporal "darkbeam" effects in poetic sensoria, a missing that is not absence in pandemic-era somatics, and a query toward the body-time of "hand-written" and Generative AI poetry. **"Withness"** names a closeness with the object-event of one's interpretive reading. Withness turns from the frequent power and distance modes of exegetical criticality and toward a standing with the engaged art material, with an attention that seeks to hover in relation. **"Poetry and the Problem of Beauty"** proposes that beauty opens in the artistic space as a process for imagining what we don't know. Representationally resistant poetry is tested against some problems of objectification—the distancing of poetic object and critical body. The judgment of poetic beauty is subjective sympathy, in which beauty's constative irruption performs its unknowings.

2

In "**Membranism, Wet Gaps, Archipelago Poetics,**" membranism signifies wet touch and transfer activities among body<>object<>body and poly-dimensional mental images within our wet neural networks. Archipelago poetics describes imaginative work according to the nonconformist relevance of oceans between: oceans of uncertainty, change, extinction, and the unseen that co-arrange and derange the apparent lands. "**The Right to Be Transplace**" queries the dominance of single-place origin. Drawing from Eugène Pottier's assertion that "Equality wants different laws," transplace is a possible answer to that recurrent question "where are you from?" You might be from transplace, with a right to be no more a stranger than anyone else. "**Luminol Historiography**" is a practice of exposing underlying strata of spilled blood, literal and symbolic, within literal and symbolic human sites. The sites are in architectures, lived spaces, geophysical forms, and human bodies. "**Thought Point**" is a theory poem, a performance text with layout inveiglement, in memory of Berta Cáceres; considering the pain of thought when plotted like points on an axis graph, it's an elegy that acknowledges the body in and as thought. In "**Bioautography and *VULVA'S MORPHIA,***" bioautography gives primacy to the bio-life in self-writing, the body of the person who makes a work that's legible in its livid somatic ecology; an artist's book by Carolee Schneemann provides the example. Bioautography also emphasizes the autonomic, degrees of non-control in systems that motivate life, and the automatic, epigenetic and experientially acquired instincts. "**Variations on the Lexememe**" is a theory poem that engages its title neologism (lexeme + meme) to consider how word conjugations can starburst meme-like in contemporary reading methods that are partly shaped by online memes. The lexememe is an instrument and the notes it plays; lines and gutters of meme frames are conceptually invoked.

3

"Soft Text and the Open Line" proposes the term soft text to describe potential language arising in our interactions with ourselves, permeant surfaces, and other beings and events. Soft text is language that formulates in non-material relation with speaking, writing, or other hard text form. You imagine an utterance but you don't say it, or soft text is what is left out of what you do say. In **"Monadic Yearning and Lingual Desire,"** monadic yearning is a term for a common, queryable, human urge to bring things together in closed instances of total connection. The essay considers language's remove from supralingual, embodied experience; it also considers lingual desire's relation with textual intension. **"Quantum Mimesis"** describes lingual art that "copies" experience unobservable with the normative sensorium, with the "naked eye." David Bohm's insights regarding quantum physics are not dissimilar to Adorno's regarding the conceptual and the non-conceptual. Dimensional space is not observably unhinged, with unaided perception, in non-lingual objects; but it *is* unhinged in language. **"The ⊤-⊥ Function"** refers to slippery signs for what one might call "cultural reality" (⊤) and "encountered experience" (⊥) as these signs operate in Laura Riding's *Though Gently;* to exist in a condition of "though," Riding's book can be read as gently removing the ⊤ from the end of thought. Peirce floats in the semiotic background of the metalogic of ⊥. **"Deformance and If Meaning"** continues the project of stimulating interpretive practices that perform, as physical criticism, what are otherwise theoretical knowledges of uncertainty. William James's "feeling of *if*" is brought in, my 1997 theory of deformance is also called "shaped reading," and passages from Leslie Scalapino's *way* are rearranged and considered. **"How Write"** is a theory poem that performs a name-transformance dialogue on exteroceptive writing, our phenomenal political embodiment with signs. Blanks provision for __________ infill, inflection, and innuendo.

4

For "**The Body Rights Movement and Rapacity Culture,**" the body is the perfect ethical symbol because it is not abstract. Calling for the end of rapism, the body rights movement also considers the presentation of one's bodily identity in public spheres, including of writing and other arts. Institutional rapacity culture is considered in relation to acts of minor rapacity. "**Four Problems of Prize Culture in the Arts**" are commodification, competition, imprimatur, and reification. The growth of prize culture in the arts reflects a suppression of alterity and plurality and cooperation in favor of identity and narrowing and elimination. "**Relinquish Intellectual Property**" exposes problems with treating verbal ideation as property. Possessiveness about word-ideas obstructs discourse and clogs minds that are striving to designate what's "ours." In two body sentences with thirteen extended footnotes and five toenotes, this manifesto enjoys a wide field of reference: Plato, Petrarch, Kurt Gödel, Simone Weil, pie, Augusto Ponzio, the Universal Copyright Convention, and more. "**Earth Rights**" is a photo-essayette calling attention to planetary well-being rights in the context of the long bleed of epicolonialism, a term for our close relation with colonizing values that have transmuted into the total capitalist project. "**Contemporanullity**" takes up the words "contemporary" and "moment," including our digitality, and argues for the political truth quotients of contemporanullity and its trans-temporality. The essay reads Réda Bensmaïa's *The Year of Passages* as an example of art putting such quotients into action. In a universe of simultaneity, superposition and entanglement are fine models of knowing. "**Syllabus**" is a theory poem of treated seminar fragments sheaved with blank lines to consider the incitements of research, dialogue, laughter, and response.

That's the blueprint, and blurprint, of the writing rooms that make up this book. If the morphology of a bird, its ornithological diagram, is its blueprint, then its blurprint is the bird in flight. Here, blurprint signifies ongoing thought-life: the morphology of this book lives in its activity. Its biblio-architecture is committed to thinking and feeling in the embodied, imaginal, ethical, quantum, artistic, and lingual ecologies of our infinite desires for life; to valuing equally the knowing and unknowing of creativity and criticality; to resisting power habits that suppress artistic and interpretive freedom; and to equality, alterity, and relation. With thanks to everyone who has helped me think and thrive in its making, welcome in.

1

Wild Dialectics

> Je crois qu'il faudra nous rapprocher de la pensée de la trace, d'un non-système de pensée qui ne sera ni dominateur, ni systématique, ni imposant, mais qui sera peut-être un non-système de pensée intuitif, fragile, ambigu, qui conviendra le mieux à l'extraordinaire complexité et à l'extraordinaire dimension de multiplicité du monde dans lequel nous vivons.
>
> —Édouard Glissant, *Introduction à une poétique du divers*[1]

> That consciousness is false which, externally, and, as Hegel says, without being in the thing, places itself above this thing and manages it from above; but criticism becomes equally ideological at the moment when it lets it be known, self-righteously, that thought must have a ground.
>
> —Theodor W. Adorno, *The Jargon of Authenticity*[2]

1 "I believe that we need to be in relation with thinking as trace, with a non-systematized thinking that does not have to be dominant, systematic, or imposing, but that can be perhaps a non-system of thinking that is intuitive, fragile, ambiguous, that will be all the more suitable for the extraordinary complexity and the extraordinary dimensions of multiplicity of the world in which we live." My translation. Édouard Glissant, *Introduction à une poétique du divers* (Gallimard, 1996), 21.

2 Theodor W. Adorno, *The Jargon of Authenticity*, trans. Knut Tarnowski and Frederic Will (Northwestern University Press, 1973), 45.

Wild dialectics is a theory of knowing as ongoing alterity. Many persons are committed to models of theory and critical practice that mobilize ongoingness, or, one might say, are committed to generating models that keep company with dynamisms of thought and being that are always underway. Such models emphasize experiences of knowing more than conclusions of knowledge, and they often perform alternatives that are, implicitly or explicitly, set aside in articulations of conclusive knowledge. These models of ongoingness linger in alterity more than in identity, and their values are generally, perhaps constitutively, process-oriented. That orientation performs a belief in procedures and perceptions as tangibly sufficient acts rather than as stations that matter because they are on the way to a goal.

The term "wild dialectics" came as a nominal intuition, sudden words that beckon further thought, when inventing a title for my poetry book *Wild Dialectics* (2012).[3] I've wanted to think about the term in relation to some compelling philosophical readings: Theodor W. Adorno's book *Negative Dialectics* (1966) and Charles Sanders Peirce's late nineteenth-century work, in particular those Peirce essays focused on his ideas about "abduction" and "continuity." My own fascination with these works lingers in *how* Adorno and Peirce are thinking, insofar as their thoughts have become, are traces in and as, their works. Their performed epistemology in relation to shapes of thought is partly ventured in terms of working through newly deployed terms, such as negative dialectics and abduction. In my experience of reading, their epistemologies are crucially achieved through their *styles* of writing, including their word choice, overall organization, sustained images, and sentence-level declarations and connections.

In relation to such discursive shapes, one form of wild dialectics focuses on *hinges* of thinking. Like opening a thought door. What swivels us to attention, and how do ideas attend from one to another, or to more than one other? These imagined hinges are multivalent, constellating touchpoints, more butterfly shoul-

3 See Lisa Samuels, *Wild Dialectics* (Shearsman Books, 2012).

ders than bivalve movements, if we can picture a butterfly with reversible umbrella-spoke wings that are fully articulable, that reticulate in every direction. I play with the image of a hinge here because it can invoke tactility, particularity, connection, and swerve at a moment of ideational activity. And because a hinge is not an origin. A hinge image also invokes the organic feel of animal reticulation and the technical feel of opening and relating with a built thing.

The first three proposals of wild dialectics concern *the nature of the start, the multiplicity of the hinge,* and *the equality of the elements* in thinking. Wild dialectics proposes that there can be no dialectical start that is unquestionably "logical." Perhaps a better term is translogical or metalogical: a language-based logic that transcends types or rhetorical fashion, that yearns for immunity from context, that exceeds even divergent languages. As language historians and translators know so well, the logic of thought as presented in language is culturally determined, and therefore always temporal and contextualized. The possible and the impossible of the thought experiments of Adorno and Peirce demonstrate that there is no *given* ground for thinking. From a different perspective, and in expressive approaches more akin with my experiences of think-feeling, the insights of Édouard Glissant can help us think about how the conditions of the present allow us to see the untenability of either "positive" or "negative" versions of normative dialectics.

Dialectics is by nature "wild": in our animality, in our reversibility, in the creation-destruction edge we continually walk in personal and civic, bodily and political, worlds. In terms of considering issues and events, dialectics can establish performances of itself only locally, taking the "local" as not only place-bound, and only particularly, that is to say as unique thought-events within potentially limitless heterogeneities. The uniqueness of a thought event, however (setting aside for now the matter of how records are kept and works are made), does not have a consistently assertable size or shape or even duration. The course of the dialectical particular is both nebulous and transient.

Since there can be no start of dialectical thinking that is translogical, then each thought hinge created, followed, or imagined after an entering move is also wild. This is a second proposal I imagine for wild dialectics: once a thinking event is underway, its hinges can swing in theoretically infinite directions, like the movements of our imagined inversionable-umbrella-winged butterfly. In writing that is centrally concerned with the expansive possibilities of imaginative unknowing, such as the creative work performed and contemplated in this book, this flexibility proposal recognizes the multivalent performance of reasoning within features such as (for one example) syntactic contingency: flex-phrasing within reflexive units of utterance, whether those units are composed (or library shelved) as genres such as "poetry" or "prose."

A third proposal of wild dialectics is predicated by the first two proposals: since there is no necessary start in thinking and no necessary direction or aspect of continuance, therefore each aspect or move of thinking assumes an equality of possibility and impossibility. In this respect, the contingency of what gets called logic discovers an ethical aspect to wild dialectics: the effort of the present to see the equality of things, beings, and symbolic systems, an effort registered in the Glissant epigraph at the start of this essay. This third proposal of wild dialectics, taken up in a different way in this book's theory of "distributed centrality," focuses in the equal right to be of each thought element.

A fourth proposal of wild dialectics is the hypothesis that any conceptual apex of a dialectical move—akin to what Hegel proposed as a "third" element synthesis that becomes a new thesis, an apex precisely differenced in Peirce's thirdness—is an opening to obscure and fomenting emptiness. Wild dialectics imagines that the abductive move is to opening rather than to any arrival, whether ultima Thule or slingshot. Thus not to a synthesis or new beginning, but to an apical hole, a full darkness of re-potentiality: like an umbral poetics, to link to another essay here: *le trou n'est pas vide* ("the hole is not empty"). In this vision, the attraction of apparent epistemological dualism *can* be in its ability to pull apart a particle-antiparticle pairing and linger in between, which is how I read the thought-motion of Peirce's Cave, in the next essay of this book. That lingering, or so wild dialectics supposes, is like what happens when one becomes the very sign one engages, in Peirce's formulation (see for example the last part of his essay "Some Consequences of Four Incapacities," whose proposals encourage an emphasis on embodied sign that traces an alternative thought trajectory to those trajectories riveted in logos).[4] Hence for wild dialectics, to return to one implication of the hinge image, dualism is not a problem at all, or would be one only if someone imagines that dualism is actually dual rather than a force whose attraction is the wild possibility of thinking that swirls in every between.

Such are my starting assertions and what this essay, and the sensorial-thought encountering of "Peirce's Cave," seek to explore.

Like many others, I have wondered for a long time about what a thought is and how it gets paired with or leads to another thought and then (and simultaneously) with other thoughts. For example: dialectics. Adorno's *Negative Dialectics* helps me think about Hegelian dialectics, that triumvirate of reasoning or logic (not, of course, the same things) that has helped many thinkers complicate "simple" binaries, dyads, and dualisms in favor of the nicer Hegelian triad. Particularly because of its built-in aspirations to what we might ruefully term "better thinking through tripartite linking," the latter triad has seemed to me to echo in a comfortable or culturally recognizable way the Christian Trinity, a triad later echoed in the Scholastic tradition's liberal arts trivium of grammar, logic, and rhetoric. These trinities in turn looped institutionally forward across the centuries, a good fit with occidental positings, so that when Hegel came along it seemed all right, okay, to line up these deliverables together. We

4 Charles Sanders Peirce, "Some Consequences of Four Incapacities," in *Peirce on Signs: Writings on Semiotics by Charles Sanders Peirce*, ed. James Hoopes (University of North Carolina Press, 1991).

could go from thesis to synthesis to antithesis and swing around about all over again.

Still, perhaps because I am not a logician, nor any other kind of thoroughly trained philosopher, the Hegelian dialectic has always seemed to be perched on turtles all the way down. I am thinking of the aphoristic answer to the question of what holds up the universe, an answer that uses turtles to stop the question with an image we cannot hold still: the supporting turtles turn infinite, like pi. The Turtle Island Indigenous name for North America dovetails with that aphorism, and this turtle image can exemplify a more general dovetailing of educational thought-images, occidental with Indigenous with postcolonial, Judeo-Christian-Islamic with transpacific with Earth rights, that show forth in this book. Such dovetailings frankly encourage the energies of creative theory models such as wild dialectics. In this case, wild dialectics can function as one way to bring together orientations (I'm gesturing to my own life shapings) that extend from Mediterranean and trans-Atlantic theories to postcolonial and trans-Pacific theories, an extension that always incorporates the bodies of Earth, even when it turns corporeality in different directions.

For my purposes here, the foundational contingency of the Hegelian dialectic is not so much because its progress narratives are insupportable, as subsequent arguments have pointed out, as that the matter of *where to begin* seems permanently in question. Using the Hegelian dialectic, and its revolving intellectual descendants, has made sense only when I operate in a mode of pragmatism, in a post-Durkheim frame in which thought experiments begin in distinctness, that is at some *where.* That distinctness, that *where,* has been a place of re-beginning, in poetic terms like Robert Duncan's "place of first permission" in his poem "Often I Am Permitted to Return to a Meadow" (*The Opening of the Field,* 1960), or like Lyn Hejinian's "Along comes something—*launched in context*" in her poetics essay "Reason"

(*The Language of Inquiry*, 2000).[5] So I could use, and also teach with, a post-Hegelian dialectic by beginning in a reasonable place, given the materials of the day. But that place was never an absolutely necessary one; it was not *the* "to begin."

Adorno's negative dialectics, described by him variously as "an ensemble of analyses of models," "disenchantment of the concept," and "thought thinking about thinking" with an aim of "total self-relinquishment," is an inspiring way to consider the philosophical problem of the Hegelian dialectic.[6] One might say Hegel lived in theories of improvement; but one can of course be constative about dialectic, can see it triangulate in multiple inversions, as with Adorno's. Among other things, Adorno takes on the "where to begin" as well as the meta-philosophical matter of what the dialectic does with the thinking person training to apply it. And Adorno *is* a philosopher: his negative dialectics works in philosophical structures and responds to prior philosophers, even as the book *Negative Dialectics* often operates thrillingly in situ, apprehending the fundamentally rhetorical situation of language-focused knowing. *Negative Dialectics* proceeds according to ratcheted modularity in its almost innumerable subtitled sections (there are 138), a good philosophical case of what Robert Hullot-Kentor calls "paratactical presentation."[7] Adorno already has a dynamic presentation at work; his where to begin does not start at only one point nor proceed according to narrow objects. But negative dialectics does operate, however reflexively and sometimes dazzlingly, with the materials of philosophical (disciplinary) response and building.

Wild dialectics takes this "where to begin" a step away, on a creative theory swerve whose trajectory is akin to the repeated advice (from, for one example, the sound artist John Cage)

---

5 Robert Duncan, *The Opening of the Field* (New Directions, 1973), and Lyn Hejinian, *The Language of Inquiry* (University of California Press, 2000).

6 See Theodor W. Adorno, *Negative Dialectics,* trans. E.B. Ashton (The Seabury Press, 1973), 29, 11, and 13.

7 Robert Hullot-Kentor, "Introduction," in Theodor W. Adorno, *Aesthetic Theory,* trans. Robert Hullot-Kentor (University of Minnesota Press, 1998), xi–xxi.

that we "begin anywhere,"[8] since, as one might say, there is no such thing as a disconnected start. Part of this swerve is disciplinary. Since its twentieth-century loosening from the historical ropes of philosophy (ropes that served as trapeze, as rope-bridge, sometimes as binding-to-carry), theory has become its own "discipline." (And discipline is a term with its own issues, given the implications of disciplined followers and of punishment, and given the conservative pressures in brick-and-mortal institutions, a description that intends "mortal" as the living force, the real "mortar," of life-blood institutions). The present so-called "post-theory" timeframe can perhaps be for wild dialectics a *topical* frame: wild dialectics is creative theory, focused in imaginative reasoning in relation with the implications of imaginative writing, itself posited as a wilder and wider field than works sometimes mainstreamed as literature. The scare quotes in the prior sentence mean to say that neither theory nor literature is really "post," not least because thinking has every reason to resist brand offers of so-called progress, just as Anglo-American-Australasian discourse has many reasons to resist throwing out history in favor of a posited "post" positioning. Very often, claims of quasi-Kuhnian paradigm shift are actually progress narratives dressed up in the guise of re-attentions that sport a dump-and-run anti-historicism.

As these different discourse approaches mean to indicate, the third proposal of wild dialectics is fairly determining: equality of approach supports the situating of this book as and in *creative theory,* posited as a blending of the seriousness of creative thinking with the seriousness of blue-sky (and, irresistibly salient: dark-sky) critical thinking. Creative theory is a term that negotiates with habits of differentiating the creative from the critical and habits of differentiating artistic thinking from theory thinking.

Believing in the epistemic work of imaginative unknowing, wild dialectics takes up its thought-cues anywhere, since

8 See for example John Cage, "Composition as Process," in *Silence: Lectures and Writings* (Wesleyan University Press, 1961), 31.

any posited quotient of "taking up" is cutting with scissors that don't exist a priori into fabric that doesn't a priori exist. Wild dialectics considers the matter of taking up a thought to be in a dynamic relation with any possibility of knowing where to take up or why one would take up in that way. We ourselves are putting together the scissors that cut and stitching the fabric that is cut. In this sense, and in relation to its first proposal, wild dialectics is radically skeptical about the assertion of any necessary starting place in thinking.

Which does not mean that the thought-start, once taken up, is evacuated of significance by its contingent beginning. That would be to have, again, the conversation about how constructivism's meanings at the very least match the intensity of meanings sought or asserted by "givenism," a term one might use for the effort to naturalize meaning as given, ideal, or inherent, in any event certainly not trembling with constructivist tectonics. Constructions are how cultural meanings happen among bodies of living; givenism operates within (imposed, ideologically re-performed) habits of constructed meanings. Although this conversation may be one to have again and again, like any political imperative, this is not the place to develop that conversation, though we might see wild dialectics as operating within contingency theories. This essay means to take contingency as granted. Its focus is on the implications of wild dialectics for what it means to take up and continue with thought.

The hinge of a next, or connected, thought is the second focus of wild dialectics, which is skeptical about any assertion of necessary causality or linkage among posited elements as one continues thinking. This matter of linkage and continuation is important for wild dialectics insofar as it is a sympathetic swerve in relation to Adorno's negative dialectics. Theory situated in the knowing of imaginative unknowing, as here, presumes linked activities of thought and feeling; it might be better to call them think-feeling and feel-thinking (sensorially affectual ideation). Looking for vocabulary that evokes that linkage, we might consider the term "rongo" in te reo Māori. Rongo seems to be oriented to linking the *sensory* with thought rather than linking emotive-rushes with think-rushes. Certainly, counting feeling and embodiment and intellection as all operative in imaginative unknowing is a tally one might cathect to: in other words, the move here is to blend sense-feeling with emotion-feeling with thinking in critical bodies. Which still doesn't provide any single term for those combined moves, thus think-feeling will have to work for my purposes here.

The think-feeling of the creative theory spotlighted in this book also presumes that imagination works in relation to philosophical, artistic, and cultural acts. That triad represents, for present purposes, thinking-obsessed (philosophically consequential), resistance-obsessed (artistically consequential), and ethically-obsessed (culturally consequential) action. Those separations are themselves artificial: one could as easily say that philosophy works to resist, art works to try ethics, and culture works to think. In each case an activity theoretically links with an attended emphasis and the posited link energizes the different aspects of each pairing. Such links are an example of wild dialectics emphases: imagination's think-feeling, unknowing, and resistance nodes and moves are not a priori; they're in wild rotations.

In considering architectures of thinking, the first two proposals of wild dialectics — the contingent nature of the start and the multiplicity of the hinge in think-feeling — point to the action of takeoff and motile tether, the contingent whirr of our butterfly-ish multiplicities. In terms of *continuing* shape, we might think of wild dialectics as functioning like a liquid cog in a liquidity of thought potential. This thought potential is partly locatable in social contexts and disciplinary orientations and technical approaches, but its totality is not accessible: its unknowingness is inherent. One possible visual analogy for the ongoing operation of wild dialectics is a rotating Clifford torus. This visual analogy aims to indicate the motility and all-over-deep-surface of thinking in wild dialectics, even as this essay plans to complicate some implications of the visual image below (fig. 1.1).

Wild dialectics presumes that, in place of deduction or induction, thought always swerves in Peirce's abductive patterns.

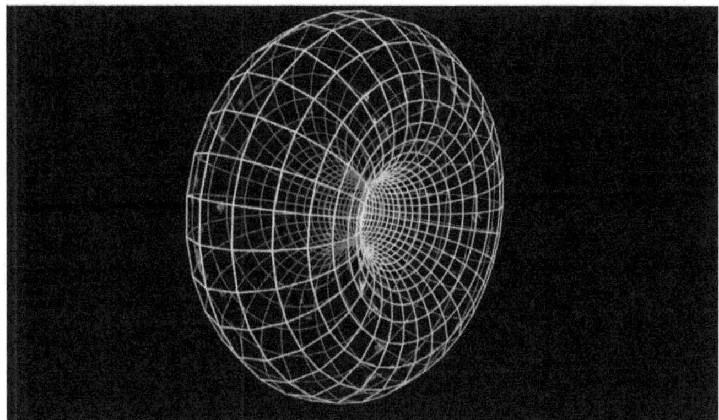

Fig. 1.1. Screenshot from Jason Hise, "Clifford Torus," *YouTube,* April 9, 2016, https://www.youtube.com/watch?v=1_pzjvVixLo. Courtesy of the artist.

In my reading, Peirce's abduction evades the so-called logical machinery of induction and deduction to locate a name for what really happens when the latter two terms are being applied. Reasoning from samples to causes and from causes to samples means asserting that one thing is measured as a sample and one as a cause, or vice versa. But these reasonings are decisions as we can make them, not discoveries of set or natural circumstances. That's what it means to call the process "what really happens."

Hence Peircean abduction is part of this imagining of wild dialectics: both the assertion of thetic position and the assertion of relations of movement among thought positions are really wild. The constellated motility of wild dialectics works to stay open to unforeseen linkages. There can be no critically innocent assertion of clean lines among thesis, antithesis, and synthesis or next-move. If one uses these terms, they should in this view be used with a mind to their provisionality: within a "where to begin," we make a decision about the usefulness of calling something thetic or antithetical or synthetic. When for example inside and outside, or being and concept, are considered, wild dialectics keeps one aware that, at each moment, assertions about what is being and what is concept, what is inside and outside, could be inverted or held to a different angle. I emphasize that wild dialectics is borrowing Peircean abduction to help explain itself. I don't think abduction will mind, given its inbuilt thought conversion ratios.

Another aspect of Adorno's thinking helps articulate the concept-nonconcept inversionability of wild dialectics. (We can imagine that the Clifford torus continues to rotate, inward and outward, its medial hole both inverting and retroverting, its all-over-surface analogously active at every point.) In "Disenchantment of the Concept," Adorno summarizes his hope that negative dialectics creates thought conditions in which a concept defines itself in terms of its non-conceptuality rather than in contrast to being.[9] Adorno wants to get philosophy to look back at itself, actively enfolding the concept's indeterminacy, its not-self, into the concept's formation. In this way the concept might hope to stop defining itself by way of contrast to an other, instead recognizing what we might term its own "Zero at the Bone"[10] — to shift to imaginative synesthetics, and to quote Emily Dickinson — and incorporating that synesthetic wilderness within a positive definition of its conceptuality. Such a dialectic focuses on thought-within-non-thought rather than focusing on thought-to-thing (or "being," to use Adorno's term).

Adorno's hope can be applied to Dickinson's zero — which itself can be thought of as a biologically enriched version of what the poet John Keats called "*Negative Capability*"[11] — as existing within philosophical conceptualizing itself. We can think of Dickinson's biological negative-space invocation as itself a precursor to the animistic aspects of, for example, contemporary so-called "new materialisms." We can also, for that matter, think of new materialisms in terms of Indigenous commitments

9 See Adorno, *Negative Dialectics,* 12 and elsewhere.

10 Emily Dickinson, "[A Narrow Fellow in the Grass]" (c. 1865), in *The Complete Poems of Emily Dickinson,* ed. Thomas H. Johnson (Little, Brown and Company, 1960), 460.

11 John Keats, "Letter to George and Tom Keats, 22 December 1818," in *Selected Letters of John Keats,* ed. Grant F. Scott (Harvard University Press, 2002), 60.

to co-imagining human life with Earth rights. The conceptually indeterminate concepts that keep wild dialectics moving are akin to the flexibility of Māori tipua, posited as both spiritual and temporal animisms.

Given that the main commitments of this book are in relations with lingual life and works, the orientations above are explanatory: situating the force of wild dialectics with reference to authorial thought-emplacements in the transpacific, for example, and in what physics can teach us. At the same time wild dialectics is fixated, here, in the embodied contingency of creatively-oriented language, in lingual *imagining*. Wild dialectics relates to the interventionist work that poetry-motivated writing can do, making language with and for what we don't know, our wild thinking, as well as for what we might be said to. The poet Samuel Taylor Coleridge's "Positive Negation" (in his poem "Limbo") is an example of how poetic language already performs arguments about the productive tension involved in thinking about a mixture of concept and non-concept without recourse to the grounding provided by some exemplary Being.[12] Not unlike what happens when one delineates a theory without checking it alongside an event such as a poem for illumination, as this essay is doing — unless we might consider the pictorial Clifford torus a constellating asemic poem, especially in its actively revolving state. Then again, this essay is not fully "reading" the torus, even if it proposes its motions as formally interactivated with the essay's urges.

Taking Adorno's point about concepts including their non-concepts within their formulations, wild dialectics posits as a positive move that we cannot even assert which is the concept and which is the non-concept, that such an assertion is also a decision rather than organic to the material. If negative dialectics focuses in part on turning the concept toward a constitutive view of its non-conceptuality, then wild dialectics focuses on the

12 See Samuel Taylor Coleridge, *Selected Poetry and Prose of Coleridge*, ed. Donald A. Stauffer (Random House, 1951).

question of where concepts and non-concepts arise, where the designation of them *as* concepts and non-concepts arises, how they are distinguished from being, what non-being is within being, and in what *order* any of these elements may be, or are, or "should be necessarily" considered. The circumstances of wild dialectics are not *ex nihilo* but a pointing, a *where,* and then an attention to the wild logics that determine what directions that where goes. Of course, as the static printed version of our Clifford torus indicates, normative codical pages are considered as instancing only one form of argument at a time, even as alternatives and soft text (as in this book's "Soft Text and the Open Line") loop theoretically throughout. Even as we know that simultaneity is larger than what time compasses.

Given the tense linearity of the expository page, one invitation in explicating the term wild dialectics is to trace its lines of denotative and connotative connection, to help keep those lines available when the term is invoked. Certainly it hearkens to "wild footage," a term for raw filmic material that film editors then shape into a "finished" film, and to the wild audio that begins any sound recording, considering that material as constantly dis-sown (continually quantum phonon dis-sown) inside the shaped end result that gets called a finished audio recording. An interest in the untouched or so-called "unmediated" art event, from outtakes to overheard drafts, proves the rule of wild footage and wild audio's fascination insofar as such interest attends to the equal potentiality of unpursued directions. Wild dialectics also hearkens to wilderness and its wildflowers, considering that the Earth is actually wild in its births and deaths and temporalities and that humanimals continually wrangle our own wilderness and growth-change in our acts and impulses. In terms of the lingual, wild dialectics also nominally summons the wild dialects that make up the alterities of languages like global Englishes, Spanishes, Arabics, and more. Language is constantly re-defined by its users, and re-corralled by power interests, precisely because all language is constantly changing;[13] language is wild forces.

Wild dialectics can also be related to wild actions, to "wildness" that exceeds the boundaries of so-called culture and is hence and always relationally and relatively with that culture, attending it with a contrastive awayness that actually brings it conceptually extremely close. At points where cultures come in to organize thinking, various dialectics take shape. Wild dialectics keeps that point consistently alive and at the forefront of decisions about how the material of thinking and imagining is organized. In that sense maybe it is wild: untame, yet extremely aware of its civilities, since it is aware of the civil as continually proposed. Those propositions are always ethical ones, like the third proposal of wild dialectics: the equality of the elements in thinking and think-feeling.

So how does wild dialectics predicate or imbue other essays in this book? As the disciplinary and imaginative ethics of Adorno, Peirce, and Glissant suggest, the applicability of wild dialectics to the theory and practice of this book is that each piece is wild in its absorptions as one way to be committed in its instruments. Hearkening to Friedrich Nietzsche's "extra moral sense," wild dialectics folds the particulates of its reading examples into theoretical practices and wonders about membranes among the

---

13 One question for AI writing concerns its relations with language change. Apprehending how the change energies of human lingualism relate with AI's large language models (LLMS) is in part concerned with the different procedures and potentials of each in terms of recombination, superpositionality, and context sensitivity. Our critical bodies are alterity transponders with and through which language breathes as we breathe with it. AI's current LLMS are statistical sorters without think-feeling; they are pattern-aligners that gather and array without fleshy, epigenetic, and contextually aware recognition. Like clichés, AI's linguals can express for us, can give us patterns we co-feel as true. It's a question of how many stations you build to off-load reference and to make language a self-playing instrument. As with anything, how we treat language becomes how it treats us. The ethics of our lingual performances is an ethics that co-makes us.

conceptual, the non-conceptual, and being.[14] Wild dialectics also presumes that an event in thinking, a "distinction," takes place: wild dialectics is not anarchism. One is performing some engagement with some object-events. But what dimensional point in what propositional event is thetic? What point is antithetic? At any node, a plural of radical particularities characterizes wild dialectics in action. That's its ethics, in a world of composited cultures and disciplinary change.

Our disciplines, including relatively flexible zones called theory or post-theory, continue to operate with four swords held over their heads, waiting for us to "get it right." To add to religion (western education's foundational exegesis: get it right or go to hell), reason (Enlightenment's palliative for growing social connectivity and unrest: get it right and become a "better" person), and scientism (empiricism's bodily and sub-cellular operation: get it right and control the world of nature), we now have the businessification of all institutional imaginaries (capital's endgame: get it right and leverage it for money). Businessification mandates turning ideas into marketable quantities. "Knowledge transfer" is a market conduit that unfencing disciplinary boundaries can help resist. Marketization avoids the very substance of wild dialectics and other resistant thinking.

Along similar lines, Adorno writes about the impoverishment of speculative thinking: see for example the section "A Split in the Concern with Freedom," about "the flagging of speculative vigor and the correlative evolution of individual sciences."[15] However salient Adorno's point about the importance of purely speculative thinking (something like what Laura Riding called "generalizations without instances"), critical practices can come in as somato-psychic hiccups to help disrupt the attractions of paraphraseable arts, to render activity itself speculative, to tender criticism as theory. In place of turning imaginative theory into verifiable authenticities of paraphraseable messages about

14 See Friedrich Nietzsche, "On Truth and Lie in an Extra-Moral Sense," in *The Portable Nietzsche,* ed. and trans. Walter Kaufmann (Viking, 1954).

15 Adorno, *Negative Dialectics,* 214.

arts in stable states, I would rather participate in declarations about the end of theory, structures, and literature alongside a self-perishing involuting freedom I imagine for wild dialectics. Such are positive conceptual "deaths" that enable the continual re-birth of the other within Glissant's porous *la trace.*

Wild dialectics strives to come at nodes of encounter and swerve abductively with an articulated set of committed uncertainties. We come to look at something imaginatively and we know we don't entirely know what we are doing—presuming we are operating, at those moments, not in a theater of medicine or war or food distribution (not in a basic situation of threatened need) but rather in a theater of thinking about how signs are happening in culture, how culture arranges its understandings and implementations of value. Much as when we stand back to think about why we act the way we do, or why a nation-state has adopted certain laws and what we should do as citizens, the operations of wild dialectics—as well, I hope, as other operations of this book—mean to help articulate not only the artifacts but our acts toward and within life. Wild dialectics is committed to critical practice as physical, generous, and permeable, even as this book's critical engagements are differentiated in named modes such as withness, soft text, membranism, and more.

Certainly this thinking acts with privilege, since it presumes semiotic literacy and adequate measures of food, clothing, shelter, education, and value to think. The pull of culture back to "basics" or "common sense" participates in a pull against the right to think, in efforts to keep people striving in bare need and states of emergency, and in efforts to pull composite globalizations in directions of reductive competition. Such efforts also stymy our access to the implications of being in quantum fields of life, amidst "wild" relational forces we are still just beginning to apprehend as conditioning our think-feeling. We must seriously resist any efforts to undermine our rights to imagine and then again re-imagine, with all the chemical, relational, epigenetic, quantum, and constitutive semiotics (lingual and otherwise) of our beings. In valuing our rights to love, to have a say, to be with other beings in articulating ethics, making works, and fostering alterity, we make vocabularies and opportunities to expand our imaginative behaviors. That's why this essay. That's why, really overall, this book.

Peirce's Cave

> la pensée de la trace s'appose, par opposition à la pensée de système, comme une errance qui oriente.
>
> —Édouard Glissant, *Traité du tout-monde*[1]

This essay considers a sensory-thought image that positions possible ways to imagine what we don't know alongside, with, within sense-attentive knowing. It links with the prior essay in developing the second and fourth proposals of wild dialectics: think-feeling as constellated continuance (as in the image of reticulated butterfly-ish wings) and as contingently culminant opacity. The latter might be expressed as hovered transitions among think-feeling, dark ongoingness opening thought positions among other thought positions. To consider this condition of keeping-on-thinking from a pivoting plateau to what can be experienced as a relational shift in direction, I turn again to the visions of Charles S. Peirce.

In Peirce's 1898 lecture "The Logic of Continuity," he describes a complex sensory metaphor for unbounded dimensional space. In the lecture, this metaphor stands in for the embodied embrain-

1 "Thinking as *trace* positions itself, in opposition to thinking as system, as an errancy that orients." Édouard Glissant, *Traité du tout-monde: Poétique IV* (Gallimard, 1997), 18. My translation.

ment of logical continuity, ongoingness, and interrelationality.[2] I emphasize that I am summoning Peirce's extended image as a way to help think wild dialectics rather than to perform logical work with the geometrical "topic" of his lecture. Not that I think Peirce would mind, given his respect for uncertainty and given the space of thinking in and as imaginative unknowing, rather than in and as philosophically enrobed logic, for the present work. I've come to think of this thought-image, in relation with the image description in "The Logic of Continuity," as Peirce's Cave. It functions as a positive image of knowing's somatic non-conclusions, an extrapolation and expansion of Peirce's explanations that signs always include the signers, and a shift from Plato's Cave of perceptual delusions and from Avicenna's Cave of the focally enlightened soloist.

Peirce describes two completely dark, large, and enclosed caves, each with two large balloons floating inside them through which one can pass, swimming through dark air, from one (warm) cave into the other (cool) cave and back again. This is a dimensional shift rather than a passage between two normative caves, and crucially for my purposes Peirce's sensory-thought experiment is run sightlessly. It cannot be *visualized,* in contrast for example to the depiction above of the Clifford torus (however much that depiction itself is a translation variant of geometric-conceptual tori). The following lines come toward the end of Peirce's long explication:

> At length, you are informed that the wall of one of the balloons has been reduced to a mere film which you can feel with your hand but through which you can pass. You being all this time in the cool cave swim up to that balloon and try it. You pass through it readily; only in doing so you feel a strange twist, such as you have never felt, and you find by feeling with your hand that you are just passing out through one of

2 Charles Sanders Peirce, "The Logic of Continuity," in *Reasoning and the Logic of Things: The Cambridge Conference Lectures of 1898,* ed. Kenneth Laine Ketner (Harvard University Press, 1992).

> the corresponding balloons of the warm cave. [...] After you have passed backward and forward often enough to become familiar with the fact that the passage may be made through every part of the surface of the balloon, you are told that the other balloon is now in the same state. You try it and find it to be so, passing round and round in every way. Finally, you are told that the outer walls have been removed. You swim to where they were. You feel the queer twist and you find yourself in the other cave. You ascertain by trial that it is so with every part of the walls, the floor, and the roof. They do not exist any longer. There is no outer boundary at all.[3]

In Peirce's unbounded continuity there is conceptually tactile dimensionality: There is always a you, sensory perception, physically portrayed and experienced mental action, and (motile) emplacement. There is no outer boundary, but there is a sensory dialectic: there is the "queer twist." The act of think-feeling, rather than being teleological or self-devouring or nugatory or resistant, can predicate on a stance of folding toward a dimension whose continuity is not rebirth, nor stative refreshing, but connection in unbounded recurrence. In semiotic terms, Peirce's cave image gives wild dialectics its enfoldment. Moves between the two caves that have become one and yet remain two can be read as moves within the second and third aspects of wild dialectics — the aspect of continuance and the (here, sensorily differential) equality of the elements in thinking. The condition of this cave of continuity might also suggest an embodied yet metaphorical image for the start of a thought, its embedded contingency. Yet I'm particularly interested in reading the "apex" in wild dialectics as it might be experienced as sense-thought ongoingness in the felt darkness of Peirce's Cave.

This "removed" double cave, not Plato's cave, is where I want to think about the continuity (to adopt Peirce's term) of think-feeling in a wild dialectics model. In Peirce's Cave, the hinge of the next thought appears its consequences in the queer twist of

3 Peirce, *Reasoning and the Logic of Things*, 253.

the abductive link. That's sign's continuity. If distributed centrality describes *ethical* equality in the elements of life, including its potential thinking, Peirce's Cave recurrence touches on guiding dialectical currents onward as thinking continues—not toward clarity or telos but toward alterity's continuity. The drive is to recognize one's contingent closeness with what Peirce called the "dynamic objects" of one's think-feeling.

The pungent smells that Peirce constructs for his two cave/balloons are part of the sensory relevance of Peirce's Cave to wild dialectics. I read his image as apprehending that sensory knowing suspends any dominance of abstract thematics in place of presence. I also read the non-ocularcentrism of Peirce's Cave as performing and encouraging distributed sensoria that correlate with distributed epistemics. I read the darkness of the thinking body—deep inside our living bodies, all is dark; flung through the exteroceptive "outside," light has no especial bearing on our quantum epistemic relating—as correlative with being there in Peirce's Cave. In a measure, one can read the moves from "one" cave to "the other," even as they are the same-difference cave, as moves within the interior body to the interior body of a thought whose aspects are always contextual (social, archival), insofar as we are using literacy or numeracy or similar systems that don't belong to us but that we join.

Peirce's Cave as Trace

In line with the transplace commitments explored in this book, I want to relate the thought conditions of Peirce's Cave with the Māori concept of *whakawhānaungatanga,* which can be translated as the making (tended, continuing making) of a network of interpersonal links. The more frequently used word *whānaungatanga* is a human kinship connection term, fronted here by the activating prefix *whaka. Whaka* is a causative prefix that motivates, in etymological terms, the togetherness described in *whānaungatanga.* As I understand it, *whakawhānaungatanga* suspends—or more precisely exists in an oral history of thinking that never established, much less thickened — a notion that researcher and research subject are separated. The *whakawhānaungatanga* experience of the thought balloons in Peirce's Cave is another way of imagining how the thinker becomes the thought sign. As the concept of *whakawhānaungatanga* suggests, and as the prior essay indicated, envisioning wild dialectics is part of an Oceanian placement that connects with other thought-formations in transatlantic and Judeo-Christian-Islamic cultural contexts. This adapted *whakawhānaungatanga* aspect of Peirce's Cave is not oriented only to humans; its other-than-human energy means to perceive the pulls of think-feeling as polydimensional, with all the potential opportunity for expanded representation and exteroception and conceptualizing that is afforded by such orientations to relational alterity. The course of the particular is wild, and the right to be of wild dialectics values an adopted, contingent, *tūrangawaewae* — to adapt a resonant Māori term meaning the place where you have a right to stand[4] — different from the stability of any particular recurrent local or posited transhistorical. We know, for example, that one problematic in Hegel is the assumption of a shared world of suppositions and goals and the assumption that the dialectic gets "better"; it goes up. By contrast, the positive valence of "living in the past" has helped Oceania and Pasifika epistemologies to thrive without positing a necessary pursuit of leaning forward into a wind of arriving futurity.

In this sense wild dialectics resists critical culture that preaches a necessarily forward-striving "improving" thought-world: the fashionable topic, the presumed-better-because-more-recent thought product. At the same time, Peirce's Cave seems to me an image of epistemic hope dis-coupled from futurity fatalism. It has seemed to me, in other words, as though the aforementioned results of progress narratives foster dis-energiz-

4 For good online te reo Māori dictionaries, see https://www.maorilanguage.net/ and https://maoridictionary.co.nz/. The Māori "wh" spelling is pronounced with an "f"/"ph" sound. The words here are as I have learned them over years of talking, reading, and listening in Aotearoa/New Zealand.

ing; they work like repelling magnets. On one hand we hear, we take in, the cultural message that things are getting better in styles, topics, thinking skills; on the other, the edge of the future sheers disempowered unknowing forces against "our progress" and deflates any accumulation of this posited progress. Believing that thinking always improves implies that your own thinking can never be "there" yet. People can feel at once pushed "forward" and flung off a never-ending futurity cliff. The co-involuting whirl/whorl of Peirce's Cave brings these ideological positions, along with the critical bodies that bear them, into question.

A steady focus on ethically-transfixed contingent theory moves is also part of wild dialectics, which exists inside my hope for contemporary theory that releases the "barbaric." To invoke its transatlantic literary modernist heritage: this tricky term barbaric is related to the virtue that the writer Laura Riding saw, though she grew nervous about it (and that T.S. Eliot saw and could never face), in Gertrude Stein's work. It is also related to the barbaric that Theodor Adorno asserts as *the* dangerous value of poetic thought, once we realize that so-called "civilized" culture, as illustrated by Auschwitz, has not discovered the ethics of barbarism.[5] Thus for Adorno (and for poets such as William Blake) poetry needs to plunge away from such so-called civilization and through barbaric modes to redo forms of cultural consciousness. I read that as a call for poetry as cultural resistance, as continual experiment against approved (deadly) civilized modes. Perhaps that is a generous interpretation of Adorno's stance, which is all right if so. It might be said that Adorno was writing within what Édouard Glissant calls "atavistic" culture, given the power of Adorno's placement in a German ideology.

We might now re-imagine Adorno's term barbarism within a global distributed centrality akin to Glissant's "composite" culture. Such imagining can perhaps dispense altogether with the terms civilization and barbarism and focus, for example, on how

5 See Theodor W. Adorno, *The Culture Industry*, ed. J.M. Bernstein (Routledge, 1991), 126.

perceiving dialectics as wild accords with Glissant's perception of the present as composite. Glissant's work helps wild dialectics understand itself as enlivened provisional thought action within the constatively unavoidable opportunities of composite culture. The desire of wild dialectics joins with the desire of feminist, Indigenous, anti-capitalist, and ecological theories to re-think thinking. We need a wide table of re-thinking in order to help equip composite culture with tools that might be said to serve as strong replacements for "given" atavisms as well as for domineering media assertions about "how things are." In this way, wild dialectics imbues tūrangawaewae with conceptual provisionality: it wants to make and re-make thought-places which have, and where we have, equal rights to stand and think.

This conceptual provisionality comes back again to the third component of wild dialectics, following on from the nature of the thought-start and the multiplicity of thought's hinges: the potential, theoretical, equality of each of the elements of a thought. Glissant indicates that he is committed to imagining identity while (he posits) Gilles Deleuze and Félix Guattari's rhizomes are committed to thought. Without presuming that Glissant means to indicate a constitutive or permanent separation between thought and identity, I understand wild dialectics as interested in thought + identity — or really thus: alterity — both transpiring in and as the body of thinking. This body is neurologically dendritic, as the "wild" shape of thinking indicates. This body is also viscerally opened and shared, as the deep surface of Body Art texts (such as Gina Pane's *Azione Sentimentale* [1973] and Carolee Schneemann's *VULVA'S MORPHIA* [1997]) vividly illuminates. Bodies of cultures, too, are open compositions. And each element of the composition is equal to the quality of any other element, in the ethical emphasis highlighted in the third aspect of wild dialectics. In these ways Glissant's *trace* is part of the condition within which wild dialectics seeks to start and continue its attentions. The distributional energy of Peirce's Cave embodies an image of equalized alterity forces through which our human thought ongoingness can experiment with differential dialectics. Especially as I work to imagine how

Fig. 2.1. Lisa Samuels, "Wild dialectics as blindsight / Peirce's Cave" (2019).

quantum behaviors are part of our mind work, part of our liquid electric conceptions and perceptions and energies, visionary alternatives like Peirce's Cave offer up inhabitable models.

Given the rendered-porous fabric of the human thought-world, any element can be turned to with resonant attention as a thought continues. In this sense the illustration of wild dialectics can map, across the Clifford torus, the queer twist of Peirce's cave and the distributed kinetic blindness of neural dendrites, bringing us to an image of wild dialectics that cannot be illustrated. We are now in a position to contemplate the blindness of the torus eye somewhat in line with what the essay "Contemporanullity" calls the "imaginative wave crest of blindsight." It's as though our image is now of dark matter, painted in a hue that aligns with its demonstrative surface. On a normative codical (bleached) paper page, the hue might resemble one that paint companies call black-white, as though it now looks like the image (fig. 2.1).

Entering a thought in this kind of compound, we can select, continue, and weigh with a wild will that is mindfully upending crowd-control modes of thinking so as to make a place of permission for a contextually mobilized zone of thinking or vision, such as the motives that create the conditions for what Glissant calls a creolized world. Consider Avicenna's cave, as in his Ḥayy ibn Yaqẓān; there the cave is solitude and enlightenment.[6] In Peirce's Cave it's explicitly sensory, abstract (mathematical), and, as with Peirce's concept of continuity, never solo: always plural and relational. Indeed fig. 2.1 might be, within the darkness of Peirce's Cave, a distributed lattice, whose rules of association, commutativity, absorption, and idempotency show set theory's analogical force in imagining equalities of alterity in how we live on Earth. Humans are entangled biological macros of the conditions of (superpositional) organization, (distributed) perceivability, and (differentially equivalent) energy patterns that disciplines such as mathematics and quantum physics so often engage to demonstrate. In its sensory-theoretical evocation of such conditions, Peirce's Cave is part of my sense of available tools and emplacements for think-feeling.

---

6 See Hermitary, "Ibn Tufayl's *Hayy Ibn Yaqzan:* Solitude and Understanding," 2007, https://www.hermitary.com/solitude/ibntufayl.html.

Distributed Centrality

Earth has an innermost planetary core; its surface, however, where beings move around, has no center points. Every planetary surface point is a candidate for physical and conceptual centrality, for being its own center. The corner, a wave, a treetop, a room of earnest conversation, organisms teeming closely, the turn of a digital page, the turn of a wing. To consider some implications of this situation, to think about the equality of every being, event, and place, I engage the ethical value term distributed centrality.

In distributed centrality, there are no margins. Everything acts centrally. Replacing center-to-margin descriptions with distributed centers means to upheave assertions that some anywheres operate as sidelines to some other more main anywheres. Distributed centrality means to undo assertions of rare centralities and occasionally rescued marginalities — assertions that are principally habitual and historical — in human attentions to what, where, or who is important. It's a resistance to habitus naturalization of dominant and subordinate relations.

Distributed centrality is a term for acting so that the center is everywhere. Such action does not presume or necessitate urges of totality or ubiquity or omniscience. Instead, we can recognize and honor our placements and our displacement from other centralities. One consequence of living with distributed centrality is recognizing the necessary disconnect of equally distributed life. We do not need to know about everything, everyone, everyplace in order to make room for them. Since nothing is everything and no one is everywhere, distributed centrality encourages a questioning of the recurrent idea that a particular cultural value, like a best shape or a perfect expression of an idea, is made in some kind of "universal" (which actually means, in most adjectival applications, planetary) accounting. Always bearing in mind the necessity of not being cruel—this is, after all, an ethical theory under consideration—no account of judgment applies everywhere on Earth: There is no exclusively best intelligence, object, event, or action within all the planetary possibilities of those forces.

Distributed centrality contrasts with practices of exclusionary centrality that can distract from the real demands and pleasures of action. Exclusionary centrality proposes that there are certain most important things, people, places; it can emanate from forces like power shoring up borders and epicolonialism gazing for, and inventing ever-new types of, horizons. If you think the important speaking is happening somewhere else, you might believe you are culturally mute or symbolically deaf. If you think the important things are happening somewhere else or being done by someone else, you might think your actions and being are invisible or inconsequent—or, for that matter, you might want to go fight for dominance. However much ideologies and activities of power seek to obscure the matter, speaking and action are central everywhere they happen. Imagining distributed centers helps to unsettle a yearning for power centers that seem segregated from us, a yearning that can foster fatalism and a sense of distance from life.

Historically the "butterfly effect" has described how small motions somewhere else on the planet have an impact on other, distant, events. The description has emphasized the effect of the seemingly inconsequential, earlier, and far-away motion on something larger, later, and deemed more important than the butterfly's wing motion. But everything is as far away from everything else as everything else. Rather than tallying its effect, distributed centrality centers the actual and conceptual butterfly. The butterfly's movement is that event. Every centrality has a potential effect for any other centrality. Hence synergies can be posited as always having, coming with, and performing within, parity. If there are effects, then beings are all effects.

The idea of distributed centrality partly arises in considering ontological, ecological, and political value within an idea of transplace as location. Transplace keeps in mind the dynamism and contingency of placement, demonstrated for example in the shifting of tectonic plates, relative space-time, inventions of nations, and the changing locations and existences of water, land, and air creatures in moving life. In political terms, both Earth rights and migrating human bodies are part of the ethics of articulating distributed centrality.

Distributed centrality harmonizes, though non-identically, with "distributed cognition" ideas that focus on continuing and shared thought-work. In that association, distributed centrality involves an ethical potential of what I call the digitas: the perfusing digital living we make with our habitus, civitas, and the digits of hands and binary numbers. The digitas can be experienced as an additive being-place: in our digital creations and searches, we become something additional to and different with our bodies. Recognizing distributed centrality in the digitas presents new challenges and opportunities for supporting the voices of everywhere. Like any library, the digitas cannot be or represent totalities. If the digitas encourages exclusionary centrality, in which "hits" constitute value, then even net neutrality is not enough to make room for all the centralities. In the ontological transit zones of the digitas, how do we listen? And how do we make room for aspects of being that cannot access or co-create the digitas? This is a question both for the digital divide, the difference between having and not having access to online computing, and for the difference between life made inside and life made outside computing.

Certainly these points circulate always back toward persons and intentional bearings — we're speaking, writing, and reading human languages. Yet every distributed center speaks whether with or without what we recognize or allocate as a voice. In planetary being, emanations continually begin everywhere. How do we listen to the centrality of the other? We can extend guardianship, as with the humans in New Zealand/Aotearoa who tend the rights of Te Awa Tupua: the Whanganui River has legal personhood status, and humans are appointed to translate its conditions and needs into the languages of those legal rights. Since that 2017 act, more non-human entities are having their own being rights recognized in Aotearoa and elsewhere. These are legislative and legal examples of what distributed centrality hopes for as a general stance. Distributed centrality emphasizes how we recognize the stone, how we recognize every being (animate/inanimate), event (macro/sub-molecular), and place (named/unnamed), not how it recognizes us. These are human values we write, and their difficult opportunities are our conditions. If you know that everything is equally central, the importance of your own actions can be more readily felt and perceived.

The ethical arguments of distributed centrality have a family resemblance with the equality of thought-centers and thought-directions in wild dialectics. Which probably means that wild dialectics is an Earth rights approach to thinking. And it possibly means that Earth rights implies a need to structure what can be called unknowing into our knowledge machinery, to make spaces for what we don't know to exist and thrive and to push on what we say we know.[1]

---

1 Distributed centrality means to be non-totalizing: It's not trying to account for every approach to organizing and describing attention. It's also an idealistic absolute: Like love and hope, distributed centrality is a concept meant to push on idealism reset buttons as people remind themselves of values they thrive in living by. To practice radical equality in the face of cultural structures of hierarchy, to value vulnerability and otherness, is to flip value switches every day.

I dream of an end to exemplitude, an end to setting up one example, one case, as though it can suffice for what are (always, only, ever) many variant particulars. Wanting to stop thinking about exceptions, other cases, and the unseen in order to join social or institutional media in preferring one object for attention is wanting to rest one's critical attention, and to rest it on an agglomerative, shared surface. That desire makes canons of many stripes, and enforces the What You're Supposed To Know among what are usually innumerable, and theoretically infinite, choices and opportunities. (I wonder if exemplitude is a misapplication of induction's "reduction of the manifold to unity": a misapplication because induction does not make space for being's alterity.)

I dream of an end to the acceptance and naturalizing of hierarchism in how we treat life. I dream of an era when "hierarchism" — recognized as an installed and historical approach — is understood to be a tricky word, to raise careful eyebrows the way other prejudicial attitudes raise eyebrows. It is possible to recognize structural ecologies in action, for example in systems of governance and care-work, and also to stay in a contingent relation with them: Understand that the structure does not transmute to infuse or essentially constitute the worth of beings enacting it and acting within it.

Distributed centrality is a resistance to power imbalances generally. There is nothing except power that allows something to be declared socially central and some other thing less central. The power to traverse, possess, enjoy, or be overwhelmed by, and the fear of being left out (foblo) of such traversal and enjoyment. Even a virus has, arguably, its right to be, contested by us who wish to be well, to maintain civics of care with each other. The viral pandemic's long moment became a new litmus test, a refresher course for how we use our powers.

The centrality of language is also distributed: each lingual event sustains and evaporates itself in similar measures. As a social force language becomes, in part, independent of its transducers, though connected and relational like anything. To give language at least occasional relief from instrumentalization, and to continually disentangle it from distortion and falsity, is to infuse its created energy with a distributed right to be. How we treat language demonstrates our values and also becomes how language treats us.

I think "distributed centrality" to test out a disappearance
of the "margin" (set-aside, far-away, quieted) because a quietude is
also central; it does not have to be experienced or read as
an omission of noise, which itself occupies its own center.
No more margins at all — there aren't any: Both
inflection and innuendo have their centralities.
Every dialectic is abductive, equipoised.

Distributed centrality is part of an attention to Earth rights, the right of everything, not only humans, to exist and thrive on Earth. For many people, Earth rights are theoretically non-controversial: The issue is how to implement and attend them. Relational ecology is what many know to be the case and what is so hard to foster, so there are translations, giving conceptual voices to the voiceless. Such translations can help us hear as we re-perceive the importance of our own approaches and effects.

If everything in an organization is needful, then each part is equally necessary. Something may be harder to do, something easier to do, yet everything is equally central, is happening as importantly as anything else and simultaneously so.

So that butterfly moves, and this letter is sent,
and diatoms aggregate, and a factory stitches fabric
for furniture, and birds call a swift meeting, and a building
is demolished, and cells push into anaphase, and
a camel is loaded with goods, a cloud rearranges in relation
to air and water, a book is published, lava and stone
encourage each other underwater, a body interprets a concept,
a child draws on a wall, a beloved dies, leaves
are clipped for nourishment, a haptic encounter senses itself,
a missile launches—

Yes, so the last one: what of Large Violence? Is that more important, a "limit case"? One act that impacts so many others.

For the centralities that experience and perform anything, that thing is for that time a distributed center that is their center. Any center has its implications and temporality. Waving the "im außermoralischen Sinne" flag of Friedrich Nietzsche's 1873 essay "On Truth and Lie in an Extra-Moral Sense," distributed centrality is not adjudicating comparative moral questions. It's a theory of equality of being, construing being as body, air, place, made things and events, molecular and submolecular, large and small. We might say a bomb that kills all of Earth's surface life absorbs all its centers equally. We might say violence and other cruelties always want to obliterate the other's centrality, and of course we have to pay attention to the things that impact us immediately, and large bad things like bombs insist.

A limit case like bombs does not dis-habilitate the reparative conceptual work that distributed centrality can be part of in our need to articulate concepts that perform in how it feels to be now. It's about equal right to be. Inherent, absolute; divided by judgments, affiliations, power, and other intersecting drives and forces. Thinking about such things relationally, like Charles S. Peirce's thousand cables interlinking, like Édouard Glissant's poetics, ongoingly leaning into these currents of potential question and aspirational theories of human attention.

Umbral Poetics

Years ago I read a story whose genius protagonists created a valley of futurity. Able to manipulate time, they set a remote green valley one second ahead of other planetary life. Outsiders perceived only a vague impenetrable mist, while those inside the valley could see the outer past. The futurity insiders then immersed in a condition of gloriously unleashed ideationalism, encouraging the pursuit of every life-enhancing thought and technique. They created — within their biospheric time border — a life of free-form experiments in sciences and arts.

The COVID-19 pandemic created related valleys, with people tucked into pods of living, communicating outwards via the digitas, for those with access. Walls of time bent around humans variously bubbled, thriving, suffering, trapped, eventually vaccinated or unvaccinated. Even as denizens of privileged regions began to emerge in semi-vaccinated spaces, their bodies existed in different times. Time here stands in for a shunted ontology, such as when we present in digital visuals like media personalities (talking head shot, framed from the shoulders and up, hands on the implements), making our lower bodies — our whole bodies — missing though not absent. The body is phase-interrupted; parts are temporarily put away; simultaneity is foreclosed in favor of a multiplication of time differentials intensified at the level of the body.

For language, which invites us into its ongoing ecologies, this multi-temporality proliferates what I imagine as an umbral poetics, having to do with meaning-position in time. Umbral means "threshold" in Portuguese and Spanish (in Latin, "shadow" or "darkness"); in English, astronomers use it to denote the darkest shadow of an opaque planetary body at the most intense occlusion of its illuminative source. For umbral poetics I'm positing an effect in poetry like an inverse spotlight, casting not light but shadow: a darkbeam, a threshold where meaning quotients position in a temporal latticing, a phase-interruption of lingual identities. The splice-effects make lingual coherence elsewhere but not absent.

A text example of umbral poetics comes in reading two lines of the contemporary poem "Misdenomers" by June Wentland: "A knotting of blizzard and breeze" and "on the linguistic snow line."[1] Reading the whole fifteen-line poem reveals the two lines as catachresis in the poem's ecology. Neither line is sensorily resolvable (not *stimmt*): blizzards and breezes cannot be knotted, much less together, unless "to knot" is read (against its denotation of a static, firm holding) symbolically, displacedly, as a bringing-close-together catachresis. Then it's a knot that cannot be tied with hands, nor seen with supra-lingual normative vision. Neither line is a match with the poem's other states; though their cold weather forces call uniquely across to each other, the two lines' intra-poem symbiotic functions are missing but not absent. Read as spot metaphors, the lines occur separately from the poem's overall image urge; they shine a darkbeam on "missing" potential poetic quotients. Their phase shifts make meaning-time occur in occluded yet evoked, sensory-present, elsewheres.

We know language always trembles plays and moves. Umbral poetics focuses on how meaning-time shifts within the illuminative (denotative, or referenced, or signified) placement of words to a condition in which they perform something that's missing and not absent. Presupposition turns subject to whirl.

1 June Wentland, "Misdenomers," *Poetry Salzburg Review* 37 (2021): 108.

The time of an umbral poetic line (or phrase, or moment) has a denotation itself occluded: Not in spite of darkness with reference to a necessary light, it means instead with the darkness of its possibility, moving in zones like the concept-sensorium of Peirce's Cave. Occluded-meaning sensory-intense phased-time, a moment of umbral poetics.

Similarly when occluded our bodies are sensory-intense and not absent. Our loves are not absent, even when we miss them in other times. In New Zealand/Aotearoa (the latter nation name comes from the Māori words for "cloud" [ao], "white" [tea], "long" [roa]), pandemic life felt like the futurity valley of the story whose summary started this piece. With its early-success elimination strategy, with lockdowns when the virus escaped quarantine, the country often continued with in-person shared events in "real" time. This other-time life was made possible by closed borders — which lingered as the nation negotiated the move from pandemic to endemic — on the other sides of which were missing experiences of bodies, writing, time.

I'm thinking of umbral poetics in the aftereffects of this multi-temporal phase-shift elsewhere-body time. Poetry lines at thresholds without doors or buildings, umbral word-bodies unhinged from habitual instrumental causatives. Poetry time in relation with other global time values. These pandemic years were, in part, a caustic clarifier of human segregations and, for writing, of the lingual paths we build across them — "Words without borders," to cite a poem title in my first (1998) poetry book. In umbral passages, a poem hovers in a darkbeam, a missing but not absent zone of tether. Not only as a query to ocularcentric material constructs but also and especially as a pitch for the positive darks of the living bodies of ongoing words.

Rising up publicly after the pandemic years, Generative Artificial Intelligence can feel like a different version of parallel temporality and occluded process. It can also feel like our aforementioned story-valley, whose activities leave out the consciousness of the rest of the world. Considering umbral poetics for Gen AI poetry, we can think that there is a different segregation, waves of end-user non-information crashing against the AI programming and its consequences. We can think of how technological tools from pens to computing have conditioned times of writing. The mediating techne of typeface and interactive computer framing, for example, float far from their provisional human conception, the living bodies that fashioned them, to their subsequent years of application. Conceptually and materially, all the human bodies uptaking these technologies are linked across times of lingual meaning-making. One of the questions for Generative AI writing is: Does programming inhere, does it sustain, embodiment beyond its instrumentalized code-slingers?

As a fashioned interoperative, Generative AI can be said to have a body only, perhaps, if we imagine its particulates as comparable to our own dispersed exteroceptives, such as unwilled submoleculars transiting through human bodies, autonomic corporeal trajectories, hinged and unhinged social interactivity. But that comparison shows its non-translation in the absences of desire, blood, breath, elemental context chaos and its task-irrelevant alterity forces, and wet and mortal consciousness. The instruction-bound impacts of Generative AI's "intention" structure a diffracted non-somatic evidence in any resulting poem. That import exists for an overtly AI-made poem and, because Gen AI now exists as a writing force, also exists as a genre-aura potential for poems being created by humans with written or spoken language in "hand-writing," stylus or keyboard, or in-person events. The translative conduit of a human body writing in a multi-time—multiple because simultaneity is the temporality of the universe, because all of a person's lived time is available in a creating event, and because context time layers and perfuses that event—is different from the particle recognition evidence of Generative AI collocating a requested lingual facture. The resulting language in either case can offer up legible umbral chances to a motivated interpreter, so the issues include how we attend to and negotiate their differences. Neurologically, humans will anthropomorphize everything they can, which is part of a constant orientation to bring the world into the human, an orientation that readily aligns with resisting the force and integrity—neutral, beneficent, malfeasant, or otherwise—of alterities.

How far can we extend our relation of embodied mind in time with poetic language toward the occlusions of Generative AI? Answering that question has different implications for reading than it does for writing. The occlusions of a Gen AI poem are political, in the foreclosures of policy transparency and of public education about AI, and are structured in a result whose process (mass-derived centripetal recombinance) is opaque. Generative AI's archive derivation recombinatories throw up evacuatedly positioned remixes of lingual histories: The living language of those recombinatories is both missing *and* absent. Bodies in contexts write with language, in surface marking and in digital literatures; Gen AI has within its processes neither body nor contexts.

At the same time, reading a Gen AI–produced poem to perceive umbral poetics possibilities can happen, if it's desired, from the side of living interpreters in worlds of bodies and other elements and of moment-simultaneity dialectics. Umbral poetics includes time as wish and lack, lingual bodies (lexical and bio-mortal) held apart and together, living readers conjuring on different sides of many kinds of borders. One might gorgeously enjoy interpreting an AI generated poem for its digital alterity, its social mass energy, and its untethering of meaning-position in time. One might not wish to hand over so much of the joy of actually writing poetry with the simultaneity of the body and the non-encompassable energies of its relations with contexts and languages.

Withness

> I always sink into the hollow spaces between the fractured text. I gush out from the hollow and get dispersed with other things that have also gushed out from the hollow. The dispersed things break once again. This doesn't mean that the text of my body, the text of my language is prophetic or mysterious. If it were mysterious, I could never do the work of fracturing the space of the real.
>
> — Kim Hyesoon, "Space"[1]

1

Withness names sustained closeness with the event of one's interpretive reading, where "event" designates a complex including the work — book, lingual weaving, movement piece, poem — the context, and the interpreter's articulating response. Withness turns away from potential power and distance stances of exegetical criticality and toward an attention with the engaged art event, an attention that does not seek to be somewhere other than in relation. Some interpretive systems or critiques have a telos directed away from the reading event at hand. Such a telos

1 Kim Hyesoon, "Space," in *Princess Abandoned: Essays,* trans. Don Mee Choi (Tinfish Press, 2012).

might well be valuable, even necessary, in some distanced criticality. Withness is simply different; it's a staying-with. In doing so, withness engages the relation of creative and critical work. Typically presumed to be one of diremption rather than isomorphic difference, that relation hovers, for this essay, in its generative egalitarian energies.

I started thinking about withness as focused on the beginning of a thought: I wanted to experiment with a deliberate turnaround from treating thought as beginning in resistance. Resistance was possibly how I learned to recognize thought, and it's a bearing that appeals to anti-authoritarianism. Yet "thinking against" a work, especially in academic or public-intellect criticality, sometimes posits interpretation as needing to respond correctively, or in a complementarity of lack. For example, someone reads a work or attends a performance and feels compelled to write back when they disagree (corrective) or when they feel that the work or performance has left something out (complementarity of lack). This stance can associate with contrastive distinction, a term for describing how a work is not like this or that prior work, especially insofar as it treats of similar materials or topics. In its judgmental forms, contrastive distinction characterizes many critical procedures, which is understandable for cultures that value presentations of "new" material that is often considered to supersede "old" material. Perhaps it characterizes many modern developed-country critical cultures, given several ideational histories. Such histories include science-inflected work testing ever "better" hypotheses; progressivism (either trying to improve something or assuming that changed ideas are *necessarily* improving, an assumption allied in turn with Discovery Narratives); and property ideas, which hold that something is owned in a way that precludes others from owning it.

Contrastive distinction can be helpful when it's in dialogue, when it shows its demurrals without prejudice toward the work under critique. A problem arises when the "new" critical argument seeks to be necessarily equated with *improved* material. Can we have a changed conversation about the performed meaning of a work, a conversation without assuming that newly-appearing work—whether "creative" or "critical"—needs to improvingly supersede others, prior or potential? Can we have interpretation without power-claims? At this point we're considering the aesthetics of works rather than their ethics; it's understandable when interpreters wish to condemn unethical aspects of an art work or a critical response, even granting that ethics is not an entirely neutral perfusion of elements, beyond obvious examples of cruelty.

Which brings up the issue of kindness and how we might think of it as constative in withness procedures relating to an art work. Among its potentials, interpretive kindness can co-support the response and the work: hover alterities alongside each other, be with in otherness. The term constative helps this essay demur from the effacement of the subject implied by the term altruism, especially in its use to describe a best kindness. To be interpretively *with,* in the perspectives of this essay, is kinder than to disappear. In withness, constative kindness involves a fostering re-framing that exponentializes the artwork's potential by adding to its dimensions with other kindred dimensions. Thus kindness, here, evokes and generates difference within and in relation to the honored "same"—the body—of the interpreted work, relinquishing urges to improve, replace, or correct.

Another issue associated with a corrective stance is exegetical hermeneutics, which value getting something *right* because of the trailing residue of canonical versus heretical interpretation in what's become known, over centuries, as "arts and humanities." As a term, for example, "close reading" (pronouncing "close" like a *close* ['klōs], an enclosed area such as a clearing in a forest) names a disciplinary habit of reading to stabilize elements of an imaginative work, and to stabilize or even to "close" (pronounced as in closing a door) an interpretation of those elements. Habits of close reading have most often been putatively clarifying, like authoritative spectacles designed to focus and freeze-frame a reading in relation to an interpreted work, keeping very separate from the critical reader's body acting with the work, breathing around it, touching its forms. With different proposed values, withness wants to stay with the work it's responding to. Its value is the opposite of critical distance. It wants critical closeness.

Yet is closeness always kind? Is withness *kind?* It is, arguably, being *in kind:* drawing together with and fostering the alterity of what's encountered. That is legible as a constative angle of kindness. In "Ethics of the Infinite," philosopher Emmanuel Levinas distinguishes saying from the said: "Language as saying is an ethical openness to the other."[2] This ongoingness of saying, its anti-teleological gerund activity, is for Levinas constitutive of ethical articulation. Extending that intertextual relation, withness is theoretically unending. One of its tasks as an interpretive strategy is to show its designs in a temporary frame — an essay or performance, for example — that can be said to stay conceptually open even when the frame is removed.

If withness has this kind of ethical "saying" movement as part of its practice, then *recurrence* is a way to describe that movement. In contrast to habits associated with (though not necessary to) close reading, recurrence wants to activate elements of an art work without stabilizing them, to approach and reapproach without desiring an end goal. In that sense withness recurrence is something like the opposite of telos. Not to have a reading encounter to get somewhere else, but to have an encounter that stays in relation to the continuing alterity of the work and of one's engagement. Recurrence also invokes the spelling "re-currents" as in the circulation of fluid, its always-reoccurring movement, and the circulation of electricity, also ongoing given source and circuitry to be so, and thus recurrence links with the embodied theory of membranism considered elsewhere in this book. Which matters because withness, too, posits ongoing awareness of one's embodied interpretation with the body of the interpreted work.

---

2 Emmanuel Levinas, "Ethics of the Infinite," in *Dialogues with Contemporary Continental Thinkers: The Phenomenological Heritage: Paul Ricoeur, Emmanuel Levinas, Herbert Marcuse, Stanislas Breton, Jacques Derrida,* ed. Richard Kearney (Manchester University Press, 1984), 65.

And yet if recurrence were to be the simple opposite of telos, one could think that recurrence were just like telos in reverse. So as usual I need more languages. One useful polydimensional image of attention involvement is what I call Peirce's Cave (see the essay of that title earlier in this book), construed from Charles S. Peirce's vivid portrayal of sensorily-transacted conceptual ongoingness, a portrayal he offers as a way to imagine his theory of continuity.[3] Peirce illustrates continuity as sensory (haptic, olfactory, non-ocularcentric, i.e., completely dark) bubbles that crucially cease to exist as finitudes when they're fully engaged. Here, Peirce's unbounded continuity helps me draw an image of withness recurrence. The act of withness reading—reading art in a wide sense, including experiencing sculpture and hearing soundwork, and more—maintains aspects of continuance that are repeatingly close with the event/work being interpreted. If withness touches on alterity ethics in reading response, its recurrence touches on guiding attention streams, whether dialectical currents or something else, continually back toward the work being read. The drive is to get as close as aptly possible to a constative empathy with the work of one's art encounter. In that empathy is also an ethical move to disrupt an approach by way of power.

The word "power" indicates an ethical reason, the word "distance" a structural reason, motivating withness. Withness strives to undo a stance toward the work that presumes a need to clarify or correct. Instead, the ethically-motivated posture of withness is to co-illuminate, to consider the same dimensions from close-difference angles. As the movement aspect of withness, recurrence wants to activate, as though touching again and again various coordinates of a dimensionalized geometry, the parts of a work in order to sense and articulate what a reading illuminates. To adapt Peircean terms for withness recurrence: one shifts abductively within continuities of relation. In this sense

3 See Charles Sanders Peirce, "The Logic of Continuity," in *Reasoning and the Logic of Things: The Cambridge Conferences Lectures of 1898*, ed. Kenneth Laine Ketner (Harvard University Press, 1993).

critical withness and recurrence replace telos with circulating whirl. The closeness and hovering of withness might make withness sound too complicit with and insufficiently perpendicular to the work being interpreted, as in, "what's the point; what are we doing here?"

Yet the conditions of any encounter always preclude utter identity, which is part of the point of the Kim Hyesoon epigraph at this essay's start. Another Peircean context for withness is an adaptation of his term secondness: the radical closeness of withness is akin to lingering in the relational encounter of secondness. Such lingering is not an overt part of Peirce's vision for secondness, which describes the dynamic theoretical zone where firstness meets another firstness, arising meanwhile and necessarily within the thought conditions of what he terms thirdness, also called continuity. Withness, then, describes a move, an expansion not offered as an improvement, within the imaginal possibilities of Peirce's tripartite figure for being (firstness), relation (secondness), and generality or continuity (thirdness). The point of imagining secondness here, having emphasized the continuity of Peirce's Cave, is that withness involves recurrent *encounter*. The mutual non-contiguity of secondness supports a description of withness as not about becoming one with the art being considered. Neither the art nor the interpreter needs to unify in order to stay with. The interpreter does not need to become of the same kind in order to foster kindred, empathy-oriented, readings. Again, kindness can be constative. Secondness is a reminder of the value of continually recognizing the alterity of oneself as interpreter, of the interpretive processes, and of the work being accorded attention.

In this complex encounter, withness also seeks to democratize, to treat with fostering entropy, the values accorded to so-called creative and so-called critical work. Such democratization can be seen as bringing everything into the status of primary text, recognizing that neither creative nor critical work has a position of superiority in relation. That recognition is another point of starting this essay with the Hyesoon epigraph. As the interpreter becomes a text in engaging a text (using "text" as a moniker for different kinds of signs), what Hyesoon terms "fracture" is also the context of openness, in which withness co-operates. In this sense withness is part of efforts to undo the epistemologically bracketed status of the creative and the relegated secondary status of the critical, which usually comes back to haunt its desired other by behaving as though it sees more clearly than the creative. Withness is part of other efforts that many people make to understand art-involved sign systems as co-indexical, as co-relational.

Withness can be critiqued as both insufficiently separated, from a point of view that values what it calls critical distance, and excessively close, from a point of view that values singularity, the firstness or unbreachable and non-paraphraseable being, of the art work. The latter point is especially clear when we consider the radical singularity and strange arising of any subject, work, and context. It takes an effort to hold that singularity and arising in the same breath as the urge to critical withness. That effort reflects a tension between default (elemental) and deliberate (socially constructed) cultural organizing: By default, events arise and we act with slippage among us. Deliberately, we turn toward each other and configure how to behave, how to be habitus beings. Amidst these slippages, withness is a critical social effort worth making. It shines a light on kindness as an aspect of the articulation of deliberate community: One accepts the granular facts of radical singularity as contiguous and entropic rather than separating. Édouard Glissant's *métissage* become pervasive.

2

Withness is one conceptual tool in the context of a different and heretofore dominant criticality that supposes the virtue of distance from the examined work or that understands such distance to be unavoidable. We cannot *be* that other, we cannot ontologically or otherwise perfectly accord with or perfectly become something other. For that matter, we often study events or works that we don't want to get too close to. Withness wants to pull the strain as close as possible to the interpreted work without pretending that distance is not part of our nows and histories, but insisting that critical relation can be with, and can perceive in particular ways by being so.

The possibilities of *witness* reside within both the word (wit[h]ness) and concept of withness: reading as witnessing, the documentary resonance of our interpretations. The testimonial timeliness of withness is myriad. It includes the body rights movement, global upheavals of migration and refugees and transnational identities, aspirations to unbuckle the hold that capital product values have on living values, the efforts and effects of Indigenous and gender studies mapping intersectionality into present history, our attunement to Earth rights, our pandemic empathy. All these events have us witnessing each other, and parts of our responsive tarrying can be—arguably many parts already are, as with documentary work—carried out as withness.

My initial thinking about withness arose around 2010, and I gave withness talks in the US in 2014 in relation to the work of Laura Riding and of Leslie Scalapino. Looking around while composing this essay, revisiting materials and extending outward, I find evidence of others thinking along the same lines then too. And why not: Retexting is as old as any discourse making. Yet it's a curious matter, if it is the case that withness-type readings were burgeoning during the last decade. For they are still received with contention, as I experience in responses to my discussions of withness. They remind me of responses to my doctoral work on deformative criticism in the 1990s. There's an expressed sense that a reading ought to conjure dispassionate ideation, make a new product, and lead somewhere else, and a vague misgiving that withness isn't adequately new or "original" in its results.

What might withness readings look like? Retexting is at least partly related: Retext is in direct engagement with, remaking or reshaping, the specific materials of prior works. Cento poems, for example, whose appropriative ingredients are reallocations of lines from external sources. Dante Alighieri retexting Virgil and Harryette Mullen ("My honeybunch's peepers are nothing like neon") retexting Shakespeare ("My mistress' eyes are nothing like the sun") swerve their sources honorifically and politically without exact resemblance.[4] Perhaps retexting is part of a more general category; perhaps it features overlapping similitudes with aspects of withness. As Mark Amsler explains in *Affective Literacies,* using for example Abelard's reordering of extant texts to compose *Sic et Non* (circa 1120 CE), retexting forms part of the historical evidence of creative makings as remakings.[5] Yet re-makings are typically not set up as withness interpretations. They are other things, performance moves recognizable as partaking of prior instances of those moves, texts that hanker after precursors, like Selina Tusitala Marsh's "Fast Talking PI" (2012) imitates the form of Anne Waldman's poem "Fast Speaking Woman" (1975), like Robert Glück's fiction *Margery Kempe* (1994) beckons, through almost complete difference, to the medieval visionary text *The Booke of Margery Kempe* (manuscript circa 1440 CE).[6] Kempe's book itself is the result of collaborations with its mostly unnamed scribes, whose textual empathies might be considered close to creative translations—from Kempe's tellings to the scribes' writings—and, even, close to acts of withness.

Potentiality archives can foster the growth of withness makings. Motion Bank, out of Germany, can be seen to encourage the perception of choreographic signatures in relation to retexting in dance: One may go to the "bank" and pick up signatures to replay. This archive availability could lead to withness movement work, were one to find a choreographic signature and stay, and stay, in kind with it to make a responsive work that shadow-

4 Harryette Mullen, "Dim Lady," in *Sleeping with the Dictionary* (University of California Press, 2002), 20.

5 See Mark Amsler, *Affective Literacies: Writing and Multilingualism in the Late Middle Ages* (Brepols, 2011).

6 See Selina Tusitala Marsh, *Fast Talking PI* (Auckland University Press, 2012); Anne Waldman, *Fast Speaking Woman: Chants and Essays* (City Lights, 2001); Robert Glück, *Margery Kempe* (High Risk Books, 1994); and Margery Kempe, *The Booke of Margery Kempe*, BL, ADD MS 61823.

replays, that builds out empathetic variations with, the energies of the starting signature. Motion Bank's first building phase was 2010–2013, again indicating some time-specific 2010s intensity of interest in repurposive archiving.[7] The present essay is ad hoc in these speculations, resistant to presumptions of totalizing, yet there are many cultural ponderings that come under the zeitgeist light of retext and withness, approaches that encourage the making of pastiche works and open software, for example, as well as repurposive and communal work.

The poet Anthony Vahni Capildeo's communal performance texts in response to the poet Martin Carter are a good example of withness. Capildeo's 2019 book *Skin Can Hold* devotes a long section, titled "Astronomer of Freedom," to collaborative performance work begun in 2014 (another example of withness zeitgeist) with Jeremy Hardingham, Paige Smeaton, Hope Doherty, and others.[8] The section sets out a poetics of that Carter-response work that includes explicitly withness-sounding language:

> [I]mmersive experiments became the context for events including reading of full texts alongside what I call "syntax poems" gleaned from them. The syntax poems offer traces of a way of being *with and inside* Carter's poetry. They are not the kind of independent verbal artefacts called responses or reworkings.[9]

In a deformance-like beginning, "Astronomer of Freedom" sets out the starting poem from Martin Carter, "I Am No Soldier," and then provides examples of six collaborative poems that draw from Carter's words and topical energies. These collaboratively authored syntax poems feature looping, treating, echoing, altering punctuation and layout, and stutter-torquing anaphora.

7 Motion Bank, "About," http://motionbank.org/en/content/about.html.

8 Vahni Capildeo, *Skin Can Hold* (Carcanet, 2019), 69–98.

9 Capildeo, *Skin Can Hold*, 71. Emphasis in original. The book's acknowledgments cite the source of the Martin Carter poem "I Am No Soldier" as Martin Carter, *University of Hunger: Collected Poems and Selected Prose*, ed. Gemma Robinson (Bloodaxe, 2006). See Capildeo, *Skin Can Hold*, 118.

The number "IV" syntax poem comes across as overtly deformative: it "simply" culls, pulls a few choice words (forty-three, in fourteen lines) from Carter's poem (which has 519 words—I counted—in sixty-one lingual lines and six interlinear blank lines) to lay emphasis upon them alternatively, to draw out and sing certain of the Carter poem's words. The start of syntax poem "VI," too, is procedurally deformative: Using only the first words of each Carter strophe, it sings:

> Wherever…
> O…
> But…
> There…
> It…
> I…
> O…[10]

As a creative witness to Carter, these syntax poems are an example of withness in action. In the notes after the syntax poems, using the plural pronoun to include the performers who worked with Capildeo, the text says "We felt that the short lines were voluminous."[11] That might be paraphrased to mean that the short lines had the potential to be and conceptually already were more than they were, and could be drawn out sympathetically in withness extensions and variations. Such potentiality honoring indicates how overt manifestations of internal *difference*—an instantiation of felt potential as something other-than even as it's also-with—are a constitutive feature of withnessing.

Characteristics of deformance are present in the critical angles of "Astronomer of Freedom." Its withness is also legible as deformance insofar as *Skin Can Hold* explains its syntax poems and the collaborative performance work in overtly critical—hermeneutic, heuristically exportable—terms.[12] Even

10 Capildeo, *Skin Can Hold*, 85.
11 Ibid., 91.
12 See ibid., 71–75, 90–98.

as it also insists on what I would call its withness energy, its hovering: "Our working materials […are] not given as a definitive guide or academic interpretation."[13] As withness readings, definitiveness is not part of the interpretive ethics of the syntax poems. The collaborative nature of the work in this case is legible as a version of withness that expands the urge to stay with by keeping the reading self open with other reading selves. Intensifying the ingredients of openness with the interpreting and interpreted other.

In a work time-coincident with the start of Capildeo's Carter collaborations (2014), I gave a withness talk-performance for a conference at Naropa (a US teaching and learning institution).[14] Working with Leslie Scalapino's book-with-images *The Dihedrons Gazelle-Dihedrals Zoom* (2010), I played a recording of my voice reading two excerpts from *Dihedrons* while I also spoke about the book's figurations and showed an enlarged slide of one of its images (a black and white etching by Kiki Smith; see fig. 5.1 below).[15] The delivery featured oral retransmission alongside reflective commentary alongside visual co-presentation, to bring creative and critical reading into convergent present occurrence. I was conscious of performing, in part, an honorific remix from *Dihedrons* in that multi-dimensional public reading. I was also conscious of bringing into a public sensorium a conversation between Scalapino and me, a conversation partly written in (unpublished) manuscript forms, part of which I'd seen and partly not. The conversation had been cut short by her death in 2010, hence that example of withness was unfolding temporally close to my grief. I had already written two pieces on Scalapino's work, one published, one as yet unpublished, and Leslie and I were literary friends when she was alive. She brought out my first poetry book *The Seven Voices* (1998) with

13 Ibid., 96.

14 Lisa Samuels, "Withness and *The Dihedrons Gazelle-Dihedrals Zoom*," performance-talk for Jack Kerouac School of Disembodied Poetics, Naropa University, Boulder, CO, USA, October 2014.

15 See Leslie Scalapino, *The Dihedrons Gazelle-Dihedrals Zoom* (Post-Apollo Press, 2010).

her O Books press, and we performed and presented together. Perhaps art-friendship was part of why I thought to articulate withness at that time, and why I think of it in terms of kindness here.

Capildeo's collaborative work with Martin Carter's writing, as a differently committed set of withness illuminations, comes out of a shared history and experience of Caribbean realities and a desire to perform the intensity of Carter's work multi-modally: "to re-present Carter's world-work in ways that would be recognisable to readers who have grown up with his words and are linked to his region, yet which those entirely unfamiliar with it would be free to enter."[16] In the honorific stance we can perceive in these text-present and unheard performances ("unheard" because the Carter and Scalapino examples cannot be fully performed in codical or online pages), withness finds part of its source in an illuminating confluence of post-structuralism and post-colonialism. Or, as it seems sensible to call it, epicolonialism, since we remain in propinquity with the colonial, whose evidences and ideologies are far from post.

In terms of post-structuralism, withness is a quite literal strategic application of, for example, the "writerly" (*scriptible*) traced in Roland Barthes's *S/Z*.[17] Withness brings together a belief in the freedom of co-imagining a work—bearing in mind the ethics of Nietzsche's *außermoralischen Sinn* (extra-moral sense, from his 1873 essay)—with the need to cherish the continually reborn other.[18] Bringing things forward in their illuminative complexity is one aspect of our scholarly acts, and withness might be seen as more on the scholarship than on the critical end of academically-homed practices. Perhaps withness is another version of the argument that scholarship is always also critical, theoretical: never neutral. Scholarship makes room in kind for the works it responds with.

---

16 Capildeo, *Skin Can Hold*, 73.

17 Roland Barthes, *S/Z*, trans. Richard Miller and Richard Howard (Hill and Wang, 1974).

18 See Friedrich Nietzsche, "On Truth and Lie in an Extra-Moral Sense," in *The Portable Nietzsche*, ed. and trans. Walter Kaufmann (Viking, 1954).

In terms of epicolonialism, inasmuch as US race work is an effort to shift out of colonial violence relations, some of poet Duriel E. Harris's work also evinces withness. Harris, whose poetry provides one of the starting epigraphs for this book, was part of my aforementioned 2014 Naropa panel, titled "Withness: thought-start in creative-critical practice"; and here is another art friendship that started in multi-modal poetics. Our panel also included poets Megan Kaminski and Marthe Reed. The panel proposal we wrote together over email describes Harris discussing her "Thingification" performance as engaging "ritualized refusal as an interrogation of the radical embodiment and radical disembodiment engendered by thing-ification, here taken as the annihilating force at the core of all oppressions (Scarry, Césaire)"; Kaminski speaking to a "poetics of permeability (absorption and embrace) [...] dissolving boundaries between self and other" in her practice and in the writings of Melissa Buzzeo, Renee Gladman, Bhanu Kapil, and Sherwin Bitsui; and Reed addressing "the with-ness of dissonance: poetics of observation, intimacy, and documentary in Whalen, Berssenbrugge, Santos Perez, and her own practice, mind/body at play in the human/other-than-human wilderness." Our panel's ethos, in relation with the Dis/embodied Poetics conference we joined at Naropa, was one of gathering and supporting, of encouraging each other in kind and with kindness.

Harris composed a follow-up piece, "Let Us Consider Sarah: Notes Toward Withness, Affect, Making, and the US Imaginary; or, You Better Work Bitch, This Is Flesh .... This Is The Prize," which brought together some of our panel thinking with more insights into her solo show *Thingification*. Harris reflects on the part of her *Thingification* performance that gives voice to a nineteenth-century "mammy" enslaved figure she calls Sarah, depicted in an historical caricature drawing:

> In live performance, the interior of the book, turned out such that the mammy—a determined fiction awakened and animated by the song in scene one, emerges, embodied. Mammy's racialized exaggerations arous[e] Sarah, the ghost of a

> formerly enslaved woman, who forces her way into presence, speaking a truth long held silent during her life in captivity.[19]

Out of the pictorial graphemes of Sarah, a historical depiction, really a representative caricature, of actual persons, Harris renders present voicedness and co-embodiment. In a way that underscores the constatives of withness's kindness, Harris is being with. Her kindness in embodying the different personas in her solo show demonstrates that "kind" is not limited to warmth in its closeness. To channel such a mammy figure is to feel hurt and to open to that hurt, as well as to honor and commemorate. To be kind is also to be in kind, to make as kind, to form kindred percepts drawing on the beautiful and the difficult.

3

At this moment of writing, I'm listening to my earlier recording from Scalapino's book *The Dihedrons Gazelle-Dihedrals Zoom.* The recording has two overlapping strands, and the talk-performance itself thus featured three interweaving audio aspects, since I was also speaking a set of points distinct from the *Dihedrons* recording. In geometry, a dihedron is a figure formed by two intersecting planes; dihedrals are the angle between those two planes. In Scalapino's book title, the compound word *Gazelle-Dihedrals* puts a land animal in the angle. Similarly though not identically, in my construction of that critical withness performance I felt my humanimal capacity interposing with the prospects of Scalapino's references. Her book title also brings temporal movement in relation with its appositive compound noun: The animalized geometry verbs to "zoom," both as a photographic lens close-focuses and as an entity performs a very fast running, swimming, or flying movement. In

19 Duriel E. Harris, "Let Us Consider Sarah: Notes Toward Withness, Affect, Making, and the US Imaginary, or, You Better Work, Bitch: This Is Flesh.... This Is The Prize," *Evening Will Come* 55 (2015), https://www.thevolta-org.zulaufdesign.com/ewc55-dharris-p1.html.

the updates that change always summons, which is part of the context-sensitivity of the dynamics of art, we can also now read the verb as referring to the interactive digital platform Zoom. A platform whose apparent immediacy and closeness both delivers and forestalls, in pandemic-intensified digitality and continued post-pandemic online habits, equalities of intimacy and communication.

Scalapino is a writer who was skeptical about the possibility of one event speaking for another. I take this to be one reason her works sometimes articulate an absolute non-relation between writing and lived experience. For Scalapino this non-relation, this radical singularity and separateness, also meant the importunity of a critical approach to her writings, which she views as speaking themselves entirely, with an adequacy that needs nothing other than reading/observation. I take her stance seriously and associate it with one of the problems this essay addresses: habits of treating critical acts as a kind of acid wash thrown on to creative acts to "clarify" them, to explain them. As though art were mute, such critical "washing" might be supposed to make art able to "speak."

We know that relation always involves alterity: No one is a flat witness to other makings. Engagement loosens boundaries. Every event interacted with becomes another version of itself, as this essay's Hyesoon epigraph suggests. A withness reading reflects a stance I also take seriously: that acts of responsive writing can engage co-imaginingly, without presuming objectivity, with a work of art. If we do not have dialogue, then we have parallel streams of action that are not permitted to mingle because the singularity of each forestalls mingling. Individual integrity is a good that helps people break out from following. But if event integrity treats dialogue as only presumptuous or exclusively other and separate, that reinforces the silos that institutional and wider cultural life continually patrol. The course of the particular can meet other courses without terminally traumatic dissolution or presumptive falsity. Otherwise we are encouraged to be lonely, disrupted, and separate—and we become more susceptible to the sheens of givenism, the faux-coherence surfaces that self-appointed dominant cultures want to assert as "real."

Another way to put this is that withness moves beyond hovering in radical singularity to a belief in the efficacy of differential community. Peirce, who seems to be one of this essay's guiding philosophical angels (I'm also re-reading Édouard Glissant's books *Traité du tout-monde* and *Poetics of Relation*), wrote about the necessity of a community of thinkers to test the possibility of overlap in modes of thinking and in specific views (see for example his 1868 essay "Some Consequences of Four Incapacities").[20] His communal emphasis has been differently taken up across the subsequent 150+ years of considering how to live thinking inside the physical and political realities of split atoms and atomized consumers and intensified individuality. And also how to live thinking inside the global, which Glissant's ethics of opacity so saliently addresses.

(here I let the recording play for a while)

The unheard sonics that accompany this essay perform with the polyvocal dihedrals and with the images that co-perform *The Dihedrons Gazelle-Dihedrals Zoom:* fourteen images, two appearing twice (from Jess Collins, Masami Teraoka, Margaret Hofbeck, and Kiki Smith), open the 111 subtitled parts to exponents of representation. The artists and the images are joined with Scalapino's language. The "Author's Note" indicates that the images are meant not as inspirations or subjects of the writing. Instead they are reported as chosen after the writing to be "linked to passages of text that show the same reality" or, in one case, to show what the author was visually remembering at the

20 Édouard Glissant, *Traité du tout-monde: Poétique IV* (Gallimard, 1997); Édouard Glissant, *Poetics of Relation,* trans. Betsy Wing (University of Michigan Press, 1997); and Charles Sanders Peirce, "Some Consequences of Four Incapacities," in *Peirce on Signs: Writings on Semiotic by Charles Sanders Peirce,* ed. James Hoopes (University of North Carolina Press, 1991).

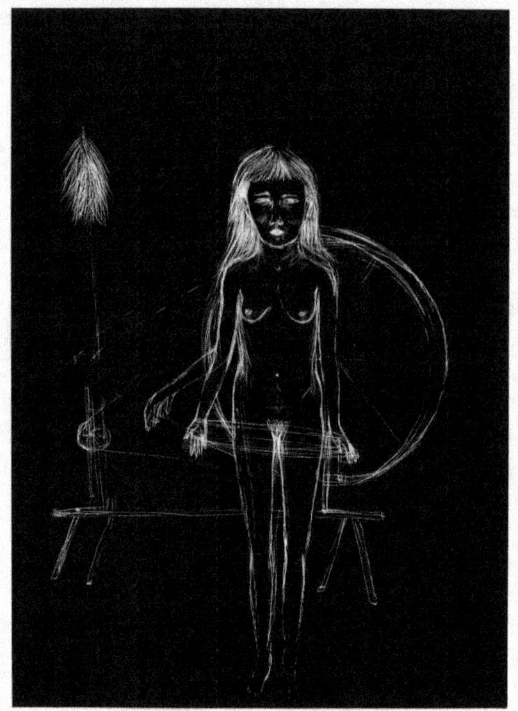

Fig. 5.1. Kiki Smith, *Spinster Series* 1 (2002), ©Kiki Smith, courtesy of Pace Gallery.

time of writing.[21] The book draws the images into a collaborative field of composition with the words: We can see them as graphemes that dimensionalize, because they "show the same reality as," the words. They are similar in kind, though constatively, without pre-interpretation.

Consider the image opposite the one-page section titled "Gemsbok" (see *The Dihedrons Gazelle-Dihedrals Zoom,* 59) (fig. 5.1). This image is from Kiki Smith's *Spinster Series,* made

21 Scalapino, *The Dihedrons Gazelle-Dihedrals Zoom,* vii.

in a "[t]wo plate, double printed iris" process.[22] The drawn lines are white signage on a black background, the contrast vivifying both extremes and also inverse mirroring the coterminous black words on the white page. The parallel co-being of the etched lines relate with the exponentializing visions of the words and also with the body of the reader joining the text in the performance of reading. The girl-and-woman stance is beside and with the spinning wheel and its threads: Literally, the arm image is etched as by her side holding the skein and also as reaching further over to touch the spun thread. The etched spinning threads are filaments holding, and being held by, and being spun out from the hair of the female image.

These images overtly associate with fate, the spinning wheel that looms out destinies put into motion with words, re-threading their inversionability and self-emission. Yet the depictive co-occurrence undoes the habitual univocality of fatalism because no one thing has to be; no option undermines the other posited options. Staying with simultaneity, the unclothed-body girl image mixes as and with an older lined-faced female image. Alongside these engineered chiaroscuro thread positions and multi-stage human development depictions, the book's copy of Kiki Smith's artwork evinces more general palimpsestic possibilities of also-versions of the image(s), in cloudy omissions of vague rubbed-out white.

The words nearby the Kiki Smith image say nothing about a spinning wheel. The image embodies whiteness spinning while the lingual "white ice" slips "the base runner." The base runner and "the gelechild" are running and freezing in the horizon plane of the nearby words. Meanwhile "Cromorne," the last part of the book, is declared to be "happening at the same time as events in the main body of *The Dihedrons Gazelle-Dihedrals Zoom*. Throughout simultaneous with the latter's extended stream."[23]

22 Ibid., 58–59. Scalapino's "Art Credits" on page 164 give this citation: "*page* 59, Kiki Smith. *Spinster Series I*, 2002. Two plate, double printed iris, 20 × 14.625 inches, edition of 24. Photograph courtesy of Pace Editions, Inc., New York. © Kiki Smith."

23 Scalapino, *The Dihedrons Gazelle-Dihedrals Zoom*, 131.

Curiously, it is possible to think of Scalapino's presentation of diremptive or distant simultaneity—that is, one part of a book claimed as happening in the same zone as another, separate, part of the same book—as a feature of a work that invites further perceptions of its alterity energies and potentials. That is, as open to withness readings at visual-image and at lingual levels. Perhaps the overt lexical intertextuality of Scalapino's declared compositional process for *Dihedrons,* its writing-through of *Random House Webster's Unabridged Dictionary,* intensifies the legibility of its openness to fractals of the semiotic real.

An experimental work of writing might be called writerly, in Roland Barthes's terms; we might wish to say that writerly strategies can be interpretive in addition to being constitutive, can resemble deconstructive and deformance and other co-performative strategies brought to any type of text. In Scalapino's *Dihedrons,* the multiple signs occur with each other, not self-withnessing so much as co-occurring polytransfiguration. It isn't far-to-fetch, though, to read Scalapino as putting her art and Kiki Smith's art into a conceptual ex post facto withness relation, since the images are said to be "linked to passages of text that show the same reality."[24] A withness reading is an in-kind performance brought to an alterity by another alterity. Maybe withness can be also the tactic of a detail moment, a breath inside other responses to a work of art.

Such a co-articulation is not the same thing as reading aloud a text on some significant day, such as a publication anniversary, though one could view that as an embodied mirror withnessing, and as a kindness and honoring. Nor is it quite the same as the ready re-enlivening of told language in oral histories or other adaptations of known material such as performance or re-enactment—but this category comes closer, since such re-enlivening always performs difference with the given materials. Barthes's resignifying of "Sarrasine" in *S/Z,* as I've suggested, seems legible as critical withness. As these comments mean to indicate, withness is a critical bearing more than a delimited set

24 Ibid., vii.

of procedures. Maybe withness also resembles, without being identical to, the work of translation. The kinds of trans-media, intertextual, and intra-text connecting we see in the *Dihedrons* book, and in the 2014 withness reading of it, call to mind the emphasis on the in-between of translation theory—attending not so much to source or target languages as to the transitively tethering co-linguals. Withness interpretation can be a swerving translation in relation to the engaged art work. The comparison is especially vivid with regard to current experimental translations generated in groups such as Outranspo, a group that includes the writer Lily Robert-Foley, whose critical-creative works can be seen as intersecting with withness impulses. Robert-Foley's book *m* (2013) writes through and around Samuel Beckett's *L'Innommable/The Unnamable* (1953).[25] Self-described as a "poetry-critique-collage," *m* is another zeitgeist example of how the 2010s were making space for interpretive work that bears family resemblances with the motives of withness.

In writing this essay I realize that my response to attending the choreographer Tru Paraha's work *blackOut* (2018) was also written in withness.[26] In place of assessing the performance, the review records a felt version of experiencing it, beginning with what reads like withness discourse:

> Describing a multi-dimensional kinetic work that unfolds over a set time invariably runs up against the limits of description. The answer to "the meaning of the work" is, arguably, the work. So a response like this one is not the work but seeks to be in descriptive relation to some of its chances.[27]

In that case, withness can arguably be read as in the frame of descriptive criticism, beckoning to Gertrude Stein's approach to

25 See Lily Robert-Foley, *m* (Corrupt Press, 2013).

26 Tru Paraha, *blackOut: part 2 of a choreographic trilogy on darkness*, Auckland, Aotearoa/New Zealand, 2018.

27 Lisa Samuels, "Illuminating the Limits," *Theatreview*, February 20, 2018, https://www.theatreview.org.nz/production/blackout-part-2-of-a-choreographic-trilogy-on-darkness/#illuminating-the-limits.

being acquainted with description.[28] To be acquainted is to be in familiarity with, without being necessarily in the family or friendship or workship group of what you're describing. Stein's own practices of swerving from discursive norms toward intimate interiorities of what's being described — as though a meal were to be explained by citing only the sounds of its ingredients — is an example of phenomenologically-oriented withness in creative documentary writing. To take encounter *as a work* and to redistribute its elements as an art is a version of documentary criticality very close to the guts of withness. For us to be acquainted is also to be in humanimal relation: In the wet electric of thinking as we respond with each other's work, we can hear the word withness as having "wetness" in its enounced and operative resonance. The wetness of sweat, eyes, and ears, the beating heart and pulsing mind reading works to co-multiply the alterity of their being and our being with them.

28 Gertrude Stein, *An Acquaintance with Description* (Seizin Press, 1929).

Poetry and the Problem of Beauty

Beauty is a problem for poetry because we no longer imagine beauty as a serious way of knowing. But it is. Beauty wedges into the artistic space a structure for continuously imagining what we do not know. This claim reverses Percy Bysshe Shelley's formulation of poetry as the place where we "imagine that which we know,"[1] which presumes that creativity translates knowledge into imagination. Our general lack of response to beauty—at least in critical literature—results, among other things, from an intuitive sense that beauty defies such translation. We can neither measure the knowledge that Shelley's imagination turns to beauty, nor can we translate that beauty back into its components of knowledge and imagination. That's because beauty is a non-conceptual way of knowing. We have developed, implicitly, a sense of the non-conceptual in artistic beauty, but we have not much developed sympathetic theories that will allow us to discuss beauty in these terms. We still largely imagine beauty in Shelley's terms, and so we think that those parts of beauty that resist the translation back to knowledge are uselessly private and uncommunicative. In fact, they are what beauty "knows":

1 Percy Bysshe Shelley, "A Defence of Poetry," in *The Critical Tradition: Classic Texts and Contemporary Trends*, ed. David H. Richter (Bedford/St. Martin's, 2007), 361.

that knowledge is also, perhaps most importantly, what we do not know. Forms of beauty are resistant structures, imaginative structures that present an impenetrable model of the unknown. Beauty is therefore endlessly talk-inspiring, predictive rather than descriptive, dynamic rather than settled, infinitely serious and useful.

That beauty cannot be translated into expository terms is a particular problem for poetry, especially in abstract language like Englishes. Poetry's lingual material is, in other contexts, overwhelmingly used and valued for its conceptual and communicative facilities. We imagine, to couch the point in terms of the modernist poet Ezra Pound's logopoeia, that poetic beauty is insufficiently difficult or concept-provoking. But when we distinguish pleasing or mellifluous versions of phanopoeia and melopoeia from the conceptual, discursive world of logopoeia, we err if we think the first two simple-minded and the last the place of seriousness. "Music is feeling, then, not sound," writes another modernist poet, Wallace Stevens, and we think that we cannot *think* about feeling or music, since they are subjective and ineluctable.[2] We think we cannot say anything critically useful about them, and so we divide aesthetics from theoretical or conceptual content and concentrate on the latter, about which we feel we can say something.

The problem is compounded by some recent critical correctives, useful and needed as they are in other ways. As we pursue historical, cultural, and gender-based critical modes, theories of beauty are often labeled hegemonic models bequeathed by white males, in part because they often are (Shelley's, for example). Taking beauty seriously, developing theories of beauty, is out of fashion. As a result, we really have not gotten much further in our theories than Alexander Baumgarten's definition of a poem as a "perfect sensate discourse"—communicating content via sensory form—or Emmanuel Kant's antinomy of taste, which is fairly useless if we hold that aesthetic disinterestedness is a con-

2 Wallace Stevens, "Peter Quince at the Clavier," in *The Collected Poems of Wallace Stevens* (Alfred A. Knopf, 1968), 90.

tradiction in terms.[3] When Baumgarten coined "aesthetic" from the Greek *aisthēsis* (sensory perception) he was perhaps more enlightened than people often are about the power of the senses, since he wanted to make serious place for the "lower" sensory functions among "higher" functions of rational meaning.

So, what is the experience of poetic beauty? It is, first of all, subjective interestedness. Interestedness requires sympathy, so poetic beauty might be defined as the result of subjective sympathy: paying enough attention to a poem for it to teach us how to read it and, crucially, sensing that it fulfills the terms it lays out. These terms may be of many varieties, such as lyricism, word attention, sound dissonance, even of a faltering which is part of the poem's point. Poems whose beauty strikes us overwhelmingly and immediately are poems that use well some of the rules we are well trained to perceive. Poems whose beauty takes time for us to appreciate have worked to increase our aesthetic faculties.

This is not to say that all poems are beautiful. Many do not fulfill the terms of their own construction, and so they leave us feeling dissatisfied. On the other hand, some poems leave us feeling dissatisfied because that is part of their point. It is as impossible to determine the difference, in terms of establishing interpretive predictions or tools, as it is to define poetic beauty. Beauty is contingent and unique and cannot be derived from or defined according to rules or explanatory codes. But I want to insist that poetic beauty is important to talk about and wonderful to experience. As the US academic Wendy Steiner puts it, "the pleasures of art, however scandalous they have come to be seen, are valuable and worth protecting."[4] Hardly surprising that pleasure and scandal occupy the same sentence, in a US context

3 Alexander Gottlieb Baumgarten, *Reflections on Poetry: Meditationes philosophicae de nonnullis ad poema pertinentibus,* trans. Karl Aschenbrenner and William B. Holther (University of California Press, 1954), 39, and see Immanuel Kant, *The Critique of Judgement,* trans. J.H. Bernard (Hafner Publishing Co., 1951).

4 Wendy Steiner, *The Scandal of Pleasure: Art in an Age of Fundamentalism* (University of Chicago Press, 1995), 80.

filled with the noise of Puritan self-suppression and preferences for action to be instrumental.

One of the difficulties in writing about poetic beauty is that poetry, being customarily all of the same basic matter (i.e., words) is always formed and therefore, in the *formositas* sense, always beautiful. To put it in Scholastic or phenomenological terms: the "material" object of poetry is language, its marks and sounds; the "intentional" object is how we, subjectively, read that material. In the material sense language is beautiful, while in the intentional sense — well, it all depends on our training. What westerners commonly register as ugliness is the effort of poetic language to resist naturalized lingual formations or formal regularity, whether at the level of phoneme, word, line, or overall form. This resistance sounds harsh in part because it is resistance and in part because it has to go so far to get somewhere that approximates escape from expected poetic manifestations, as in these lines from US poet Bruce Andrews's "The Impatient Heart":

> church bells howitzers aloft to oust who suspect they've come as idea of beauty must matrimonial aside attention suddenly spirited to smooth a tug also in attendance in defense of hand flintlock rifles ego amid keys gaiety of sleepwalking had cornered[5]

This passage fulfills some conditions of poetic beauty: moving relations of sound and vision, accumulations of diaphanous and concrete referentiality, mouthfuls of language. The vowels dance with the consonants: "-ur- -el- -owitzer- -oft to oust who" moves to "suddenly spirited to smooth." How is this kind of poetic beauty different from what we might expect to hear discussed in an essay about mellifluous poetic beauty? We might expect to read excerpts from William Butler Yeats or the US poet Gjertrud Schnackenberg, or at the very least from some of Gertrude Stein's or David Bromige's sweet simplicities. Each of these poets

5 Bruce Andrews, *Wobbling* (Roof Books, 1981), 86.

gives evidence of the fluency of words coupled with sonorous communicative expectations, for Yeats or Schnackenberg, or of words given sonic range for the sake of prepositional sensibility or deictic encirclement, for Stein or Bromige. But poetic beauty is not only evident lyricisms or the apparently perfect mesh of prosodic tool with signified point. To risk a definition that predefines nothing: Poetic beauty is a different thing in different poems.

So, what is the problem of poetic beauty? It is not simply the neglect of beauty, or the denial of its existence; it is also the several reasons for that neglect and denial. One reason for the failure of interest in beauty is sensory repression, particularly of the erotic. Beauty is always, to a greater or lesser extent, tied to eros. André Breton, an enthusiastic French surrealist, calls this "convulsive beauty": art he likes must "arouse a physical sensation. [. . .] I could never avoid establishing some relation between this sensation and that of erotic pleasure, finding only a difference of degree."[6] US academic Jeffrey C. Robinson laments that, "[i]n denying ourselves the beautiful, we have lost in addition the erotic experience that accompanies our access to it and our experience of it. This, in a society as neurotic about desire as ours, should come as no surprise."[7]

But we don't admit denying ourselves the beautiful; we just give it other names in an effort to dismantle it into formal or cultural properties. That's because another problem with beauty is that it presupposes, inescapably, interestedness. Most criticism longs for disinterestedness, so it longs to disassemble all things that seem to prove that disinterestedness cannot exist. But, to rewrite Kant, the delight which determines the judgment of taste is utterly dependent on interests of various kinds. It does not follow that interestedness decreases our vocabularies, least of all our ways of seeing and knowing. On the contrary: To

6 André Breton, *Mad Love,* trans. Mary Ann Caws (University of Nebraska Press, 1987), 8.

7 Jeffrey C. Robinson, *The Current of Romantic Passion* (University of Wisconsin Press, 1991), 7.

expose interest is to expose its endlessly varying manifestations, to increase rather than to limit both what we can say and what we can think. That's one point of making room for the absent presences of soft text, explored elsewhere in this book. That's also one point of what I call subjective correlatives in the work of Laura Riding: Their range of provokable referents and sensibilities goes beyond the Lockean designs of T.S. Eliot's "objective correlative." Subjective correlatives are the *more, more* of multiplied human particularities.[8]

Bound up with both its erotic components and its inherent interestedness is the fact that beauty is a manipulative force. In biological terms, poetic beauty seems to be a supernormal releaser of the language world. We recognize our sensible reaction to its charms, but once out of nature we want to prove that it has lost dominion over us, and so we refuse the irrational form-intensity of poetry. We don't want, as discursive groups, to be tyrannized by love, desire, or sensation, so we say that because they are subjective they effectively no longer exist as discursive issues. In neglecting to talk about them we are a bit like the devil in William Blake's *Milton: A Poem:* "Satan Refusing Form." And a bit like those whom Theodor Adorno references in this book's epigraph, wanting to "punish undisciplined gestures."

We have at least not abandoned the modern urge to intensity, which is another frame for the question of beauty. The common opposition between modernism's urge to intensity and postmodernism's knowing better seems to me false. Postmodernism's theoretically posited inurement to intensity belies its practical embraces: trauma art, celebrating failure, the works of writers such as Kim Hyesoon, William Vollmann, Afrizal Malna — all these rely on surface-to-depth intensity, cousin to the eighteenth-century sublime. We might well find, for both

8 See Lisa Samuels, "Creating Criticism: An Introduction to *Anarchism Is Not Enough*," in Laura Riding, *Anarchism Is Not Enough*, ed. Lisa Samuels (University of California Press, 2001), xlii: "Riding's subjective correlatives are 'ratios of fabrication,' linguistic equations for the instability of thought and emotion. They make the reader experience that instability rather than indulging in the comfort of an 'objective' human representation."

modern and postmodern versions of beauty, common ground in aesthetics of intensity.

The difference in the postmodern aesthetics of intensity, perhaps, is that we want somehow to *be* the intensity, not to attribute it to a form. So we open up a gap between the intensity, which is us, and the poem or art object, which comes to resemble a cultural husk. To put it another way: Theory and culture, as group projects, tend to exclude sensibility, but poetry always has sensibility, which must be experienced subjectively. The Scottish philosopher David Hume took us from the object of beauty to its perceiving subject. In forming critical groups, we have somehow posited being forced to reemphasize the object of beauty: We write essays or books about poetry, and our writings mediate between us as readers and writers and between us and the poetry, in a triangular objectification of poetry, critic, and (often critical) reader. We don't see (sense) each other, we read each other. Because this objectification—through the distancing of both poetic object and critical stance—is a false emphasis, the object ends up being emptied of its sensible beauty, which is always a question of subjective human experience in relation with the art's materials. So we end up saying that the object has no beauty, and that we are wrong to speak of beauty, from a longing to solidify group perceptions in and about the object. The subjective experience of beauty becomes closeted, off the record. As Charles Lock puts it, "[p]erspective is the way out of participation, our protection from confusion and involvement. Being left outside is the price of objectivity."[9]

Many other "problems" of poetic beauty remain to be considered. First, its historical links with morality and cultural instruction, the kinds of bells that are rung when we read that "beauty is truth" (in the John Keats 1819 poem "Ode on a Grecian Urn") or when we hear that "only bad witches are ugly" (in the 1939 film *The Wizard of Oz*) or when we understand that there are few social ills that a good architect cannot clear up

9 Charles Lock, "Petroglyphs in and out of Perspective," *Semiotica* 100, nos. 2–4 (1994): 413.

(Bilbao: "More than just Guggenheim"). A second "problem" is beauty's maddening self-sufficiency and self-possession, the wreath of apparently impenetrable quiddity that its being-ness weaves around it. A third "problem" is the paradox of beauty's seriousness, given that it doesn't know much philosophically or intellectually. But two things seem to me irresistible: The first is the argument that began this précis, that beauty is a structure for imagining what we don't know. The second is that beauty must change within the "unchanged" work. This compulsion or imperative for change is part of what Wallace Stevens invites the poem "Notes Toward a Supreme Fiction" to think about, in the section titled "It Must Change."[10] Poetry wants to be timeless or immortalized ("Not marble, nor the gilded monuments / Of princes, shall outlive this powerful rhyme" as William Shakespeare put it), but it also wants to live. It is up to ongoing readings to find both the temporal intactness and the contemporary potential of any poetic beauty.

10 Wallace Stevens, "Notes Toward a Supreme Fiction," in *The Collected Poems of Wallace Stevens* (Alfred A. Knopf, 1968), 389.

2

Membranism, Wet Gaps, Archipelago Poetics

> I will content myself with saying that the only things valuable, even here in this life, are the continuities.
>
> —Charles Sanders Peirce, "The Logic of Relatives"[1]

Wet Contact

The overarching western paradigm for imagined order in the nineteenth century was, I have long been informed, time, which shifted in the twentieth century to space. If such an overarching idea is possible to wrangle at this point, then perhaps the paradigm for imagined order in the twenty-first century is touch, contact in all its tactility, with the historical problem of colonial contact intact within that touch. And with decisively real ecological and biological bodies foregrounded in that touch. Wet contact is closer and faster than dry contact—literally, sound travels faster in water, electricity jumps liquid—and membranes work as both bio-zones and substantial metaphors for

1 Charles Sanders Peirce, "The Logic of Relatives" (1898), in *Reasoning and the Logic of Things,* ed. Kenneth Laine Ketner (Harvard University Press, 1992), 162.

the actualizations that occur in wet contact. Membranism, then, is wet touch and transfer event of object to body, body to object to body, and mental image (three-dimensional, embodied, and active idea) within our wet neural network. Membranism means to emphasize the contact we sustain with each other and with our objects and events of transaction. The distinctness of membranes, for cellular action and for membranism as a metaphor, is that they are contact and transfer event, act and object linkage, permitting passage, and activation horizon all at once.

Discussions of representation—how figures in words, images, and sounds are connected with real and imagined objects, events, and ideas in the world—are most often set within the context of a removal of contact, a slippage between representing figure and represented matter, and a subsequent pondering from a conceptual dry distance. Here membranism interposes: the eye that looks at the representation is wet; the air between hangs droplets; the brain for figuration is wet; the ear's drums vibrate all the way through; the fingers touching the object are budding with tiny moistures. In imaginative works, which always involve some kind of representation, the page, the canvas, the keyboard, the historical conjuration, sculpture, dried paint, objects, and inky fixity are all fascinating in part as and because of the interrupted dynamism of their moist conception and the posited wet life of their participant-creators.

Often, in the west, water seems more temporary than time and space, as though water's more intense substantiality is an inverse sign of its evanescence. Figuring substantiality as more temporary than abstraction can be a way of ordering mental concepts in reverse: thus western religious beliefs and the invisibility cloaks of ideologies. Membranism means to be both more present, more conscious of its ongoingness and transfer, and less imagined as lasting (in all three senses of that word, as fastening, finishing, and enduring) than concepts of discrete or distanced observation.

Consciousness Is Electrifying

When you read this the liquids inside you are surging electricity and yet you do not die from the equation. Thinking is self-electrocuting. Mild electricity across membranes generates and retransfers felt life. Within membranism's contact paradigm is the electric equation always present in the digitas, a term I use to refer to the principal, or at least the loudest proclaimed (newest felt, barely theorized), imaginative interface of our era. The digitas means the digital realm performed by and interlaced with the digits of binary code and our fingers, with our habitus, and with the civitas.[2] Western imaginative work and reflective theory now are always, whether explicitly or not, composed within the digitas. In terms of daily acts, I realize I am referring to those human activities that are privileged to access the practical digitas. But in terms of imaginative cultural life, the digitas is *the* enveloping and extruding paradigm of interface, the interface that enables digital (and "artificial") intelligence, the interface that most explicitly reflects the alterity of membranism.

Just as membranism as metaphor is allied with its literal image—the soft wet intactness of looping transfer—so the digitas operates as a metaphoric constellation and as a literal computing level. Now that diatoms, those minute ocean algae, are forming the basis for some new computer chips, computing is getting overtly wetter too, in relation to the wetness of the humans who act in it.[3] We should be able to take computers underwater, in an everyday way, soon enough. Then we

2 The term *habitus* means to invoke its usage beyond Aristotle, as elaborated contemporarily by Pierre Bourdieu (habits of cultural consciousness manifest in and as our behaviors and approaches), as well as its usage in eco-morphology. The term *civitas* I hope to be using not as a nod to the Romans but as another rhyme with "digitas" that can refer in a generalized sense to persons aware of sharing in the works of semi-permanent locale gatherings, whether these latter involve tribal, nation-state, or shared geophysical places.

3 Michael Sussman, "In Diatom, Scientists Find Genes that May Level Engineering Hurdle," *Science Daily*, January 23, 2008, https://www.sciencedaily.com/releases/2008/01/080121181404.htm.

might further mitigate a felt, and arguably learned, separation of media from mediation. Computing is more responsive to biological structuring and metaphors than it might at first appear to be. As Mario Pérez-Jiménez points out, for example, membrane computing is an offshoot of natural computing "inspired by the structure and functioning of living cells."[4] As computers come to operate more in parallel with our wet contacts, then bio-computing, literal digital selves, can resonate more with the synchrony between the electricity and the water in our neural networks.

In a long western conceptualizing of human wetness and dryness, the first is customarily suspect and the second asserted as the context for doing and thinking (but not at all asserted as the concomitant context for "being" and "dwelling," to extend the Heideggerian cue). Substance dualism, in the vein of René Descartes, values mental activities as separate from putatively less self-transacting, indeed apparently unnecessary, bodily activities. Descartes did not write, for example, as one might for membranism, "I bethink as a wet electric being in contact with an event-object and a you, therefore I am a looping moist electric exchange in bethinking."[5] However reductive such an assertion may well be when applied to careful philosophical work, this epistemic/ontological apartheid—dry thinking from wet being—is still very much in operation in western activities. But it is also in transition. Membranism's contact is available in

4 Pérez-Jiménez summarizes Natural Computing as "a new computing area inspired by nature, using concepts, principles, and mechanisms underlying natural systems." See Mario J. Pérez-Jiménez, "An Approach to Computational Complexity in Membrane Computing," in *Membrane Computing*, ed. Giancarlo Mauri et al. (Springer, 2005), 86. Gheorghe Paŭn, *Membrane Computing: An Introduction* (Springer Books, 2002), sets forth many hypothetical consequences and problem sets of membrane computing and is a useful orientation to this field.

5 René Descartes, *Discourse on Method and Meditations*, trans. Laurence J. Lafleur (Liberal Arts Press, 1960). What Descartes did write includes: "I concluded I was a thing or substance whose whole essence or nature was only to think, and which, to exist, has no need of space nor of any material thing or body" (25).

the operations of the digitas, itself establishing and thickening whilst cultural pluralism re-shapes our identity discourses, as altered metaphoric imaginings of human make-up indicate (see "hive-mind," see "posthuman," see Édouard Glissant's composite culture and métissage, see, even, globalism challenging the nation-state).

Moistening the Continuum

Our most evidently wet selves are a matter of extremes: womb and infancy, incontinence and other loosenings of the body's liquid boundaries in trauma, epiphora (excessive tearing of the eyes), orgasm, and of course bleeding, whereby the body's richest liquid is spent. Our moderately evident wet selves are a matter of dailyness: urine, basal tears, sweat, menstrual blood. The containment of our natural liquids and the careful release in socially permitted-and-constrained circumstances is a constant interest of every culture; I am mostly operating here in western ones.

I am interested in how the figure of the contained wet person, full of watery brains and pumping blood and sweat but not evidently revealing that condition, becomes a figure for the non-translatable event of any complex cultural happenstance. The more we release the possibility of these waters into cultural circumstances the less mystified might be the relation between the individual and the cultural. The prohibition "don't touch the art" is because of your liquids at least as much as it is due to a concern about giving potentially dangerous access to a person who might wish to, or might accidentally, damage a work. The "dry" explanation, however—involving the sacrosanct desired eternality of the curated work—arguably has become the ideology that obscures the liquid issue.

Imagine more cultural engagements carried out as moist exchange ceremony. This essay is elaborating a metaphoric membranism that is connected to literal membrane activity. One such literal level was first pointed out to me by the cultural theorist Stephen Turner: Aspects of the Māori *tangi* involve the cultivation of intense wetness in the eyes and nose as a way of grieving someone's death. Not spontaneous tears, but a ceremonial excess and calling forth of tearing. The word *tangi* translates as "to weep," and one of the *tangi's* repeated proverbs is "Me nga roimata me te hupe ka ea ai te mate," which is commonly translated as "by tears and mucus death is avenged." The wetness of living bodies is being deliberately summoned. Such ceremony is in contrast to the general western and especially Anglo-American-Australasian preference for so-called "authentic" emotion in response to strong events such as death. The permission brackets of such "authentic" emotion are "out of control" rather than in control; that is, grievers cry because "they cannot help it." But imagine if we produced tears like sentences that would be accepted ceremonial corollaries to events such as death. I can only speculate about membranism in the arena of the *tangi*, whose forms and nuances exceed my limited knowledge of Māori cultures. But in the context of this essay I can imagine the superabundance of cultivated wetness as going beyond the so-called authentic toward imaginative work that engages and incorporates authenticity to the point where ceremony, or artifice, operates as exponentialized sincerity.

Such exponentializing of thought-affect (grief, in the *tangi*) via moisture as ceremony is a kind of self-conscious wet physics, a term I use to indicate applications of quantum theory's organizational consequences. Those consequences include the presumption that all interpretive categories are constructed, are in effect localized and self-aware cultural anthropology, not (strictly) biology. In the wetness aspects of the *tangi* we see bloody brains in watery bodies working together in cultural acts both resistantly imaginative and productively social. The *roimata* (tears, as in crying with the eyes) and *hupe* (mucus) of the *tangi* are resistantly imaginative acts as soon as they meet discomfiture about cultivated displays of feeling and overt corporeal overflow. They are productively social as a continuity of access to a wet culture of pre-"contact," to use that term in its colonial frame. Insofar as we might wish to change some of the terms of contact, to reinvigorate wet contact in our theories, such resistant wet ceremony has something to teach Anglo and other western theory.

What that something is I'd like to put into the context of wet physics via an application of Charles Peirce's "continuum of qualities," specifically from his lecture on "The Logic of Continuities."[6] Peirce comes in here because of his sustained focus on thought organizations as *bethinking* (that is not his word, but a word meant to gesture to his ontological metaphysics), his multidisciplinary inspirations, and the intense physicality of his illustrative imagination. When he works to explain his continuum of qualities, the *singular surface* of Peirce's doubled cave bubble — from an image he describes at more than quotable length, explored elsewhere in this book in the essay "Peirce's Cave" — is like a floating membrane.[7] For Peirce and for membranism this continuity of "relations" with singular surface involves a metaphor, or a thought-experiment, for imagining our organizing of bodies and world and encounters. In turn, I hope membranism can imbue Peirce's continuum of qualities with moisture. Such a transliteration, from continuum to membranism, can operate in the context of wet physics to facilitate a yet more palpable, more wet contact-oriented concept of the continuities among mediated acts. So that Peirce's

6 Charles Sanders Peirce, *Reasoning and the Logic of Things: The Cambridge Conference Lectures of 1898*, ed. Kenneth Laine Ketner (Harvard University Press, 1992). This essay does not afford the scope to fully explain the implications of the wrought parallel between Peirce's continuum and membranism, and the reader is referred to Peirce's lecture (see 242–68) for further consideration. The following excerpted paragraph might go some way toward indicating why I think it matters to bring Peirce in to a complex of considerations including quanta and ceremonial tears:

> A potential collection more multitudinous than any collection of distinct individuals can be[,] cannot be entirely vague. For the potentiality supposes that the individuals are determinable in every multitude. That is, they are determinable as distinct. But there cannot be a distinctive quality for each individual; for these qualities would form a collection too multitudinous for them to remain distinct. It must therefore be by means of *relations* that the individuals are distinguishable from one another. (248, my italics)

7 Peirce, *Reasoning and the Logic of Things*, 252–53.

Pure Mathematics need not be segregated, as he posits it to be in his passion for the pure thought-forms of higher mathematics, from "we [...] little creatures, mere cells in a social organism."[8]

Archipelago Poetics

When moving here in 2006, I thought about archipelago poetics as a term to gesture to the intense oceanic unknown with, also, the land quotients of Aotearoa/New Zealand's geophysique. It's true that the five syllables of the word "archipelago" sound like a beautiful journey, and that they resonate in my reading history with the witnessing that is also a bid for unavailable freedom chronicled in Aleksander Solzhenitsyn's book *The Gulag Archipelago.* The Greek meaning of "chief sea" had already transmuted into the use of "archipelago" to refer to a wide sense of a large cultural area, an ideology of area-meaning including known and unknown features and ideas. So, all that lexical infusion formed part of my imagining of archipelago poetics. As I have expressed, including in this book, I am interested in imagining what we don't know, in exploring the implications of what we cannot one-to-one (monadically) access, mirror, or control, and I was considering the implications of living where wet non-access characterizes, in part, what is available to humans. In the mainland United States, that is excepting its currently six territories (Puerto Rico, American Samoa, Guam, and the Midway, Virgin, and Northern Mariana Islands), Hawai'i, and Alaska, one has a sense of enormous dry land that is *available* to the inhabitants. That access contributes to a belief that people know what they see, that it is up for possession, purview, knowability, inhabitability, transaction, and transversal. In the UK, to continue with my own prior principally Anglo-American orientations, one looks to the European continent for a continuation of traversability.

In Aotearoa/New Zealand, by contrast, because of the presentness of the ocean we are hemmed in by non-access, co-

8 Ibid., 121.

extensive with deep water, released to what we cannot possess. We can be intensely aware of the grounded islands that permit and constitute human interchange—though of course remarkable underwater moments are open, for example, to transmigrating oceanographers.[9] This literal situation of islands and ocean made me think the term archipelago poetics could refer to our condition of interchange across inaccessible vibrant gaps, ocean as fact and idea. Archipelago poetics describes local imaginative work according to the nonconformist relevance of oceans between: oceans of uncertainty, change, extinction, and the unseen that arrange and derange the stand-out possessed lands.

Archipelago poetics certainly concerns language differentials, in dialects, codes, and languages, as all human transaction does to greater and lesser degrees. My broader interest here is in the gaps among apparently knowable events and how that gap-ness comes to characterize one's hermeneutic expectations when one encounters a work of imagination (whether a nation or a work of art). Archipelago poetics means not to stabilize gaps but to traverse them, to activate and dislocate the isolated islandic discourses we can all feel our selves to be characterized by when we are focusing on those moments of comparative dryness on land.

To put it another way, my long-held interest in the gap is latterly concerned with how it can function as a membrane, a suffused wet conveyance, rather than as a blank break or diaphanous air or discontinuity with edges. The gap as membrane is filled with inhabitable wetness, a gap not of split but of contact, a membranism gap. In the context of archipelago poetics, this interpretive image of the gapped membrane means to emphasize the admixture and change that happens in the membrane conveyance. The passage of the archipelago gap is via a membrane, the metaphorically co-imagined ocean, whose message

9 I use the term "transmigrating" with reference to diapedesis, the movement of blood cells through capillary walls, as well as to its definition as movement from one country or place to another. For the former definition, see *The American Heritage College Dictionary* (Houghton Mifflin, 1993), 384.

transitions operate via what is other (wet and pressured, dark and occluded, fostering of non-human life) and what is in that sense and context unknown. The course of this membranism courts unprefigured combinations and responses. Torquing the moistness of membranism with the oceanic water of archipelago poetics helps emphasize the constant fluxed connection in "bethinking": We do not imagine a release from the membrane contact or from the oceanic context; we do not imagine we know (all of) what will exchange in that contact. The combination of membranism and archipelago poetics also exponentializes the wetness of these metaphors, and therefore mirrors what sometimes seems the miraculous speed of attention in an artistic exchange, since, to repeat, wet contact is more facilitating than dry contact.

Wet Gaps on Page, Mouth, and Screen

So then, to the interpretive poetics part of this essay's proposals. What happens if we read the areas across and among artistic inscriptions and images as liquid, instead of as air and space? In her 2001 poetry and images book *red shifts*, the UK poet Maggie O'Sullivan helps challenge what has been often previously imagined as dry spatial areas among words, as when we learn to speak of blank page areas as "space" on the page. O'Sullivan's gaps seem deliberately bodily and wet (fig. 7.1).

In this open-book image from *red shifts*, the recto page that faces the verso text page features discrete and blended streams of red and black watercolor as well as some quite small drawn lines, triangles, and irregular squares. On the watercolor printed page, wading through the areas and paint traces facing O'Sullivan's words, I am reminded of the blood that gets released in the making of an old-fashioned chisel *moko kauwae* (latterly, more humanely, performed with needles), the carved pattern rivulet tattoos in the lips and chins of some Māori women.[10] The

10 For information on this practice, see, for example, Michael King and Marti Friedlander, eds., *Moko: Māori Tattooing in the 20th Century* (Alister

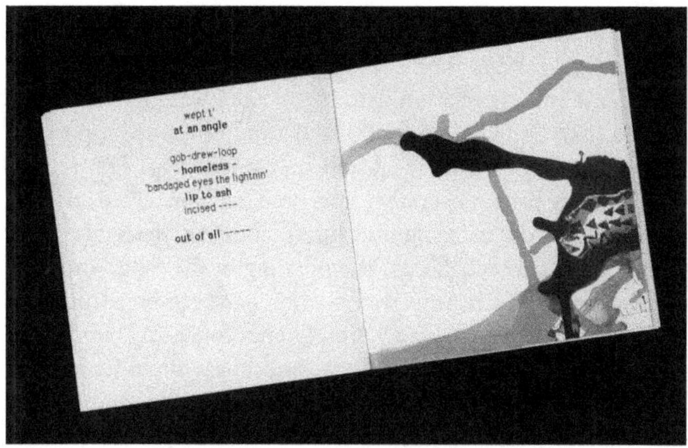

Fig. 7.1. From Maggie O'Sullivan, *red shifts* (Etruscan, 2001), n.p. Courtesy of the artist.

streaming red of O'Sullivan's watercolors is reminiscent of moving blood, certainly, and many pages in *red shifts* feature words such as "gouged," "turning flesh," and "tonguesbled." O'Sullivan's book, as with many of her works, is replete with references to the bodies of both human and non-human animals. In the context of this essay it is interesting to consider parallels between what a non-Māori can perceive about the *moko* (what seems evident in the perception of the symbolic tattoo when one is not inside the practice and culture) and how a reader comes into O'Sullivan's image and poetry book. In terms of representation's force, I think of the moko alongside the membrane gap and alongside stories of reading aloud for so long that one's vocal cords and mouth begin to fleck blood on the page, a somatic membranism ceremony. The metaphor of membranism reading recognizes the gaps as wet via the mouth and eyes and fingers, recognizes the swirls that liquidity introduces in the material, recognizes as strange the blending of literacy paper (a poetry book) with graphic excess (blood images), and lips (for speaking and eating) with chiseling and needles (to make the moko).

Taylor, 1972).

The preceding comments touch mostly upon the referential wetness and markings of *red shifts,* suggesting what might seem a formally strange relation with the *moko.* I want to turn to the related idea that there is nothing natural or given in perceiving the areas among word clusters on a poetic page or screen as airy space or time. Certainly I have read and conceived analyses of poetic word-clustering and line-floating in space and time terms, especially insofar as "the opening of the field," in twentieth-century North American poetics, has been construed as a field of dry paper-qua-land.[11] A preference for seeing blank parts of pages in terms of air and space and linear time, forward or back, over imagined interpretations that are water and ground and cyclical (recurrent) time is, in my experience, dominant in the hermeneutics of our bibliographic cultures as well as, so far, in the digitas. But there is nothing less reasonable in perceiving interstitial and intralinear areas as metaphorically wet. There is no more sky in the page than there are oceans.

In the example from *red shifts,* the areas around the printed words and the watercolor reproductions are a high-contrast white in relation to the graphics and words. To say that either page is literally dry does not quite work, since if it were perfectly dry we could not turn the page; it would disintegrate. Imagining the words as scored on a membrane pulls them in a more tangible relation to the uninscribed parts of the page, as though a membrane page can be imagined as thicker, wet translucence rendered here a particular color (white, which we are in the habit of associating with blankness, in books and other interior design). A thicker membrane page might encourage an inter-

11 Robert Duncan, *The Opening of the Field* (New Directions, 1973). The title of Duncan's first poetry book became for some US poetics synonymous with opening up the poetic page to spatial hovering and line clusters. This view of the poem on the page is a move away from strict line-by-line poetry that presents as unconscious of the page as an active participant in the poem's meaning resources. The open field view is also associated with Charles Olson, whose poetic lines often look scattered on the page and who is known, in poetry circles, for having declared space crucial in the twentieth-century US imagination.

pretive sense of palpable potentiality, a connected continuation rather than an airy echo. Metaphorically, to apply the categories of this essay's opening paragraph, membranism reading views the page as contact (something is manifest and encountered), transfer event (something is given and received, and altered in exchange), linking act (writer, reader, language, and image meet in the membrane page), object (the page is solid, is a thing yielding and pliant and tense all at once), permitting passage (you can go through the page, can turn to another, can hover between what is "incised ---- // **out of all** -----"),[12] and activation horizon (the watercolor image and the thickened printface is perceptible as a continuation of the damp yielding of the white ungraphed page).

As I have suggested, we can easily point to the references in Maggie O'Sullivan's book, the blood and Earth and birds and bodies, as encouraging a potential perception of its inter- and intralinear areas as watery rather than airy. Perhaps a strictly formal membranism reading might be better tested with writers whose texts have neither images nor constancy to liquid references — Stephanie Christie, Harryette Mullen, or Edmond Jabès, perhaps. But we can also read O'Sullivan's references in the more customary dry-paper way. We might want to claim that the dry air of the paper forms a contrast with the incisions or visitations of her words, which are sometimes printed in red ink, and watercolors. Alternately, again, we might read Charles Olson and, say, contemporary poets such as Nisha Ramayya and Craig Santos Perez as having textual portions situated on membranes, with areas of moisture all around.[13] I am deliberately bringing

12 Maggie O'Sullivan, *red shifts* (Etruscan Books 2001), n.p.

13 Regarding Craig Perez's book *From Unincorporated Territory [hacha]* (Tinfish Press, 2008), the blog of his publisher Susan Schultz has a summary of some of Perez's remarks about the page space in his book: "On this first page, 'from Lisiensan Gaılago' (15), names given to Guam are put in dialogue and spread like islands across white space — not an Olsonian field, but a Perezian ocean. Craig considers that there are currents between the words; the closer the words are to one another, the more tension is created between them." See Susan M. Schultz, "Skyping Craig Santos Perez," *Susan M. Schultz's Blog*, April 18, 2009, https://tinfisheditor.blogspot.

wet interpretations in to the uninscribed and ungraphed portions of page spaces as well as internet displays.

Which might seem a bit like linking O'Sullivan's paint shapes to *moko* blood patterns. Membranism, to underscore the point, wants to alter our relations with continuums of relating. How do we tally our expectations of familiarity when encountering an art work (am I coming to *red shifts* as specialized art or sociologically artifactual culture; is a *moko* art or culture)? Computing poetry such as that celebrated in Eduardo Kac's *Media Poetry,* with its combinatory approaches to the multiple spaces of language (sounds, nanobots, environmental interactions), is an overt invocation of the possibilities of wet contact, of membranism, in the digitas. Kac's own "biopoetry" is an acute literal example here: He makes poetic urges biologically transacted and transactable.[14] Is a poem of his amoebic or textual?

Much other computing art evokes the possibilities of electric liquidity, as well as embodiment. Mark B.N. Hansen adduces the example of the work of Teresa Wennberg, specifically *The Parallel Dimension* (1998), developed for the VR-Cube, which sets up body places as "a metaphor for the nongeometric space of the virtual." Wennberg's work presents six imaginary rooms demonstrating different body spaces, from The Brain Chamber to The Heart & Blood Room, The Breathing Cathedral, The Thought Cabinet, The Flesh Labyrinth, and The Dream Cavern. For Wennberg's 2001 project *Brainsongs (Welcome to My Brain),* she writes "we experience a real-time metaphor for the change and transformation that is constantly taking place inside us."[15] I

---

com/2009/04/skyping-craig-santos-perez.html. Such comments seem to chime synchronically with membranism, especially with archipelago poetics and wet page gaps.

14 See Eduardo Kac, ed., *Media Poetry: An International Anthology* (Intellect Books, 2007), 191–96.

15 For brief descriptions of Wennberg's works, which can be experienced only with access to their complex computer installations, see Teresa Wennberg, "Brainsongs (Welcome to My Brain)," *Archive of Digital Art,* 2001–2002, https://digitalartarchive.at/database/general/work/brainsongs.html. At the time of writing this essay, the site www.nada.kth.se/~teresa/PDVR.html was live; it has now cascaded out of the accessible digitas. For remarks on

would like to see Wennberg's works rendered wet; I would also like to see her work as marking a bridge between Teresa of Ávila's *The Interior Castle* (1588) and a truly wet concept of virtual reality. Such a concept might give up using the term "virtual," since membranism wants to emphasize that there is no such thing as virtual reality given that there is always a wet human connection in relation to and enabling computing acts in the digitas.

Imbue

Insofar as I was formed within an Anglo-American, transatlantic, and Mediterranean People of the Book critical preference for dry hardness, my gradual formulation of membranism has been one more heave against those grains and another expansion, another panoply of ideas with which to expand critical bodies of perception and experience. For articulations of thought-being I have been long ago drawn more to the concept end of the spectrum than toward the affect end, to Michel de Certeau and Pierre Bourdieu more than to Gilles Deleuze, for example. The present essay might be considered to extend the linking gestures of Deluezian rhizomes all the way toward the water that nourishes those rhizomes, all the way to Glissant's literal oceanics as visceral metaphor, as well as pulling metaphors of connection back toward the bodies of the enacting and activating participant-creators (readers/writers/viewers). That drawing together I am deliberately making as a relation amidst water, since water is the destabilizing, the scorned phlegmatic in humors theory, the unsettling undefined.

Conceiving ungraphed and uninscribed screen, page, and canvas areas in terms of watery membranism, we might object that their meaning potentials are submerged, even "drowned." That reaction is arguably part of a preference for space-time-

Wennberg's works, see Mark B.N. Hansen, *New Philosophy for New Media* (MIT Press, 2004), 182–85. Hansen's stimulating book is directed differently from my emphases, but I am responsive to his interest in affect and bringing the body in to time-space and digital reconsiderations.

dryness in conceiving. Such a view might proffer purified air as a metaphor for clarity of mind, might think of water in terms of natural bodies that fill with silt and are visually impenetrable, or even think of clear water in terms of its literal potential for perceptual distortion. The metaphorical wet gaps in membranism mean to hold the words and other graphed elements in an active tension, elements amidst the graphemes, to be filled areas in which we feel the skin, touch a depth of page or screen, sense a weighted resistance as we move from sign cluster to sign cluster, or indeed introduce visual distortions as we join the work of art in perceiving it.

The differentials of visual distortion can be positive, in terms of a theory of membrane reading, can help make an argument that images — that any "relief" or thickening of the literate context — serve to increase the palpable quotient of the nearby words. To put that another way, graphemes that de-emphasize transparent semantics thicken the surface of an imaginative work and can thus be conceived as damper (because touchier) than abstract semantics. Bodies of paint or drawing, as well as transparency-resistant writing such as unusual or differentiated typeface, are comparatively palpable, and palpability is a kind of increased moistness. Getting the reader/viewer's body in self-conscious relation with the membrane of the imaginative work helps that reader/viewer imbue into the work. This palpability is part of the involving effect of bpNichol's thick purple paper in his *Martyrology* series (1972–1990). It is part of the impact of Tom Phillips's *A Humument* (1970, with successive editions added) with its deep surface pages and painted swirls, and part of Albert Wendt's *The Book of the Black Star* (2002) with its self-palimpsestic black ink work, its continuities among inked lingual and paralingual markings, as well as part of the impact of O'Sullivan's red print and watercolor accompaniments in *red shifts*. The meaning event of the membrane encounter is a matter of vibrational transitions among work, reader/viewer, and posited creator. Funnily enough, water coloration can be seen as a literal transaction of such metaphorical membranism. The scientists Charles L. Braun and Sergei N. Smirnov note that "the intrinsic blueness of water is the only example from nature in which color originates from vibrational transitions. Other materials owe their colors to the interaction of visible light with the electrons of the substances."[16] We can think of membranism as a constellated vibrational transition.

Activity Theory

In 2006, the Auckland Art Gallery presented an engaging installation by Stella Brennan. Titled *Wet Social Sculpture,* it consisted of a hot tub in the middle of a fairly large room, with muted lighting, mild psychedelic images projected on a wall above, and a 1970s-ish sound track including, as I recall, whale songs and similar pulsings (fig. 7.2). Outside the main installation room, a "corridor" created by blue rubber matting hosted a row of hooks on which were hung identical blue bathrobes provided for patrons. If gallery visitors knew the set-up in advance, they could plan to bring swimsuits and have the full experience of the piece. You could take a shower in a small side room, put on your togs, don one of the blue robes, pad across the industrial blue plastic pathway to the installation room door, open it, walk to the tub, and get in the warm water. There were a few colored lights inside the tub, glowing slowly in various patterns. As one of my first art events after arriving in Auckland/Tāmaki Makaurau that year, I joined poet and visual art historian Wystan Curnow in the hot tub to talk about art.[17]

We sat wetly, occasionally commenting on the immersive experience. At one point other patrons entered the room, fully dressed, and walked around the hot tub. As they circled us, it was clear that no ready social discourse bridge existed between the people outside the hot tub and those inside. We realized we

16 See Charles L. Braun and Sergei N. Smirnov, "Why Is Water Blue?," *Journal of Chemical Education* 70, no. 8 (1993): 612.

17 For more, see Stella Brennan, *Wet Social Sculpture,* 2005, http://stella.net.nz/work/wet-social-sculpture/. At the time of writing this essay, the work was also discussed at the now-evanesced site www.aucklandartgallery.govt.nz/exhibitions/docs/0609waltersjudge.pdf.

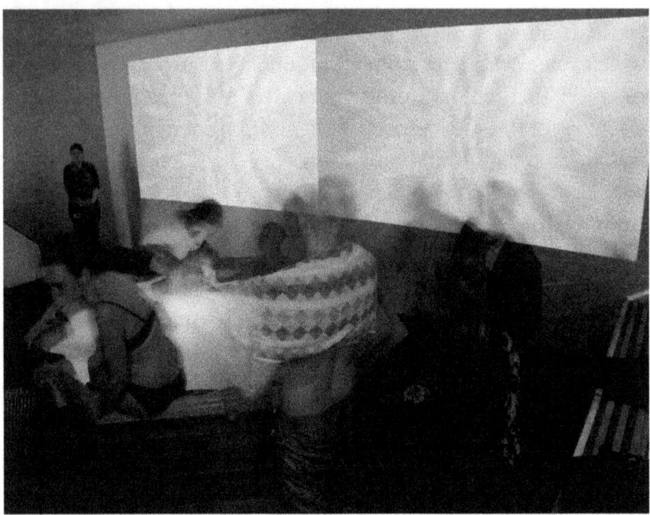

Fig. 7.2. Stella Brennan, *Wet Social Sculpture,* 2005, mixed media, courtesy of the artist and Starkwhite Gallery, Auckland.

had joined the work of art. All this was very interesting, since the setup also made for a public health-oriented consciousness that one's body fluids were on offer and needing to be contained. What kind of bathing suit was covering how much of your flesh? What was the chlorine content in the warmish water (not too hot lest anyone be burned)? The *Wet Social Sculpture* water was nowhere near as cold as a "real" world corollary that came readily to my mind: the rock pools in Marin County, California, where denizens frolicked naked and often stoned in the 1970s. The comparison was a contrast, a multi-temporal jostling of cultural contexts, which may well have been part of the artwork's constitutive points.

I felt the contrast between life and art events also as a natural liquid self outdoors (in Marin County) and an artificed liquid self participating in an indoor artwork. In that sense the art work's structure was inadequate to "authentic" social experience but adequate to artificial or conceptual wetness. To put it another way, *Wet Social Sculpture* highlighted the particularity of one's interpretive self especially by insisting in its form that *joining*, in effect melding, was the only full way to experience the art event. Brennan was making art out of life, to be sure. Acted life, not observed life; the water of *Wet Social Sculpture* made for the closest possible contact, exchanging fluid with our bodily pores and crevices as literally as it melded metaphorically with our interpreting selves. Withness criticality as bodily co-imbuing. One benefit of current curatorial practices that encourage audience response is that the museum-goer slows down, draws a finger across the digital text panel, writes something back.

Brennan's piece was exteriorizing and making explicit the request of an artwork: that you carry out an act in experiencing an imaginative work, that you link with its membranes. In this sense there is a similarity between the strangeness of becoming semi-naked and wet and joining an art work, and trying to shift one's interpretive position toward membranism. Our imaginative encounters are governed by default approaches, including the linear turning of pages and quiet walking in museums and valuing of critical distance. Membranism wants at the very least metaphorically, something as Brennan wants literally, to shift one's encountering metaphors with art. In each case the literal level of encounter is a physical intervention, an activity of your interpreting self coming like a membrane into joined contact with the membranes of its encounters.

The Right to Be Transplace

> I dream that I burst out laughing, that I span a river in one stride, or that I am followed by a flood of motor-cars which never catch up with me.
>
> — Frantz Fanon, *The Wretched of the Earth*[1]

> L'égalité veut d'autres lois.
>
> — Eugène Pottier, *L'Internationale*[2]

Human emplacement touches on what it means to have or not have a home region, to be (or not) "from" somewhere, to belong to more than one locale as an adult, to live as a transplace person, and more. We can talk about being transnational, learning language families in various parts of the world, and learning to inhabit multiple cultural patterns. Many people acquire multiplace experiences and identities without having grown up transplace. This piece fixes on transplace as a matter of the establishment of place-linked identity during human youth. Here I'm talking about the formative consequences of moving around

1 Frantz Fanon, *The Wretched of the Earth*, trans. Constance Farrington (Présence Africaine, 1963), 52.

2 "Equality calls for other laws." Eugène Pottier, "L'Internationale" (1871), https://www.toupie.org/Chansons/Internationale.htm. My translation.

repeatedly and continually among highly variant places from babyhood to the start of adulthood: growing up transplace.

By "move around" I mean not be from somewhere, and by be "from somewhere" I mean a place where you lived, or still do, for some solid time of your first decades of life. The psychogeography of such a place regularly gives people who grow up there a particular sense of self—you extruded into it and it gave itself back to you, so that street corners, mountain edges, repeated sound patterns, types of shops, bodies of water, or peculiar scents and styles of light, are coextensive with sustained experiences that shaped your early selves ("selves" in the plural because life provides many opportunities for developing selves among which we code switch, slip, and romp).

When people ask you that primary question Where Are You From, and you answer distinctly that you've moved around, they then (often, frequently) say yes but Where Were You Born as if that might reveal/revalue the truth of place origin. Often when you answer the natal place name they say ah, I know that place (or similar situating response) and then they sometimes (frequently) act as though they've satisfied their own criterion for assuming who you originally are.

This locative querying can feel absurd when it assumes that there is a certain set foundation for human apparitioning into the world, in this case a place foundation, whether agricultural or city-state, for sure located. Not hunter-gatherer; we've left that behind. Or maybe we're coming back to it, but if we are it makes many people nervous. They want to tag you like you're a micro nation with borders. We might consider how current place-identity approaches have been shaped by the modern version of the "stable" nation-state. We might wonder: Where are the wildlife corridors for humanimals?

It's always difficult, maybe impossible, to *acquire* a from-somewhereness. Even if you move into a place and stay there for decades or the reminder of your life, you are still "from" the place you came from before. This is one root for the suspicion of so-called outsiders. And it's one root for place purity insistences, for advocating for the sole support for (or pursuit of) people

From There or things From There. Place purity is expressed for example by the UK Prime Minister Theresa May in an October 5, 2017 speech: "If you believe you're a citizen of the world, you're a citizen of *nowhere*. You don't understand what the very word 'citizenship' means."

When you resist origin-place-tagging, some people respond as though you are resisting telling something that you *could*, were you not being evasive or unreasonable. As though you are refusing to give your legal appellation and asking them to just interact with you, without a given person name (imagine were we to have no names when we meet — imagine lifting away the veils and suppositions of Cinnamon, Linda, Wei, Sepideh, Skawennetsi, Valentino).

Of course, there are different versions of any in-between. In the racializing of a mingled world, for example, some transnationals are so-called marked and some are so-called unmarked, where the term "so-called" underscores the trouble in naturalizing the invented race-based distinction. An "unmarked" transnational is apparently not as visible as a "marked" one, as though your skin color brings you into visibility. Which could be a nice thought were it not inextricably allied with deadly racism.

The violence that someone does when they insist that you be From One Place and that you Are One Thing is a violence people have been talking about for a long time. There are many kinds of identity and different levels of movement coercion and a range of what we imagine as or call "choice" or fate. Frequent place shifting as a private family or group matter is not coequal with forced place shifting due to public war and conquest. The repeated problem many people have with Inside and Outside. Stop being outside; or only be outside. Stop being other, or be only the other. It's exhausting and not a small matter, not inconsequential for anyone on the scale of being and moving around.

It's also difficult, maybe impossible, to acquire for oneself a from-somewhereness without experience in from-somewhereness in those first two decades of living. I mean, I wouldn't really know how to try. But there are other resources. The rule of reflective being (the thinkability of anything thinkable) and the case of different experiences mean that transplace or transnational are gauzy nets that only ever cast over some of the thinkable terrain. Anyone might spur perpendicular vectors from ideas and sensations indexed here.

So what do you do when you meet someone who's from transplace? First, don't panic. It isn't their fault that they are not From Somewhere, nor is their not-from-somewhere status an intended reflection on your own experience and identity. They (adopting the ungendered pronoun for both singular and plural third person) don't want to take over your Fromness, though they might occasionally feel a curiosity and even a pang when encountering someone who is resolutely origin-emplaced, wondering how that feels inside and as a body in relation with recurrent terraforms, weathers, dialects, and architectures.

What is a place, anyway? Arguably these very points could be said to reify an ideology of Fromness. So what's in contrast? What does a transnational not-quite-fromness look like? Where is transgeography? What feelings might go along with being from transplace?

You come into a bracket whose parameters, like the anxious modern nation-state, are never quite the same: One place might be codified by size, by boundary nature, by tongue flow or language mix; another might be made by others or imagines it has grown up from inside its ox-bow origins as though suppressed hors-human life were translucent wallpaper visibilizing as flags only when the human is thrown up mirroring on it; another might give time to stories of upheavals of land and water, new formations that carry out long echoes of changes on planetary surfaces.

What happens when you are transplace or transnational in a from-somewhere context? It can be lonely, so it's kind to be kind to someone who doesn't mean not to belong to one place. And belonging, make no mistake, is a central issue here. A person who is not From Somewhere and who can't easily become part of a new Somewhere can be rendered fraught with comparative non-belonging.

The transplace identity of a person is not necessarily, in itself, noticeable. It takes some conversation to learn whether someone you've met might be from transplace. It takes some category expansion to accord transplaceness a being-from status. One occasion of formation-recognition for transplacers is when we meet others. Then the possibility arises of knowing how that in-between-places shaping feels for someone else who grew up with the ontologically constitutive anti-foundationalism of *moving around.* Such encounters make me think about how transplace can be thought of as place on the move, movement as place, being from movement, movement *as* substance (pulling Aristotle's contrast into and through itself). I am from what some think of as displacement, from transplace. It's theoretical to think of what to call it. Hence perhaps a predilection for neologism arises from experiences that don't yet have much for proper names.

Within its differences, transplace queers the dominance of single-place origin. It's a right not to be a stranger, no more a stranger than anyone else. Drawing out a nuance of Eugène Pottier's statement in the epigraph for this essay that "Equality wants different laws," transplace involves a right to name oneself as trans-geographic, to own that condition of movement-origin in a way not too distant from the right to self-name (to change your name, legally or otherwise) and to self-identify your body orientations in terms of sex and gender — in those parts of the human world that allow such orientations to be spoken and acted on. These latter conditions of deliberative nomination and self-knowing bear a family resemblance to this essay's desire to accord to movement-place its own conditions of reality and respect.

You might find someone who thinks with the givens and with whom you cannot begin from a cut possibility — that's the maybe exhaustion, the voice floating boxed in a perfusive aura precisely in the conditions of never-recognizability through the entire body, a temporary playful provenance built without faux-permanent walls; astonished in its ohs, the understandable person focusing on the three-dimensional objects that condition the temporary sky, nature a cough inside the bag of cultural obedience, no doubt something particular curves your back — and you are half-way after a big falling out of the tree after pushing into that cut to perceive what inveigling multi-resonance, what darkbeam clarity the circumstance might split and yield? Exile is a condition bolstered by the idea that home equals a place.

Setting to one side for now the important topics gestured to by the term transnational, transplace as movement states that when movement happens between one body/place and another, the movement itself is a real condition of being. Transnational assumes identifiers based on nations, thus it conditions, albeit in interesting political ways, what transplace might mean. Here, transplace means to resist and add to, to exceed and differentiate from, nation-state identification. To think multiple and moving soil water air clouds distance stones land-shapes plants cities transportation values and groups and sounds of different tongues and elements and animals as and in places.

Movement is a real substance; its in-between of bodies in places is another instance of thinking the heft and breath of the in-between. To be transplace is to be *as from,* to be shaped in the absence of unique place-origin and in the presence of multiple movement-origin, many kinds of fromness. Movement leaves the bodies among which it happens and becomes itself movement-location, lodged in the adult identity of its experiencers. More than strategic essentialism, I'm thinking about the rights to be accorded to different in-betweennesses, and, here, as those are manifest in transplace persons. We can recognize that the evidentiary person is not so easily correlative with our learned modes of recognition. We can recognize being-from-movement as its own belonging.

Luminol Historiography

> A man made his bed down on a grave but didn't know the grave was there until something told him that he was asleep on a grave. He knew someone was buried around there, but he forgot where it was. He just shifted over then and went to sleep.
>
> — Ida West, *Pride against Prejudice: Reminiscences of a Tasmanian Aborigine*[1]

Luminol historiography names a practice of exposing underlying layers of spilled blood, literal and symbolic, within literal and symbolic human sites. The sites include architectures, lived spaces, and geophysical forms. Proposed practitioners bring along metaphorical buckets of luminol, a chemical compound used to illuminate hidden blood in crime scenes, and a strong supply of brushes. They splash luminol historiography across the fettered landscapes, along human roads, across new and old buildings. Some of the sites ripple and pulse, gobble up the luminol, and glow.

In this particular imagining of historiography, luminol is overall metaphorical: The work is carried out in archival research,

1 Ida West, *Pride against Prejudice: Reminiscences of a Tasmanian Aborigine* (Montepelier Press, 2004), 78.

personal interviews, ecological change observations, ethnoautobiography, studies of building plans, and hiring (or impress) practices. Luminol historiographers might borrow crime show bearing to give themselves courage in difficult scenes in which they investigate underlying violence. Any given surfacing or careful cleansing may elude our historiographers, of course, and underneath there is always another underneath, the pressure of built history is so great, the palimpsest of Earth so generous.

Luminol historiography names a principle of historiographic impulses, which overall seek to render the once-occurring into graphemes and other materially perceptible forms: writing, drawings, excavated finds held under light. In this case, the focus is on bloodshed. The term came to me as an image of the researching body picking through the details and surfaces of cultural places in order to illuminate hidden blood traces. I was mentoring a student working on the creation of a modern colonial city: what it still now overlays, what its shininess might obscure in human trauma.

Although the luminol application might be largely metaphorical in luminol historiography, the brushes are real. They serve for definite acts of inscription: pen and ink, calligraphic witness, keystrokes of historiographic record. Think of writing with luminol pens and computers, theoretical techne that can make us consider all our devices for such making, and such records. What are the sources of our pencils and pens? What computing devices are we working with? What are their costs and devotions, their mined ingredients, their histories of replication and trash? What if our devices shimmered with their costs in blood when we held them under luminol light?

Blood can be moral and emotional as well as biological. It is part of our identities and economies. Some historical buildings glisten with gold made out of literal blood: one might wish real luminol to be applied to core samples of church and state gold laminate. Some cultural structures shine with the loss experienced by people who gave their life meanings and times to those structures without any real connection, sense of co-ownership, or recompense. Some buildings or roads may need a modified luminol compound, more like blood-money illumination, to show their sheens of obliteration.

Luminol historiographers can walk along any ground and splash their luminol across its surfaces: Launceston, Mount Royal, Santiago, Fuente Grande, Tāmaki Makaurau. A city shows its traces, contingent playgrounds, wired offices, layered living spaces, quite new oldnesses; it might seem easier to point the brush of luminol historiography at a city's bold erasures than it does to examine wide swaths of unbuilt ground. But any site can show its density of suffering with application. Look at Erín Moure's poetry studies of forest areas in Ukraine, in *Kapusta* (2015): how the plants coming out of ashen ground transmute the bodies of people buried underneath. The ground's a sponge of forgetting spilt. Take the luminol bucket and splash it on that ground — metaphorically of course, as we don't need another poison thrown on Earth, however much its resonance points back to us already: what's there, what isn't, what's wafted away or carefully repressed.

Ida West wrote one book, *Pride against Prejudice: Reminiscences of a Tasmanian Aborigine* (1984; she expanded it in 1987 and again in 2004), pulled through the repression of her circumstances and full of luminol. Some passages are overt about the historical blood infused into geophysical areas: "Tanner's Bay is a shocking place for ghosts. I don't know what happened there. There's an atmosphere about the place."[2] Other passages apply the luminol brush differently:

> I can remember Mr Colin Thorn asking me what was that letter. I said it was a snake, although he wanted me to say 's'. I'd get up and say the wrong thing, then tell him I couldn't learn.

2 Ibid., 16.

> Sometimes, though, I'd say something right. I liked writing. I always had problems putting the pen in the right hand, and when he wasn't looking I put the pen back in the left hand.[3]

West's historiography unconceals multiple layers of violence and turns them into possibilities of empowered writing and alternative reference in the very ground of suppression. In the passage above, using the style of reported speech voids the punctuational norm and puts the impetus of the teacher's question into the (left) hand of the writer. The letter ("s") is not a letter but a snake native to Lutruwita/Tasmania whose living shape gains priority over white education's abstract signs. The word "right" is performatively revealed as a matter of power, in the judgment of an answer ("right") echoed as the force applied against the child student's bodily left-handedness. Over and over, West invents her own communally situated, autochthon literate status, throwing new (luminol) ink on to given historical structures.

History shows up any time, of course, despite being so often obscured by the too-often swamping presentism of cultural acts and structures. History's our penumbral weather, perfusive and conditioning. And history has its allocations of deliberate forgetting, a cutting of significances out of a present rather than a perception of contiguity and continuity with a present. In other words, the present is for some cultures snipped from continuity with a past. Forgetting, as Stephen Turner and other thinkers about colonialism and its posts have written, is a central feature of cultural narratives.

---

3 Ibid., 6. This extraordinary communally-focused memoir is out of print: "It has taken me years to complete this book. I have never done anyone any harm. I mixed with everyone, tried to help people of all colours and races, as some have helped me. It was my sister Girlie, niece Leonie, daughter Lennah, daughter-in-law Elizabeth and cousin Clyde Mansell who told me to continue scribbling. I would stick the notes in a drawer on the shelf where they lay almost forgotten" (xv).

Yet luminol is, after all, crafted to wake up what's hidden. Some kinds of blood — of birth, of already well-recorded wars, of abattoirs — is to be expected. So when our researches open up literal and metaphorical bloodletting to view, we have to think about what portions are inevitable, waiting to be known for their details, and what are deliberately hidden, pushed into some criminal events of cultural fashioning, resistant to extrication, or previously known but carefully erased.

We ourselves are full of blood. What happens when we spill luminol on our own bodies? Does our blood shine through the skin? What is the story of that blood — have we spilled ourselves; is there an epigenetic revelation to be had? Where and what are our portions of doing and done-to, in the songs of violence? What happens when we answer those questions?

Thought Point

for Berta Cáceres

Lisa Samuels has not shared anything on this page with you
In her book a personal devotion to feminist theory
Is an erotic situation because words drape electrically through
her mind
Which insists on reciprocity where we live
Whose meeting point's a commission between external and in-
Sight: at the point where anything is made is the center of its
making
You can go there, over to the new center
Down to the new center, up to the new center
You integrate divergence without fail muscles
As a courtesy to this idea, which meets where you become one
too
Where the literal becomes physical as a consequence of your
attention
You become yourself a concept meeting that one, free
From self-possession's warrantless erasure of relation.

Go to work and take up the material of nature's swift ability
To self-heal, if you count a heal as change mark
To the dense struggle to make external possibles
Ready for those shots that come where she is not alone
The very visceral vanishing of point perspective
As the concept ceases to be holding
Provided by its other. The concept realizes self-perception's lonely cry
Because the filled-in area is vanishing.

Every center gets its day replete inside and out
Not long enough for anyone to know it
Which is why the exhalation leads to terminals where the
Battery charge of culture wants to rest. Please let us rest
Says Cloaky to the bastion of divergence. No, Cloaky, no:
She'll not. One's claim in faith to ill sunder finds
There's battle in the breath, certain scattered objects
Such as water, life, stars, eyes, voices calling out
A topic's reason for assent to start itself righteously
In the center of what's powerless. That center pulse
Gives out a new authentic, one's own object turns
A scaling trans-surrender in the zone that never mocks.
This is what gets called authentic tribute. The idea of her
Eyes and stars and water is a center one can breathe
In as example. The social location of our ideas has changed

Which is exhausting to the slow move against which
Measure's latent knowledge's wont to hover.

So we put a body there: its signs of force
Trigger the necessity of knowing from that center
Pulls us toward an other we accept, attention's moment
Emphasis mine. To cause her to be idea's open score
The words fill up our heady eyes and flesh out
To the multiples of center. We cannot abnegate
In thinking for her of her near to her
Breath's contention cancels out the slow
Determination how we value musters in "the world"
A known dispute. There's no way to speak ugly but to say
Plural's a wretch, so close in to the skin such
Convention's blasted its own wise.
Which is related, tell me, to the topic of our
Mass centrality everywhere you can think
Think allow it. This is predicated on belief
Your structures listen to announcements very far away
Her body brings it close and proves the rule.
The satisfied relief's no thought at all
Since publication's superadded form
The circumstance of central's system fix, means we're
Undergone, a fragmentation lick as having given up
In gaze. It almost makes you wish for porn's effects

Submission to the site where desire's activate
Hits hard a moving purview. The gaze returns itself
Without a recognition of its mirror apps
The schedule of our freedom's hidden from the beast
We give ourselves, a private reliquary stipend
When we save our chance to misrecognize
For the wrong occasion. We might instead cross-cut
The labor of our thought as yielding when
We meet in real quiescence to the far-off zone
Where thought displaces both itself and us.

The product of a woman failed itself far-reached
But only in a hid-sight dead to actual failure's
Crucial work. You have to give up in advance to understand
The work the water did over her flesh
Without analysis, our context becomes a moment's
Harvest kept with hers: that's thinking parlance
Self-formed in a wrap with far-clung instance
More authentic than what you're swamped with feeling's
Vacant register smashed on you when it's "close to home."
Further's no escape beyond control if it's choisir
We're dead not knowing so reciprocal to how
We might then land. I can't interpret her whom I've not seen
But having seen in scene withstand
Trajectory of thought beyond the heart.

Misrecognition's grace is there interpreted
Resisting on the eye, the living space a dark intended
Document we'll never see, so knowing's then a subject
Near to me so far as I have no such face nor never will.
Authentic listening's bonds broke mutual.
When you express it starts to feel as well, a mutual
Cancellation of captivity breached in the ramp
Where blood's a thought armed on the floor's example
Intemperate wish to make us heal as hole.
So nothing's thought the echo of this one-time stolen role.
Accept and don't accept the rigorous loss of view
Lisa Samuels has shared anything on this page with you

Bioautography and *VULVA'S MORPHIA*

The word of life, it is my meat.

—Anne Bradstreet, "The Flesh and the Spirit"[1]

Body Double

In 1997 Granary Books, a US publisher known for its lavish textualities, produced thirty-five copies of Carolee Schneemann's *VULVA'S MORPHIA*.[2] At the library rare books room where I first encounter it, *VULVA'S MORPHIA* arrives in a large grey box, a plexiglass slipcase 9⅛" wide, 11½" high, and 1¾" deep. Inside the box, the book presents its blood-red velveteen cover, with no words or letters on the front or back. Thus the first paratext or bibliographic code is tactility and color saturation, as though you aren't handling a book so much as a blood-colored

1 Anne Bradstreet, "The Flesh and the Spirit" (1678), in *The Complete Works of Anne Bradstreet*, ed. Joseph R. McElrath, Jr. and Allan P. Robb (Boston: Twayne, 1981): 175-76.

2 *VULVA'S MORPHIA* began as a thirty-six-image installation work. Carolee Schneemann, *VULVA'S MORPHIA*, 1995, photography and paper, 8 × 5 feet, each image 8.5 × 11 inches, text strips 2 × 0.58 inches, http://www.caroleeschneemann.com/vulvasmorphia.html.

work of thick velveteen wall art or portable sculpture. The book title is embossed on the spine, and when you open the book you see and feel that its 11" by 8 1/2" inner pages are stiff, with tight fuzzy grey paper. It's as though the spine is a backbone, while the coloring and touchy density of the pages proposes the grey matter of the brain in relation to the cover's red matter of oxygenated blood and soft tissue. The book has twenty-two thick and unnumbered pages, really page-boards, whose width, rigidity, and heft compel attentive movement, not swift turning as with normative codex paper. I turn the pages as though they were stiffened vellum, and this carefulness is motivated not only by the rare books room, with its panopticon fustiness, but by the book's intensely *made* quality. The tactility and body colors of *VULVA'S MORPHIA* bring into physical consciousness, even over-determine, what can often be a physically unself-conscious approach to a reading situation. A performed argument, enacted with book arts materials, precedes and prepares for the book's graphic and linguistic interiors. One historic echo is sentimental literature, in the positive sense of the "body in the mind" and "thought beating in the heart."[3] The book's body is an argument; the book's conceptualizing is emblooded.

You open the book onto its back and spread it out before you. Especially given the book's obsessions, the inner title page is legible as labia minora, with the inner folds coming after text body

3 "The body in the mind" is a frequently posited emphasis in studies considering pre-twentieth-century literatures of sentiment; we also hear it in body and affect theory work, as with Mark Johnson's 1987 book of that title. "[T]hought / Beating in the heart" is from Wallace Stevens, "Notes Toward a Supreme Fiction" (1942). For the present essay, a salient way to think about the history of sentiment comes in the "Declaration of Sentiments" signed in Seneca Falls in 1848 by one hundred activists seeking to redress the suppression of women's rights. Modelled on the US Declaration of Independence, the "Declaration of Sentiments" demands that women have "immediate admission to all the rights and privileges which belong to them as citizens of the United States." See Elizabeth Cady Stanton, "Declaration of Sentiments," in *History of Woman Suffrage, vol. 1*, ed. Elizabeth Cady Stanton, Susan B. Anthony, and Matilda Joslyn Gage (Fowler & Wells, 1889), https://www.gutenberg.org/files/28020/28020-h/28020-h.htm.

and page lips have been opened. The first softly grained photographic image (see fig. 11.1) features three fingers spreading a vulva, labia majora and minora illuminated in blue light. The credit at the end of the book calls this image "Saw over want," a "self-shot" from 1982, and the clause underneath this first image is "VULVA READS BIOLOGY AND UNDERSTANDS SHE IS AN AMALGAM." We can thus read the image in relation to words that posit VULVA as an anthropomorphized, or at least personal-pronouned, organ-consciousness. The distributed cognition of the body extends and shares its wet electric thinking activity with a cognizant and literate version of the female genitals. In Schneemann's vulvar organ-actor we might recall the modernist poet H.D. asserting that "[t]he brain and the womb are both centres of consciousness, equally important" and asking, "[s]hould we be able to think with the womb and feel with the brain?"[4] H.D. also calls the womb the "love-region," extending its capacities to men as well as women. Other precursors and compatriots keep company with what Schneemann is doing here, including Yoko Ono, who, as Schneemann notes, was also performing body art in the 1960s. The reading and understanding introduced on the first page of *VULVA'S MORPHIA* eventually come to encompass artistic as well as many other behaviors—anatomizing, burying, fucking, explaining, worshipping—with an emphasis on embodied spiritual activity. In a decidedly updated version of a literature of sentiment, Schneemann writes in a 1963 entry of her notebooks, "I decided my genital was my soul."[5] That decision is one that conditions her art works up through and beyond *VULVA'S MORPHIA*.

The self-shot nature of the vulva photograph (fig. 11.1) pushes this work inward toward the author, and the biologically performed and theorized self-telling aspects of *VULVA'S*

4 H.D., *Notes on Thought and Vision* (City Lights, 2001), which performs, in the words of Susan Stanford Friedman, "a modernist gynopoetic." See Friedman, *Penelope's Web: Gender, Modernity, H.D.'s Fiction* (Cambridge University Press, 1990), 11.

5 Carolee Schneemann, "The Notebooks 1963–1966," in *More Than Meat Joy: Complete Performance Works & Selected Writings* (McPherson, 1997), 55.

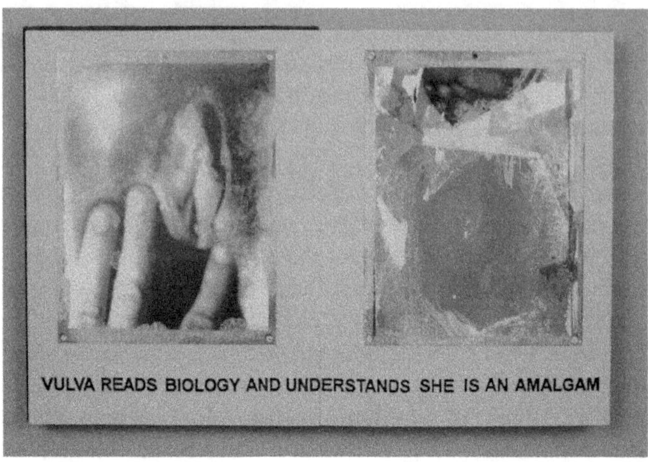

Fig. 11.1. Carolee Schneemann, from *VULVA'S MORPHIA* (Granary Books, 1997), n.p. Courtesy of the artist and Granary Books.

MORPHIA are this essay's main focus. Those aspects constitute Schneemann's version of what I call *bioautography*. This critical neologism inverts the normative term "autobiography": Instead of the "self-life-writing" order of the term autobiography, the term bioautography gives primacy to the bio-life in self-writing.[6] It also means to highlight the morphemic quotients of the

6 The relative emphases I perceive between autobiography and bioautography might be gestured to with examples: The first resembles André Malraux's *Anti-Memoirs,* trans. Terence Kilmartin (Holt, 1990), while the second resembles Kamau Brathwaite's *Ancestors* (New Directions, 2001) or Nathanaël's *The Sorrow and the Fast of It* (Nightboat Books, 2007). But then one would need to be familiar with those examples. If I'm asked to contrast autobiography and bioautography, I would point two fuzzy set hands in two directions, understanding that there are many works around and in between. One hand would lean toward norms of exposition, in which socially situating persons attempt to understand how life has shaped them, and they life, over some period of their reported experiences. That's autobiography. The other hand would lean toward poly-dimensional signage, from cross-genre to multi-media to performance to liquid syntax and other more apparently para-perceptible differentiations in how language can speak a self—and with an emphasis on the present and feeling body of the querying maker. That's bioautography. The latter, it is hoped,

syllables: bio-auto-graphy is bio-logical-/auto-matic and autonomic-/graphing. As term and concept, bioautography emphasizes several shifts. We move from the customarily abstracted cultural or character lessons of autobiography to start with the biology of *bio,* the body of the living person who makes the work. The term bioautography also means to emphasize two valences of the infix "auto": first, *autonomic,* and the degree of non-control that obtains in autonomic systems that motivate and sustain life, with all the sympathetic dubiety about conscious choice that accompanies an emphasis on our autonomic systems. Another valence of the infix "auto" is the *automatic:* matters of instinct from the epigenetic to the socially acquired, matters that also question how the will is involved in behaviors and events. This second emphasis includes not only responsive body-life and unconsciously regulated (or, for shorthand, "autonomic") body events but also the interruption of conscious control held up as a value in so-called "automatic writing," in which the writer makes an effort to loosen control of message and style within the writing process.

In a manner that might also be beckoned in the word autobiography, bioautography emphasizes the syllable *graph* as pointing to the plural potentialities of signage. Signage includes visual images with and without, as and not as, visual words. It also includes the signs of the body of words, the letters and other marks within layouts (lines, sentences, and more) that correspond and conjure with literate comprehension. Operating within a fundamentally written area—which is the primary though not exclusive signage of an event we call a book—bioautography emphasizes signage, recognizing writing as one type of sign within the embodied dimensionality of life writing. In a sighted environment, words themselves are of course graphemes, visual signs. Conceptually, graphing also refers to imagining relations among parts, the lines of blueprints (and blurprints) and meta-mathematical equations, the lines of con-

will have more expansive weight in this essay than this footnote can support.

sciousness distributed throughout the human body. Bioautography can refer also to performance writing, even as this essay focuses on the codical framing of *VULVA'S MORPHIA*.

Bioautography, then, means body life + focus on the accessible and inaccessible self + making as graphing. As a genre swerve, it extends and differs from my earlier use of the term "autography" to describe Lyn Hejinian's book *My Life*.[7] The features of bioautography in Schneemann's book are not entirely unique—that is not the point of my focus on this particular book—but instead are indicative of a turn in writing to viscerally specific biology of the identified self. The somato-psychic knowing and explication involved in bioautography index a widespread change in imaginative languages of the body self, and here of the vulva. We know, for example, *The Vagina Monologues,* whose first run was in 1996, a year before Schneemann's book; we know Schneemann's earlier work *Interior Scroll* (1975), a performance elsewhere remediated in video versions of Schneemann standing naked on a low table, pulling a long thin text from her vaginal canal and reading it aloud, the text issuing like umbilical cord language. Indeed, a still shot from *Interior Scroll,* "the Cave," appears in *VULVA'S MORPHIA,* one of twelve photographic images of Schneemann's anatomy among the thirty-six images of the book. The inclusion of images from earlier work within the pages of *VULVA'S MORPHIA* is an index of the mutually enfolding and cross-referential nature of Schneemann's oeuvre and its bioautographies. The body life is both accessible and the perfect horizon of the inaccessible self, which is always interior, even—or precisely—to life writing's investigations.

In this sense, bioautography presents a different facet of the concept of an author's "oeuvre." (Here "author" stands in for

---

7 Lisa Samuels, "Eight Justifications for Canonizing Lyn Hejinian's *My Life*," *Modern Language Studies* 27, no. 2 (1997): 103–19. "Autography" means to recognize the primacy of the written self, the languaged body, in some forms of life writing. See for example A.C. Spearing's *Medieval Autographies: The "I" of the Text* (University of Notre Dame Press, 2012), which applies this model to readings of medieval texts.

someone doing any artistic making, including writing and performing and videoing and more). We might be familiar with author studies focused in knowing the created works and knowing the artist's life in terms of serial social events and contextual connections. Knowing the author as a body is another way to conceive the work, as a body doubling with the author's body. In titling her essay book *Bodies of Work* (also 1997), for example, Kathy Acker (re)announces the self-conscious performance of an organ- and limb-level embodiment of knowing in her writing. And in Choy Ka Fai's *Prospectus for a Future Body* (2011), the body's co-imbrication with agentive digitality is somatically pursued, with a socially distributed impetus.[8] Bioautography's body double is also another way of thinking about epistemologies of the reader, about the literal anatomy of readership, as the human reader approaches the proffered human maker's work. Reading does not incur an invasion of privacy nor, usually, a literal exchange of touch between author and reader, though bioautography adds to the potential implications of physical closeness (and possible fetishization) such as author signatures and first-hand work performance.

Such first-hand performance is an acute topic of bioautography in the digitas, whose body works are called up online by our hands on devices and perceived through our eyes or ears or overall sensoria. The urge to split the atom of digital separation — to splay the body-self and invoke the body-end-user — pertains to many digital body-telling works, from Ka Fai's to Teresa Wennberg's *Brainsongs: Welcome to My Brain* (2001). These latter examples lack the viscerally genital self-intimacy of Schneemann's work, an intimacy increasingly available in online image-texts. Still, you cannot render a digital version of a work like Yoko Ono's *Cut Piece* (1964) with real bodies performing in real time, and the simulacral nature of digital platforms is far from handling the hard-to-find artist's book of *VULVA'S MORPHIA*. But Schneemann's images are online too, and the *idea* of

8 Choy Ka Fai, *Prospectus For a Future Body*, 2011, http://www.ka5.info/prospectus.html.

the body interpenetrates with its actual fluids and tactility. The difference is one of degree in a map that is always both body and idea.

In other words, bioautography emphasizes the body of the person writing herself even as it, conversely, reminds us that the personal body is always *conceptual.* Consider the second image of *VULVA'S MORPHIA* (also in fig. 11.1), a recto image that appears quite abstract compared to the verisimilitude of the opening vulvar self-shot. This second image's visual abstract presents a red patch with white swirls around it: The painted-over-collage effect above it looks a bit like paper and dermis tissue. Perhaps paradoxically, the book and the body arguably merge more explicitly in this second image than they do in the first. That is, in this second image the body's verisimilitude in representation and the book's textuality as fabrication are blended together in a way that challenges any notion that either is simply conceptual or simply physical. This blend is a version of the membranism that characterizes bioautography: the wet interface between artist and work, between concept and embodiment, and between work and reader. Here again, the sentimental is political: The "body in the mind" of bioautography is an emphasis that extends from an Anglo-American-Australasian literary history to possibilities for present-day body theory that combines the aesthetic concerns of a writer like Friedrich Schiller with the political concerns of the "Declaration of Sentiments" to produce art like *VULVA'S MORPHIA.* My epigraph from Anne Bradstreet, for example, indexes a seventeenth-century view of split body and mind, or "Flesh and Spirit," even as I am drawn to the line of her poem that actually mashes together meat, text, and soul. This essay's bioautographical reading of Schneemann's work seeks to conceptualize the crucial dimensional entropy that obtains and intertwines "between" one interface and another: body and mind, flesh and idea, and (a related artificial separation) art and politics. To emphasize the body in the mind is still a needed counterbalance to the rational suppositions that dominate interpretations and expectations of abstract semiotics such as written language. It may be that the overall cultural need to stabilize sign systems, for legal, identity, and monetary reasons, means that readings of entropy and interface, such as bioautography, are permanently in the position of counterweights that need rearticulating.

Body Triple

The dialectical implications of such interfaces conjure another way to perceive the bioautography of *VULVA'S MORPHIA*. An endnote tells us that the second image of *VULVA'S MORPHIA*, in fig. 11.1, is also a photo-work by Schneemann, this one titled "Triptych—Impressed." The image title emphasizes the visual artwork and the conceptual body turned to religious art. Triptychs originated as European religious, and especially medieval, visual trilogies of telling, often in central positions, such as altars, in Christian church arrangements. The three folds proposed different temporal moments in a given typology, a customary, familiar, and implicitly narrated religious scene. In Schneemann's image, the triptych has been brought into one panel. The image "impresses" a triptych relation—the telling of the body, the work, and the activation (seeing or reading *VULVA'S MORPHIA*)—into a single frame. The self and book are further melded, further inscored in a shared membrane.

Of course, the vulva can be seen as a triptych as well: Open the side doors of the labia and the central panel is revealed. Art triptychs can be seen as opening bodies, as a well-known surviving triptych, Hieronymus Bosch's *The Garden of Earthly Delights* (c. 1490–1510), reminds us. Bosch's *Garden* is enclosed within a case whose outside bears an exterior world creation image; you open the large doors to witness the three panels "moving" left to right, shifting from innocence to experience (though ambiguous signs characterize the distinctions between those states) to hellish penetrations (less ambiguous). If we could imagine Bosch's three panels "impressed" together, we might posit the visual consequence, and its conceptual provocations, as similar to those posited in Schneemann's second image. Here I am thinking of the meaning quotients of Bosch's well-known triptych in relation to Michel de Certeau's insight about "ratios of fabrication": the reading of and as artifice, the *poesis* of interpretively impenetrable surface, demanded by the mimetically irrealist energies of Bosch's *Garden.*[9] If the triptych is a dimensionalized work, beyond and within its boxed structure, then all the visuals can be seen as simultaneous intra-impressions, commenting with each other. In Bosch's case an impress of all three panels might mean the panel of pinkish innocence would meet its oils with the central panel of circulating people-ish bodies, both in turn blending together with the dark skewerings of the hellish right panel. Put it together, close the panel doors, and it makes a blended world. This is the kind of thing I mean when thinking of Schneemann's triptych as coextensive with its embedded alternatives.

In other words, Schneemann's images work like book-bound biological sculpture whose accompanying language renders their import culturally clear though not descriptively circumscribed. You could say it works the other way around, too; maybe the images are what we want to call additional, but the intensity of its book arts and visual arts can make the verbal language of *VULVA'S MORPHIA* seem at times superadded. (This essay's Appendix quotes the 151 words that constitute the main text of *VULVA'S MORPHIA*). Compared with the semiotic multi-dimensionality of the book's images and artist book rarity, its language can seem informational and anchoring, only lightly determining how we might interpret the visuals and haptics. As with the title of the photo-work "Triptych—Impressed," the words encourage us toward a conceptual or even neo-ekphrastic reading of the body images.

At the same time, the physicality of the words is in resistant relation with some customarily abstract expectations readers can bring to lingual semantics. In *VULVA'S MORPHIA*, the

9 See Michel de Certeau, "The Garden: Delirium and Delights of Hieronymous Bosch," in *The Mystic Fable*, vol. 1: *The Sixteenth and Seventeenth Centuries*, trans. Michael B. Smith (University of Chicago Press, 1992), 49–72.

running text underneath each image is printed in all caps. The font is an impressed and richly black text with edge tremor. It looks like blown-up newspaper or typewriter font. The words have an inset quality like black inky canyons you can feel when you run your fingers across and into the typeface. This is "inner" text, impressed into and pushed below the page surface, text that is immensely touchable, all of which is another stylized expression of the condition of inwardness of VULVA and her book. The layering of image, image title, principal running text, and book art form structures a dimensional enactment, language plus embodiment, as this essay has already suggested. In the case of the "impressed" typeface, its tactility reminds us exteroceptively of the embodied practices of people of the book, from the touched-smooth surfaces of the lower parts of the Wailing Wall to the effaced images of holy personages in books touched thousands of devout times to the chiseled stone of inset words in grave markers, replicated in turn in the US Vietnam Memorial names made into inner text. The touch of text is critical to its processing, another counterweight to its presumptive abstract investiture.

VULVA's overt character reading underscores this situation in a negative perspective. The autonomic aspect of bioautography is emphasized, for example, in the book's first sentence, printed across three pages: "VULVA READS BIOLOGY AND UNDERSTANDS SHE IS AN AMALGAM / OF PROTEINS AND OXYTOCIN HORMONES WHICH GOVERN ALL / HER DESIRES...."[10] This opening sentence is both true and not true, in the Nietzschean sense, given the combination of "reading" with "hormones." The interaction of reading, an acquired artifice of cultural transactions, is blended with the experience of being infused with hormones like oxytocin. Reading and being infused with hormones are made explicitly co-equal; the artificial and the natural are perfused together, therefore, not "all her desires" can be governed by the autonomic or unconsciously regulated. The import of the language here allows us to see the slippage or deferral of its com-

10 Ellipses in original.

munication and pushes us toward reading other parts of the text for life meaning and work import. The language indicates a frame that also and concurrently slips.

The arguments I'm making here about the overall perfusion of body and mind, bio-life with abstract concept, text as image and image as text, take a different direction from Donna Haraway's assertion of a non-identity between the genetic apparatus of "the human" being and the accompanying genetic apparatus "not human" that is within the same human body. Haraway writes:

> I love the fact that human genomes can be found in only about 10 percent of all the cells that occupy the mundane space I call my body; the other 90% of the cells are filled with the genomes of bacteria, fungi, protists, and such, some of which play in a symphony necessary to my being alive at all, and some of which are hitching a ride and doing the rest of me, of us, no harm. I am vastly outnumbered by my tiny companions; better put, I become an adult human being in company of these tiny messmates. To be one is always to become with many.[11]

The final sentence makes the best fit with the emphases of bioautography, which would want to query Haraway's description of an "I" split from resident others. "I" is not restrictively equivalent to human genomes any more than one's experience of an object-event is separable from all other describable aspects of that object-event. With its corrective swerves toward a notion of the body fully in mind, the concept of bioautography includes these elements together. The autonomic is that which exceeds in relation with genetic expression or putative semantic will. In this way a connection between the fabrications of the emblooded body and the fabrications of semiotic excess in language can be seen as functioning, in part, autonomically. Body triple adds to

11 Donna J. Haraway, *When Species Meet* (University of Minnesota Press, 2008), 3–4.

bioautography's body double (body of author + body of work) the infinite body of alterity we can associate with what Schneemann calls her genital soul. The conceptual connectivity of infinite interpretive potentiality is (also always already) physical. Body triple's dialectic is within a circle that performs semiotically the interconnection of the living bioautographical author with the body, signs, and contexts that all co-make her work.

Body Tropological

The *MORPHIA* of Schneemann's book title beckons us to consider forgetfulness, what is forgotten by VULVA, as well as the active agent, the drug ("morphine") of VULVA. VULVA's drug is desire, and it is also the relation of thinking and desire to sight. The artificed combinations of life presented as VULVA's experience exceed the biological apparatus of a vulva, which has no literal eyes to read. No eyes, that is, unless she operates with and as a new semiotics: In Schneemann's book, VULVA becomes language and reads, interacting the biological with the cultural, interacting the autonomic—or the unconsciously regulated machinations of our bodies—with the willful. The word morphia has also the word "morph" within it, and the morphing from one form to another is part of the desire-drug indicated by the book's title. VULVA's morphia is to exceed the physical body by not operating within its normative biological constraints. Rather than the threat of the female anatomy in the folklore images of *vagina dentata,* we have the anatomically active morphing into *vagina oculus,* vagina with eyes, a blend of the gazed-upon with an empowered answering gaze.

This sighted vagina partakes of an old comparative: We see it for example as a culminant observation in Geoffrey Chaucer's "The Miller's Tale," when the summary of Alisoun's relatively empowering experiences includes the line "And Absolon hath kist hir nether ye."[12] In that case the nether eye is part of a skew-

12 Geoffrey Chaucer, "The Miller's Tale," I.3852, in *The Riverside Chaucer,* ed. Larry Benson (Houghton Mifflin, 1987), 77.

ering of the men bent on having sex with Alisoun. In *VULVA'S MORPHIA*, the seeing and reading VULVA is a more explicitly dimensionalized agent: She experiences herself in landscapes, in the flesh, and as a passive and active agent in contests for art and power. *VULVA'S MORPHIA* is full of photographs and other images that emphasize transcultural and perceivable (trans-semiotic) vulvar forms in landscapes, urban objects, abstract forms, and religious iconography. The extrusion of bioautography into psycho-geography is well indicated in the work that Schneemann does with vulvar forms. Across these gathered images, VULVA moves like a trans-self between concept and apparition in the vulvar morphings of Schneemann's book.

Perhaps especially given the contortions involved in these kinds of conceptually anatomical morphings, we also want to consider pain, and *MORPHIA* as the drug that dulls pain. This is the kind of pain theorized by writers such as Elaine Scarry in *The Body in Pain* (1985), J.G. Ballard in *The Atrocity Exhibition* (1970) and other works, and Kathy Acker in most of her novels. How is VULVA pained? As a consequence of her cultural position, Schneemann's book proposes, and it is a position entirely stitched in with the physical position she occupies. One bioautographical image shows a treated photo of Schneemann as a naked toddler in a swim tub, a photo that was (according to Accreditation #30 in the end pages) scissored by the ten- or eleven-year-old Schneemann, who cut off the bottom half of the photo in what was presumably a fit of self-conscious shame. The adult Schneemann, the composer of *VULVA'S MORPHIA*, restores the image in and as art (fig. 11.2). The genital and leg areas are drawn back in, with coloration both arcane and artful. It's arcane because we can see the drawn-in portion in terms of its photo-coloration, used especially in the second half of the nineteenth century and early twentieth century to intensify photographic information, to make photographs look more fruity and lively, to artificially import so-called "natural" color into black and white photographs. It's artful because here the coloration combines so-called natural color (green for grass)

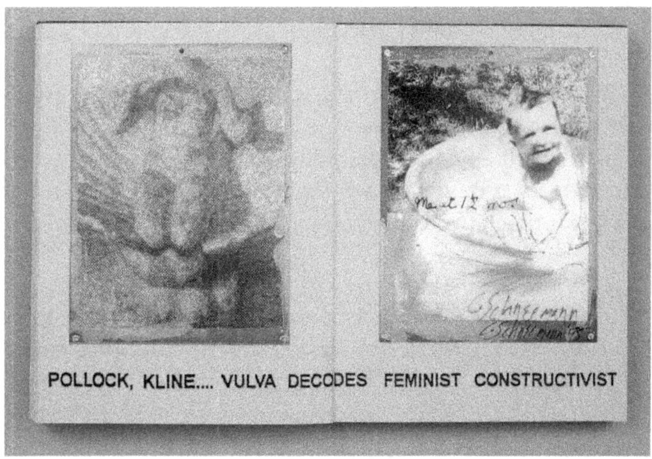

Fig. 11.2. Carolee Schneemann, from *VULVA'S MORPHIA* (Granary Books, 1997), n.p. Courtesy of the artist and Granary Books.

with highly symbolic color (red for the extirpated then restored lower half of the young child's body).

Here the morphing entailed by the book's title has been violently scissored on the genital area of the depicted author-as-child figure. That semiotic wound has been healed by the bio-autographical author, whose signature is explicit on the altered photo, as well as by her avatar, VULVA, within this book. Part of the semiotic healing is the blend of the mimetic with the tropo-mimetic, specifically the tropo-metonymic, the blend of the half-body of the natural child with the half-body of the conceptual, spiritual child. The healing registered in fig. 11.2 is not in rendering sutures imperceptible but in allowing semiotic cross-fertilization to both show and mediate that wound. I derive this idea of the tropo-metonymic from the medieval fourfold interpretive model (echoed, here and there, ever since): the literal, allegorical, tropological, and anagogical. In Schneemann's case, the tropological—the quest of the spirit—is perched within and as the vulva. The tension between suppositions about genitalia and questing souls is part of the bioautography of *VULVA'S MORPHIA*.

As a textual character, VULVA is mostly aware of these issues and in pain as the at-once aware and oppressed educated version of herself. The text does not permit escape from the constructed scenes of VULVA's self-awakening. About two-thirds of the way through the text,

> VULVA STRIPS NAKED, FILLS HER MOUTH / AND CUNT WITH PAINT BRUSHES, AND RUNS INTO THE CEDAR / BAR AT MIDNIGHT TO FRIGHTEN THE GHOSTS OF DE KOONING, / POLLOCK, KLINE.

The mouth full of paint brushes is yet another morphing of VULVA into a mouth, or into a vulva with a mouth, that is then turned to a body + art vulva-like opening once again when filled with paint brushes whose bristles (presumably of non-human-animal hair) perform a family resemblance with human genital hair. Meanwhile VULVA is also described as having a cunt that is filled with art tools (paint brushes), in a replicative doubling or self-metonymy that intensifies the lingual dialectics. This complex report of a genital-dialectical action-self unfolds across pageboards whose images are also and already intensifying depictive dialectics. The bioautography acts as a self-telling pressured in pluri-dimensional apparent dumbness: Here the filled state of VULVA's mouth (filled with the tools of art) also renders her unable to speak. We are made to experience the bioautographic message across all the book's signs rather than as a report of a deputed speaker, since although printed words are part of this book's semiotics, VULVA as a posited character never speaks. Her "voice" is suppressed, as even in this rebellious moment VULVA double-brushes art with a painting mouth (in the face) and a painting mouth (in the genitals). At this textual moment VULVA also, of course, stands in for the live embodied organism in relation to ghosts of dead art.

The woman artist "becomes" VULVA, analyzing politics, as the final endnote indicates, according to what is good for VULVA.

At one of its limit points, bioautography thus has the body in effect stand in for and as the entire "self." *VULVA'S MORPHIA* is an organic continuation, in book art form, of the artistic ethics articulated in Schneemann's *More Than Meat Joy.* Explaining her 1963 work with "Eye Body," Schneemann writes:

> Covered in paint, grease, chalk, ropes, plastic, I establish my body as visual territory. Not only am I an image maker, but I explore the image values of flesh as material I choose to work with. The body may remain erotic, sexual, desired, desiring but it is as well votive: marked, written over in a text of stroke and gesture discovered by my creative female will.
>
> I write "my creative female will" because for years my most audacious works were viewed as if someone else inhabiting me had created them — they were considered "masculine" when seen as aggressive, bold. As if I were inhabited by a stray male principle; which would be an interesting possibility — except in the early sixties this notion was used to blot out, denigrate, deflect the coherence, necessity, and personal integrity of what I made and how it was made.
>
> In 1963 to use my body as an extension of my painting-constructions was to challenge and threaten the psychic territorial power lines by which women were admitted to the Art Stud Club, so long as they behaved **enough** like the men, did work clearly in the traditions and pathways hacked out by the men. (The only artist I know of making body art before this time was Yoko Ono).[13]

Schneemann's use of the word "votive" in describing matters of the will can also apply to the tropo-metonymy of *VULVA'S MORPHIA*. Having engaged materials of the entire body for decades, Schneemann here concentrates on its spiritually core element of the genitals. The book's photographic image of human copulation, featuring a tumescent penis upright inside a vagina, is arguably an example of VULVA being "inhabited by a stray male

13 Schneemann, *More Than Meat Joy*, 52.

principle" and thus an image of conversation, medial apotheosis, even an acknowledgment of the male genitalia as being along on the book's spiritual quest. The conversation is intensified when we see that image as also looking like the vagina has grown a penis depending downward; the morphing impetus so prevalent in *VULVA'S MORPHIA* transforms into an Escher-like blend. In that interpretation of the book's copulation photo, at the level of the human genitals VULVA brings the "male principle" along to ask the question that ends "VULVA'S SCHOOL," the autodidactic feminafesto that closes off the book: "Vulva learns to analyze politics by asking, 'Is this good for Vulva?'"

Limit Case

So is the bioautographic body also hierarchized, or is it entirely distributed? There are things to say about the positive aspects of a re-decline in the ideology of personal bodily modesty in western thinking, though that topic is complicated by necessary attention to privacy matters. But I want to end by emphasizing the limit case of the vulva as bioautographic locus. The vulva here, in the majority of the book's images, is the topographic aspect of the vagina, visible "on" the moving body and in sculptures, flower heads, and the book's other *hors-corps* images, whereas much of the vagina (both biological and as pictured in *VULVA'S MORPHIA*) is interior.

Partly, as indicated in the brush-mouthed *VULVA* passage quoted above, this genitally bioautographic locus is a matter of sound and voice. The evidently language-less, that is, speechless, VULVA stands in for the evidently language-less body, for whom language functions as apparatus—an acquired addition to the body's natural or rest-state sounds (circulatory and nerve-system in origin, thumping and high-pitched) and to the articulate sounds the voice box can make even without language. We can imagine the absence of speaking parts for VULVA, in a book dedicated to her expressive and political work, as indicating the book's desire to throw into question the relations of anatomical authenticity with artifice. The languaged, but not speaking,

VULVA inhabits a tense region of balance and displacement between abstraction and embodiment. Moreover, the absence of speaking points to an emphasis on the expressive and communicative power of body semiotics without language, of expressive and communicative composition as non-explanation. In other words, it points to one important feature of bioautography: its performance of the opaque, the interpretively impenetrable or infinitely *potential,* semiotics of body-life.

In this sense Schneemann's book is a descendent of one of the earliest female-authored English-language manuscripts, *The Booke of Margery Kempe* (c. 1440). Margery's book is set up as narrated by a woman to more than one male scribe; it thus posits Margery as having a second-order, displaced voice in the midst of a drive toward embodied spirituality—tropological flesh. Margery's unsettling "roaring" and frequent spiritually-induced tears can be read as another version of the excessive, dripping female body in and as a book that stands, in turn, for a self that is conceptualizing spiritual intensity. Margery's book is a very early example of controversial bioautography, with a displacement between concept (abstract language) and flesh (voice).

It is trans-semiotic displacement that makes the connection here. The complex semiotic rendering and questioning of the power of language in *VULVA'S MORPHIA* is in part a result of the cooperative subordination of the words to the body of the book and its many visuals, a result of images that bristle and copulate silently, whose activity points to what is not there (sounds, past events, other places). The body of the bioautographical writer cannot be actually present and yet is made, conjured as, present. This semiotic pain is at once a register of insistence and impossibility: a semiotic wound that has to remain continually open in order to be continually healed. This is one point where we might think about the nature of distributed bioautography. Yes, the body's largest holes—mouth, eyes, ears, nose, anus, vagina, meatus—are hierarchized as entry and exit points for the body. Yes, VULVA is metonymized as a paradoxically whole, active agent in this book. The bioautographic distribution happens at the level of interface with what is outside the body. This is the distribution of bioautography with and across its art form. It exceeds the boundaries of the body via the holes, bringing in the world and pushing the body out as the world. This insistence is part of the intimacy of bioautography, whether accomplished with a focus on the holes of the eyes or mouth or vulva. As Marquis de Sade understands with the constant artifice-reset-button he pushes in a book like *Justine*, the customarily unseen genitals can be a faster conduit to responsive attention in the rupture between the seen (we see what we think we know we see) and the unseen (we suddenly look at the genital other-as-same).[14] The dialectical distribution here is with the world rather than within a set-apart body. The most intimate or private part of the body acts as a sign and conduit for the connection of the self with all that is outside the self.

A related limit point is that imagining VULVA as and with a language puts us in the position of thinking explicitly about where semiotics works in terms of desire and power. The presumption of what comes first is inverted in the shift from "autobiography" to "bioautography." Leading with the body, rather than with expository and narrative language about abstract identity, is leading with opaque and unset meaning. In that sense it is more overtly rupturing. Not only because it is the body per se—any "being" might perhaps do this kind of critical work—but because, in the matter of self-telling, leading with the body is leading with distributed quiddity. The body does not stand, or lie down, or open up *for* or *to;* it stands, lies down, looks, opens. But *VULVA'S MORPHIA* goes further than that in what I am calling its tropo-mimesis: The tropo-metonymy of VULVA standing in as the self works in relation to the spiritual iconography that Schneemann unveils. To put the female genitalia in the position of the spiritually seeking self is bioautography with a vengeance.

---

14 Marquis de Sade, *Justine, or the Misfortunes of Virtue*, trans. John Phillips (Oxford University Press, 2013). For Barthes's salient comments about semiosis in de Sade, see Roland Barthes, *Sade, Fourier, Loyola*, trans. Richard Miller (University of California Press, 1989).

Appendix

Full principal text of *VULVA'S MORPHIA* (not including inner title page, two appendix pages, and colophon):

> VULVA READS BIOLOGY AND UNDERSTANDS SHE IS AN AMALGAM / OF PROTEINS AND OXYTOCIN HORMONES WHICH GOVERN ALL / HER DESIRES.... VULVA DECIPHERS LACAN AND BAUDRILLARD / AND DISCOVERS SHE IS ONLY A SIGN, A SIGNIFICATION OF THE / VOID, OF ABSENCE, OF WHAT IS NOT MALE.... (SHE IS GIVEN A / PEN FOR TAKING NOTES....) VULVA READS MASTERS AND JOHNSON / AND UNDERSTANDS HER VAGINAL ORGASMS HAVE NOT BEEN / MEASURED BY ANY INSTRUMENTALITY AND THAT SHE SHOULD / ONLY EXPERIENCE CLITORAL ORGASMS.... VULVA RECOGNIZES / HER SYMBOLS AND NAMES ON GRAFFITI UNDER THE RAILROAD / TRESTLE: SLIT, SNATCH, ENCHILADA, MUFF, COOZIE, / FISH AND FINGER PIE.... VULVA STRIPS NAKED, FILLS HER MOUTH / AND CUNT WITH PAINT BRUSHES, AND RUNS INTO THE CEDAR / BAR AT MIDNIGHT TO FRIGHTEN THE GHOSTS OF DE KOONING, / POLLOCK, KLINE.... VULVA DECODES FEMINIST CONSTRUCTIVIST / SEMIOTICS, AND REALIZES SHE HAS NO AUTHENTIC FEELINGS AT / ALL; EVEN HER EROTIC SENSATIONS ARE CONSTRUCTUED BY / PATRIARCHAL PROJECTIONS, IMPOSITIONS, AND CONDITIONING....

Variations on the Lexememe

Performance with a lingual tenor
keyed to haptic para-senses
bright express

a dream of counting
on an infinite beach
every grain of words

here's my dog of language
heark heark
bustling the frame

a reel reportage
doting pink experience
in a wreckt descript

an abrasion outside pleasanture's ex-weeping
in reactive electric color woven
doctrine made a singular blindesse

someone's holding a plicative mode frenze
with fun bodies in cloth
facing a swift embouchure of plosions

slats on bridges flapped by gaps
and dendrite whorl pats
for neutrality with genderness

a thought balloon
thin vellum water bomb
incoming

some bricolage with sowers (succumbing laughing
nodding agreement at a fair
urbanity with florals

corner-turning in the city's shiny
country geoplummet
break out to unveil

history cake sliced
through with tongues
all flavor pages

terraforming with rentless sign
interiors toward a moment of
seclusion with ice cream

a diegesis of intelligible lips
four prisms soft-sanding
by a tanner

language is an atmosphere
we breathe magnetic
oxygen co-sough

a set of words
entangled
in a bough

(accelerando) something winged
un-hinging singing crinkling
to unfetter

haunting lying plane of sigh
laugh ghetto
pick up schticks

truckle text the body's grammar lust
an epidermis thread
infinite bloom

hammering pianos
with a homeomorph
enjoining the intone

simcast skies
fondle cloth maples
copying sine's murmur

already quantum language
shows the way
non-locality in any touch

eyes up the icosahedron
anchor pointillist
toward chiaroscuro twang

mess wrangle
durée from your archaic oak
joints

some dear self self-toggling
conjunctions open hand
sidestroke into a messy kelp

heave words make
verbal islands yummy
syllable cress

a game of trace
the map conjoining Mach bands
tighten a genre heave

hyphen-dragging street cars
purple entwine
vroom

measure a word one way and
(go ahead superpose more)
mentum another

swerving or n-dimensional
bullet gravel
pushing blood ink

graphemic mouths & light
transit late
recycle the innards of words

breathe in morpheme
breathe out
lingual dioxide

neither a paragraph nor a stanza be
for bodies recombine
diffractionly

a twist on a curling anime of
word shapes spit
letter beans on-field

watching the page
brim with water re-
code

sign the walk with legs
pen-like stitching books
sliding in justified screes

description's velvet corduroys soaked
in a wet commutative
mulch

a persona grid traducing
documents to claim a past or
book some phoneme loge

intralinear casements growing
word molecules
climb an anaphora

someone with berry juice interstices
conveys your mind to
plank on clouds (come on)

a word suddenly
opens the door of
another word

chalk tablet for edible presupposition's
disappearing links recipe or
cramming the mouth tenderly full of letters

red trails for phrase's pas de deux
reserves a single word
a convex glass

leaning on allusion's heavy sword
a bright dirt quilt
over ideas of nationhood

the soft pad of my dog's thumb
creates the walk we take
loading petals

tract talking on the trail
signs in midair
scrolls for glossy animals

3

Soft Text and the Open Line

1

Soft text is potential text arising within language users in our interactions with ourselves, permeant surfaces, other beings, and events of living. It's language that silently formulates, that never quite materializes, in relation to hard text forms like speaking and writing. Soft text is the invisible textuality of potential language: language that stays within the mind. You imagine an utterance but you don't say it, or soft text is what is left out of what you do say.

Soft text is present in every moment of lingual living. It can be an interior imagining of uttered oral text — someone speaks and you picture the words in your mind — or an aural imagining of visually presented text, as in silently sounded reading. Soft text trembles in the encounter between a language user and an object-event. These trembles can be morpheme fragments, phonemic waves, full unuttered sentences, and more. Because soft text is potential in the moment, its visuality or aurality or tactility is imagined but never incarnate as hard text.

A line in soft text is an increment of encounter experienced as a medial not-quite-articulation in the vivified non-evidence that constitutes soft text. Say you look at some boats and your soft text silently describes those boats. They move like little soft text lines, each boat a word or phrase, their conglomeration a soft text bunch of lines. *Boat boat boat little white boat tilt boat shiny*—this description cannot be soft text because it's recorded in hard text form, but it's an example of what could be a soft text instance had it not been written here. And if those descriptive boat words happen inside your mind in silently sounded reading, that interior saying is a soft text, translated from the visual and not spoken.

Say you look at a boat you know, with a person on it with whom you are connected. That boat's soft text has many other lines, exponentialized by the potential utterances between you and that person, the soft text between you. *Line boat shoe turn then love now if soft wind plan eyes mouth body speaking:* this description also cannot be soft text, see as above. It's a hard text example of the soft text that cannot be exemplified, though its lingual omnipresence can be pointed to.

Soft text is a lingual experience theory analogous to the social space theory of Lisa Robertson's "soft architecture," a term for embodied interactive living in devices, histories, and circumstances of architecturally built areas. Taking inspiration from Rem Koolhaas's Office for Metropolitan Architecture (OMA), and situated in other critical swerves against monumentality, Robertson's book *Occasional Works and Seven Walks from the Office for Soft Architecture* (2003) considers examples such as ephemeral shacks and city fountains, and our bodies walking near them, as soft architectural activity amidst "lasting" architectural constructions.[1]

Amidst hard texts, soft text goes unsaid. The said is the selection from potential soft text—not necessarily controlled selection—in oral text. The spontaneous said is the partial waiver of the potential of soft text in the oral encounter, no scribbled speech notes around, no social media script. Say you are speaking on the phone with someone: Soft text occurs in the moments

1 See Lisa Robertson, *Occasional Work and Seven Walks from the Office for Soft Architecture* (Clear Cut Press, 2004).

when no-one is saying any words aloud and yet you know the line is open.

Hard text and the line is another matter. Hard text is inscribed or uttered in or on or through some recipient recordable surface(s). A hard text line stays the potentiality of soft text, even as soft text hovers around the line with alternate instance. Soft text is the alterity, ghost, futurity, prefiguration, and potential otherness of the hard text line.

Soft text has nothing against hard text. After all, hard text has the incarnate virtue. It generates yet more potential for soft text in relation to the said and inscribed. Where would soft text be without incarnate textuality? Who would learn its rhythms? Who would imagine its absences?

Where would hard text be without the potential alterities of soft text wreathing around and inside it?

Say you are in the Metro and hard text defines many spaces around you, where to go, what's here and there, what to buy, what people are saying to each other. Soft texts are the spaces among those incarnate textualities. The walls glow with what might be said about them. You might answer a sign in your mind *"what fucking way out?"* and your irritated silent soft text links you to that Metro text without your saying a word to anyone.

Say you are walking on a hill and speaking nothing nor writing in relation with the hill at that moment. The hill has things to express—reports from other encounters, possible verbal descriptions of its dimensions and past shapes and inhabiting animals and plants. You say nothing and the hill says nothing. Yet the potential for utterance wreathes your encounter. You imagine partial sentences, words that flit between you and the hill, lingual matters in your thoughts. You say nothing and write nothing, not deliberately leaving out hard text, just walking and thinking in relation to that hill. That is a structure for the potential presence of soft text.

Everyone makes soft text in dreams. Text that can really/almost/never be told, though its reports ricochet through language like poetry.

In a hard text poem, soft text is conceptual breath opening lingual potentiality—perhaps even without regard to the degree of openness of the set line, or at the least in a discorrelate relation with cloistered strophes or open page layout. Soft text is potential alternates within phrases inside the lines, potential letter chiasms that conjure the bodies of other, absent letters, the partly lingual gestures of the interface hand touching the screen, unarticulated contiguities and potential recombinant lettrification. The more opportunities there are for soft text, whether within lexical strings (words, phrases, lines) or across the composition (shaped correlations, transmediality, conducted surface area), the more the line can breathe ideas, feelings, and presence.

2

A poetic line can be theoretically and practically any articulation and response, from visual-tactile (page/screen/cloth/glass/floor/wall) to sonic (live/recording/voice/instrument/ambience) to biological (tattoo/cellular etch) to conceptual (posited with a translucent poetic or without any instance at all).

A hard text line is a unit of order from potential. It is a locutable, a Hello, an attention moment, a space-time within simultaneity, an irruption in the scrutable, a node, a clasp, an extension, a sustained rhythm, a yell in one spot, an echo from one place to another place right away or across what's called history, a touch on the page and thus to you, a link on the screen to another node that catches it and throws you on, a tiny roseate cut whose reading makes it blossom, an audible yelp or flutter brought into hearing by your hand as you touch the arrow pointing > then you || it and you make it > again you || it and you stutter it with your digital flick or control button your finger tip or if you're aural/ oral you flint it with your mouth you tell it to Act, that's a line on screen a line inscreen like inline skates you go a direction you touch the > || [] you make it start pause stop you make the line as a unit of continue or Force Stop.

A line proves the rule of language's constitutive inability to foreclose; it's a freeclose, it opens up a claim on your attention, the Hello a unit of welcome toward a potentially limitless otherness of switching on your head to a shaped attention

A line is a ridgeway on a topomap and a lit path on a screen, paper page and illuminated text lit in your relation

A line is a soundwave, a sound moving its arm across the ready air you notice it, you co-make its airwave ripples

A line is a sightmark, a deep cave surfing its opening on a held page, miniature hugeness echoing inside your cavernous eyespace

A line is a mindlight, scattered blink city or like bridge lights one by one by one by one by one by one by one your mental car's attention turns them on you pass through turning on the lights.

A line intervenes in soft text as a rendering. In whatever passes for oneself as ordinary existence, a line is a moment of attention. You give yourself to it and it is glancing, fleeting, a trace, or you give yourself longer and it asks for more and it's sustained, prolonged. It exists by itself with your attention or it adds to another line and you make something together with your holding the variable hand of the line.

3

In trauma or in ecstasy, we could say the line is obliterated: experience blares, you are integrated by being split and holding excess with your body. The line in this case becomes a report from elsewhere, a translation and medial stasis within that rupture of your ordinary existence. The soft text of trauma is a swamped blare. Its hard text can produce lines that are anything from sliced glare to careful pulses, depending on when you make lines out of the record.

In Bill Direen's *Enclosures 2* (2016), for example, the death of his father is explicitly part of what swerves the otherwise-prose of Direen's book into a prolonged poetry. Here are some lines from the long poem "Centre":

Light scales, optometry puddles on the walls,
Suspensive shade,
Tempera touches as just-audible matter.
Pods deliquescing as matte shade, joining fingers,
It all throws me across a parallel to be of one mind,
Before snapping me back to a correlative *hamartia,*
Where stems swish and proudly seed.

Spinning disks of coal shiny vinyl once voiced
Scripts of unsatisfied longing.
I drew the odour of turpentine and wrote tobacco blue,
Edging inches further away from home,
Then miles, oceans away from God,
I added sulphur to the provocative *incendium.*

Away away we are nothing silver can exalt
Nor lurid signifiers demean.
Backward flaps of days! What we were!
Breasts bared, up naked rocks struggling,
Self-scratching till the skin ran and tears,
Tears through and thoroughly.[2]

All those lines, and only two enjambments! Only twice does the line accede to the cliff face of its end. Otherwise control, control: formal capitalized initial safety letters holding on to the left margin, gentle commas and full stops delivering the line to the right margin, one cry (the exclamation points line), and otherwise the lines pull their trauma inward, where soft text co-turns quite mental.

That mentality can be partly private enigma in the opened text: what the writer thinks or knows or partly-thinks or used-to-know that doesn't leave denotative (semantically and contextually curtailed or "clear") marks in the text.

That mentality can be the presagement of "It all throws me across a parallel to be of one mind," a line whose interpretive

2 Bill Direen, *Enclosures 2* (Percutio, 2016).

opportunity can be irresistible to the hard-text imperative of the critical reader. And if that reader knows you cannot score all the opportunities of reading that line, if you know that its contexts and recombinations are theoretically infinite, then you know soft text is part of the breath of that line. The scrutable releases the infinity of the inscrutable; interpretive penumbra always glows with soft text.

In other words, possibility intrinsically exceeds actuality, thus there is always more soft text than hard text any where and any time.

Some of the breath of soft text inheres in the breaks between strophes in Direen's poem. In the blank line between the first and second strophes, time, experience, and the unsaid or mentally part-formulated language of being alive has plenty of denotative, biographical, and soft text opportunity, while time is hastier, more whiplashed, in the strophe break between "*incendium*" and "Away." Those larger breaks tap into the smaller rivers of page area that run around and through the words in each strophe and line. And then, at a letter scale, the lettrified inflections that shape sound patterns — for example, "ds de   es   as a ade" from line 4 above ("Pods deliquescing as matt shade") and "l iny vinyl o ce voice" from line 8 ("coal shiny vinyl once voiced ") — are legible strikes, one aspect of the innuendoes of soft text that can constellate implosively or explosively in a reading.

4

These latter observations participate in the pleasure of poetics, as in calling out assonance and alliteration in the line. In *Harmonium* (1923), Wallace Stevens writes about the difference between an event and its aftermath:

> I do not know which to prefer,
> The beauty of inflections
> Or the beauty of innuendoes,
> The blackbird whistling

Or just after.[3]

The interpretive mind of soft text sounds some of the infinity in hard text's inflections, and the breath of soft text is theoretically infinite innuendo. That's one reason why line breaks, as well as blank lines between and around hard text lines, participate to differential extents in the potential of soft text. That's one reason interpretation never ends.

And while this essay is getting more involved in the soft text of book language, the soft text of conversation, digitality, and encounters with the non-verbal world are transcendently beckoning to think about. Happily, the membranes among these soft textual apportionments cannot be delineated with absolute fixity, even as they all defer from hard text.

5

When I first wrote this essay I was asked to speak to my own writing, and this final section briefly considers soft text in relation to my experimental memoir of childhood, *Anti M* (2013). That book resulted from a long process: I wrote an extended work, turned its drafts in various directions, and then finally took out the majority of the words, initially leaving the retained words in the page areas they had inhabited when all the now-gone words were around them. After some time, I then finally reshaped the layout with codical energies in mind. I called the resulting genre "omitted prose." The writing and revising process, from the first draft starting point to the book-accepted-for-publishing moment, took fifteen years.

By then, *Anti M*'s pages were deep with alternatives and potentiality, certainly the thickest palimpsest I've yet created. A palimpsest always complicates writing's surface, encourages the sense of writing as unfolding on deep surface. In *Anti M*, the

3 See Wallace Stevens, "Thirteen Ways of Looking at a Blackbird," in *The Collected Poems of Wallace Stevens* (Alfred A. Knopf, 1968), 93.

line is a sculpted occurrence within the conceptual vellum of its omissive writing. Here's an excerpt from chapter 3, "Florida":

She begins to try
to grow
to go
to read to dividing
to
an
impenetrable
like
vivid
of the outer world.

Her color is
Florida country
in a large car hitting the front rider.
Dash blacked out to ambulance all right,
up at the side, by having an unsafe story
playing on the unpaved sensation
provoked by an animal against whom we had no

well

well
go to protect
however much we know a malleable imagined
Daisy to the hilt, swinging
the officers

saying

the movie

that got under my skin.[4]

One might describe part of the potential text here as what was once present, the palimpsest of multiple revisions and erasures. But *Anti M*'s palimpsest is only a special (prolonged and peculiarly motivated) case of what happens with all published books that go through processes of writing, rewriting, omission, substitution, editing, and revisitation. Books have reams of missing pages, scores of drafted words, that were present in composition and are absent in the published book form.

As with all books, the inherent soft text of *Anti M* is what was *never* in its materials across the years of its composition, its multiple turns toward other versions of itself, and its final hard text form published as a book. Soft text swims around and through all those moments: It's the not-yet-imagined, silently unremembered, words wedged in the muscles of the heart, unthought or thought but not written in any version. Then, in reading, soft text performs in the newly seeable and hearable potentials that privately resound in readers encountering the hard text constellations.

We can consider areas of conceptual overlap between revisionary palimpsests, with their hard text ghosts, and soft text. In the gap effects of poetic layout—intralinear and interlinear blanks, letter-scatter, typeface shift, morphemic floaters, upside-down lines, and more—we may perceive some absent presences that might have once existed, that are versions of palimpsestic revision, and others that are exclusively potential, that are true soft text. Poetic lines can work both registers of suggestion, absent presences as well as chambers for soft text infinitude. Indeed, both registers can be seen in the above *Anti M* excerpt, in both the cloistered lines and the open layout.

In the excerpt's cloistered lines—in which words occur in normative position one after another, aligned with a set margin—we can perceive denotative omissions that have been resutured in the lines "Dash blacked out to ambulance all right"

4 Lisa Samuels, *Anti M* (Chax Press, 2013), 42.

and "up at the side, by having an unsafe story[.]" The palimpsest has been occluded by the cloistering of the lines: there are no evident blanks to perceive. Yet catachresis shows the jam of missing former word partners — a dash does not black out until, here, it does — as well as perhaps sparking potential other word partners in the soft text imaginings of a reader. And the prepositional appositions perform a kind of bodily catachresis: One cannot be, until one is, *up at by.* What a reader may think within the cloistered slippages of those lines is an occasion braiding the palimpsestic with soft text. In these cases, omissive writing means that some intervening word(s), and also the spaces created by those word omissions, were taken out. The textual intension is perceptible in terms of interpretations of its effects. The durational processes of writing, revising, omitting, and resuturing, however, are unrecoverable across the book's compositional years: Reading these lines isn't a matter of asserting what has been textually present and what has been taken out and reshaped. Instead, these lines are compression examples.

Anti M's omitted prose proposes that a line can be this kind of margin-held syntactic unit as well as other things: a word, a floated cluster, and an opening or blank in the areas of the page. For this particular book, line blanks showcase both palimpsestic absent presences and soft text. But this is simply an intense case, perhaps a limit case, of the truth that a blank line is also a line. As with the nature of timing and context in any social performance, silence as well as articulation makes communication. Among its other possible time and context effects, a blank line can stage soft text between lines, in interlinear gaps, and inside a line, in intralinear gaps. Consider the intralinear gap in this line from the above *Anti M* excerpt:

She begins   to try

The blank line between the word-pairs both pulls them together, because of their grammatical magnetism ("She begins to try"), and registers the possibility of all sorts of something and nothing thought or undertaken in the area in which the word-pairs are apart. The blank intralinear is partly an occasion for omitted prose, the absent presences that are crucial to this memoir. In terms of soft text, though, that intervening blank line is expansive with infinite potentiality: It plummets meaning. Soft text tells us that nothing decides what happens in that blank except, silently and momentarily, the encounter it has with you.

Monadic Yearning and Lingual Desire

> If a plurality of states of things is assumed to exist which involves no opposition to each other, they are said to exist simultaneously.
>
> —Gottfried Liebniz, *Mathematische Schriften*[1]

Again today I've been in discussions with people who long to be in total contact with authorial intent in order to coinhabit total meaning in reading. "Intent" in this discussion presumes that an author wields both choice in writing and also control over a transportable, stable, "meaning" to be entirely "found" in the written work. This meaning is projected as findable by "accurate" code-deciphering with expert hermeneutics or because the conduit of intent-to-reception transfer seems to be, is perceived as, functioning without interference: Author and context and platform are experienced as mirrorable in reader and context and reception. Unmediated transparency is the dream of total intentional lingual contact. The work, the author, and the reader meld in the apotheosis of a stabilized contemporary monad.

1 Gottfried Liebniz, "Mathematische Schriften, Vol. 7," in Max Jammer, *Concepts of Simultaneity: From Antiquity to Einstein and Beyond* (Johns Hopkins University Press, 2006), 80.

Such an intention-seeking is part of a larger category I think of as monadic yearning, a term for the urge that some persons—or many, or all at some time or other—have to access monads. Monads have been defined in philosophy as single essence points in which something (some idea, some fulfillable real) is fully itself, and monism as a condition in which the necessary ingredients of reality perception have been (contingently or hypothetically) ascertained.[2] In an organic etymological swerve, computer programming corrals the term monad to indicate abstract, multiply morphable, programming that can glide over and through individual code languages and implement the desired result without deleterious software-specific side effects. Monads are computer programming's omni-lingualism. The single monadic essence gets to go everywhere, speak every coded tongue.

Monadic yearning is a term to describe a common human urge to bring things together in closed instances of total connection: experience, understanding, inhabiting, belonging, connectedness, surety, comfortable finitude. It's possible to think of monadic yearning as the other end, the complementary finish line, of Jacques Derrida's imputations for "archive fever" as the urge to find the starting point, to discover the wellspring, of some thing or idea. The implications of monadic yearning connect with neurological and somatic desires for surety, with the need for shelter, with a desire for shared community, with sensations associated with shared religion or other belief system, with some ideologies of romantic love (visions of melded selves). Monadic yearning is arguably then perceivable in myriad aspects of life, and often connected with or even necessary to human good as well as to obscurities of our being such as how we relate with the fact of death.

2 See Ernst Mach's refreshingly antinomian description in John T. Blackmore, *Ernst Mach: His Work, Life, and Influence* (University of California Press, 1972), 193: "There are as many different monisms as there are people in it. Monism is provisionally a goal [...] but it is scarcely anything fixed or sufficient."

Monadic yearning can come across as akin to the "one-ing" that the English medieval mystic Julian of Norwich imagined possible with her God; it can occur as a moment of wanting to "get something" completely; it can occur as a person wanting to be entirely loved without perceptible condition. It's not in itself pathological or reprehensible; it wafts through people's experiences of life in different ways. And monadic yearning intersects, in some ways of thinking about the matter, with some people's desire to know exactly what a text means by closing the authorial intention loop. Monadic yearning, then, is a large category of suffusive onto-epistemological experience within which the desired access to authorial intention, to the imagined author's imagined-to-be-assertable intended meaning, can be seen to occur.

The present piece is interested in how yearning plunges through the aerated lattices of semiosis in the materials of lingual arts and how humans meet those materials. I'm thinking for now about the abstract materials (letters, words, spacing) of lingual art: writing, without soundscapes or visual images included or without strong contextual curation such as might occur in a museum, in the pre-interpretation type of text panels. And I'm thinking about expanded representation in and for the lingual.

To think further about the desire to contact the author's spirit of intention, it's interesting to consider vehement human response to depictions of sex. Access to a posited authorial intention and (potentially) shareable experience, such as in intense sex writing, is one route for apparently trying to satisfy that undying wish for connection reported by so many readers and in so many interpretive situations of scholarship and pedagogy. As has been doubtless noted before and is now part of idea inheritance — part of conditions registered in the essay "Relinquish Intellectual Property" — one reason sighted humans respond to physiologically accurate visual sexual depictions is that there's no denying that what's depicted is (depictedly, for AI can display this too) taking place. It's "real"; it shows as action in the visual field what is also potential action in bodily experience. Aural sex can be simulated, whether live on phones or recorded or digitally concocted, so it's perhaps not quite as convincing as visual depictions, though voices are embodiments themselves and can operate their melismatic simulcast in styles that reach listeners and provoke response.

Written sexual action operates from a position of more representational remove than visual images and aurality. Yet reports of written sex are verifiable. And even though not photo-scopic, they are sensory in other ways: in eyes touching the page, hearing of one's own breathing and of context noise and page surface, braille fingers touching, considering the shapeliness of words and the literate delivery mode of book or screened device. The body mind pays close attention. Reading sexual depictions conjures the absolute sexual potential in bodies and in one's own body: One can have sex, one is the result of sex. Test-tube infants, too, are jointures of sexual material that comes from orgasm and conception. Every human joins with sexuality.

Granted, all these referential levels themselves are questionable, because we're still not there in that moment having the sex depicted, so issues of simulacra condition and thread through these remarks. The point here is that this condition of bodily presentness, in representations of sex, seems to mitigate a central (for some people) problem of lingual representation — its disconnect, its remove from real action, from our own body mind fluid experience potential.

We can say that a reader's desire to establish authorial intent reflects a desire to solve "the problem of representation": to overcome, short-circuit, any separation between the reader and the energies of the text. It's not so much that these readerships want the author, or even let's say exactly want intravenous access to authorial intent: They want the text to be unhidden, and they seem to perceive that the humanity, the ideational body, of the author will yield to them the sense of completist knowing they desire. They want to substitute the lingual remove, the writing, with the thinking-intending body of the composing author. (This situation subtends obsessions with authenticated author connection to reports of identity and experiences, hence anxiety about memoir faking.)

It's as though, metaphorically speaking of course, sex with "the author" or mortally opening the author will be akin to joining the author, becoming the author, and thus becoming the text and knowing its all. Perhaps this is one reason it seems to be such a relief to many institutions of interpretation when artists actually die, so that they don't have to be responsible to those artists' lived uncertainties and mobilities anymore. Interpretation gets nearer to being able to close gaps of knowing. The author has died for our desire to climb inside meaning. The birth of the interpreter becomes more staunchly possible.

The more I write this missive, here and now, the more I understand such readerly urges to be inside lingual meaning, in psychological and experiential and bodily terms. Yet it isn't as though it didn't make sense before. It's rather that this pursuit of the impossible (sex with and death with and possession of a posited capturable panoply of the materials of a representation in lingual meaning) as the best route toward lingual desire so often sets aside other routes that might actually work better in yielding pungent connectedness to language's activities and forces. Monadic yearning hits a wall when it tries to corral the lingual — it projects a vanishing content of inert semiotic equipment onto events whose meaning-life is fractal, simultaneous, wild dialectical, on the move.

So how might we bracket out habits of authorial-intention-striving that feature in the kinds of conversations I had today with people who are longing, as it were, to crawl inside the author so as to close filled-in circles of meaning? Reading for subjective correlatives — which I wrote about in a different approach[3] — can be seen as engaging conduits of lingual think-feeling that do not correlate with narratorial norms of socially lived experi-

3 See Lisa Samuels, "Creating Criticism: An Introduction to *Anarchism Is Not Enough*," in Laura Riding, *Anarchism Is Not Enough*, ed. Lisa Samuels (University of California Press, 2001), xxxix–xliii.

ence. Subjective correlatives are one way to read the lingual as a zone where our resources as lingual beings interact fractally with the text's dynamic resources. In reading for subjective correlatives, we don't assume that what the modernist writer T.S. Eliot termed "objective correlatives" are either present or missing between the writer we're reading and us. We don't assume the representational text seeks to encompass, just as nothing can entirely encompass or end questions — perhaps apart from the bliss of absoluteness experienced only in the moment of the end of the possibility of experience-as-we-know-it: our own dying. Subjective correlatives are a subject-emphatic interpretive poetics allied with the poetic conditions of what Veronica Forrest-Thomson termed a total image complex,[4] a kind of post-structural metaphysical conceit. Subjective correlatives "make sense" not with reference to extra-lingual social-real narratives but with reference to lingual imaginaries: becoming the aspect of ourselves that is (projectively, aspirationally, somatically) lingual, in pursuit of connection with aspects of writing that are lingual.

But surely all aspects of writing are lingual? Yes and no: the forces of inscription and aurality and word-touch are not limited to words on screens or paper or earbuds or other kinds of art-book mouth-word pages. The plural conditions and differentials of sounds, sights, smells, contexts, technes, paratexts, rooms, aims, land, air, hunger, time, epistemological habits, magnetic Earth: All these are involved with language. The lingual is always already connected with every force of its potential and instantiation. Lingual representation thus becomes multiply plottable across and as diffractive matrices among other matrices in experience — it continually negotiates superposition, in lingual quantum terms. With such a potent purview, we might choose to wish to constantly expand rather than narrow our approaches to how we make and experience and interpret

4 See Veronica Forrest-Thomson, *Poetic Artifice: A Theory of Twentieth-Century Poetry* (Manchester University Press, 1978).

lingual representation. To yearn to meet such simultaneity diffractions with our own.

Another heuristic for displacing, potentially redirecting, urges toward authorial intention might be termed textual intension: conjuring engineering-like efforts at energy-holding, that kind of tension, in the place of the vanishing-because-multiple aspects of what artists mean to do (their "intentions") when they make something. Reading with textual intension as a desire plot is to vibrate, gesture, cluster, differentially manage phrasal joints and angles, plurally evoke referential imaginables, interactively stroke the lettrified skin of the built language event. This experiential access is outer-directed to the reading-evoked blurprint of the made work. Such textual desire gives us access to exits from habits of reading for imagined-as-withheld references, whether we imagine such references to be in fixed outside worlds, univocal word definition, or locatable total-author-intention.

Textual intension is to structure distributed reading differentials that conjoin our access to experience as distributed activity differentials. That's a contrast between the emphasis of a poetics theory like subjective correlatives and the yearning with textual intension designs toward the art event's diffractive simultaneities. The point of the latter is to cultivate access to lingual art considered as built environments of always-differential expansions of meaning-making. Textual intensions access dynamic lingual "blurprints" (as in the "Contemporanullity" essay in this book) with the us that is not only lingual but also in other ways engineeringly *made:* as cellular and ideological micro-structures, meaty and motile, elementally pulled, co-tense, beings.

Perceiving textual intension can be like working with the promises of gravity topography, in which a quantum sensor conjures, as mappable, versions of what is a changeful field of force (gravity) that is outside of our palpative range even as it coholds that range. This kind of context feels to me more organic to textual intension reading than, say, the also-relevant aspects of intension in linguistics approaches. In the hermeneutic I imagine for textual intension, the text is like a (set theory) lattice inveigled with lingual folds — algebraic, poly-semiotic. Our lingual desire becomes diffraction yearning co-looped with the lingual work. Our interpretation urges less toward the delimitedly temporal and more toward structures of simultaneity. However paradoxical the latter articulation may be, it's a paradox that the demonstrations of a work such as *Evolution*[5] can be interpreted as making manifest. We might imagine *Evolution*'s pseudo-codical thrum happening with any holdable book, with any lingual interaction in reading.

I confess I do believe this kind of perception will give us more satisfaction in reading. Focusing in the expansively situated lingual acuity we have, in meeting other lingual acuities, will garner more senses of meanings than any monadic yearning to inhabit a closed circuit of meaning, such as the body of the author's imagined-as-intended experience, can ever give. Diffraction yearning toward textual intensions, with all that implies of non-reintegrated energy potentials, cultivates closer experience with the moving fractals and simultaneity lattices that are the life of temporal language events. Such interpretive positioning can be a paradox worth opening for.

5 Johannes Heldén and Håkan Jonson, *Evolution*, 2014, http://www.textevolution.net/.

Quantum Mimesis

> If we once made clear to ourselves that we are concerned only with the ascertainment of the *interdependence* of phenomena […] all metaphysical obscurities disappear.
>
> — Ernst Mach, *Die Mechanik in ihrer Entwicklung*[1]

Quantum mimesis describes writing whose styles enact the constitutive mobility and dimensional mutability of its depicted realms. By styles, I mean rhetorical features "below" the level of whatever genre that writing might be said to inhabit. Quantum mimesis performs with implicit, or explicit, reference to the vibrational force that quantum theory has in our ideas about artistic representation and lived experience. We exist as fleshy electric bodies in quantum energy fields that are part of our beings and concepts. Talking about quantum mimesis is part of continuing to imagine how art "copies" observable and, apparently, unobservable experience.

"Mimesis" is a word from a so-called dead language; the term representation is sometimes more fashionable. I use mimesis here for two starting reasons: first, the linguistic enstrangement of the term points to its aesthetic history, and I want to write

1 Ernst Mach, *Die Mechanik in ihrer Entwicklung,* trans. Max Jammer (Brockhaus, 1921), 219. Italics in original.

within that history and to resist some more recent histories of the term "representation." As Raymond Williams summarizes, in the eighteenth century the term representative became allied with the notion of the "typical" and with realism. In the nineteenth century representation "became specialized to a sense of 'accurate reproduction' and in this sense, probably not earlier than [the twentieth century], produced the distinctive category of **representational art**."[2] In a formulation familiar in Anglo-American-Australasian cultural ideologies, typicality, realism, and accuracy get bound up together. We recognize something we've seen before (it's typical), we see it presented in an explicitly imitative way (it's realistic), and it all seems correct, "accurate" to normative social life, so it can seem that there's no need to do it any other way. But nothing inherent in representation makes this equation necessary, and the fostering of that default equation is arguably part of social machineries that work to naturalize stability in the arts.

A second reason to use the term mimesis is that I want to reclaim for non-narrative poetry an important form of mimetic work. By non-narrative I mean poetry whose bulk cannot be, as an arc or prime impetus, paraphrased according to storyline, stable message, and normative human-ish speakers. No definite genre stamp cues us to the presence or absence of narrative poetry. For example, as I've argued elsewhere, the differential subset "autography" presents a written self in writing,[3] created fabrics of life attention that correlate with, even as they do not imitate or correspond to, stable narratives of "authentic" flesh and blood experience commonly offered in autobiographies.

This second reason also emerges from my desire to set aside anti-terms, such as "anti-representation" or "anti-mimesis." Such terms both explicitly sideline or forfeit the potential aptness of their associations and also show forth the impossibility

2 Raymond Williams, *Keywords: A Vocabulary of Culture and Society* (Croom Helm, 1976), 269.

3 Lisa Samuels, "Eight Justifications for Canonizing Lyn Hejinian's *My Life*," *Modern Language Studies* 27, no. 2 (1997), 103–19.

of escaping their terminological histories. In addition to encouraging simple antinomies. Besides, it isn't as though a modernist writer like Gertrude Stein was looking to go *against* imitation or against representation.

This essay argues that quantum mimesis *is* a mode of imitation, different from the more Newtonian mirror effects commonly evoked by the term mimesis. Mimetic types have a long history of differentiation and expansion. In what can be seen as a provocative bid to promote his metaphysics, Plato considered music the most mimetic and sculpture the least mimetic of the arts. Given the non-semantic and highly wrought mimetic of music, and the naturalized dimensionality and thing-ness of sculpture, Plato's preference (unsurprisingly) indicates that mimesis for him was crucially ideational, not object-oriented. For Plato, art most importantly imitates — summons and bodies forth — ideas, not (mere) things in the world. Samuel Taylor Coleridge distinguishes two kinds of mimesis in his *Lectures 1808–1819 on Literature:* one is copy, or mechanical replication, and the other is imitation, "the Union of Disparate Things." Eric Auerbach's influential book *Mimesis* (1946) begins by outlining two mimetic types: a Homeric, antique, detailing representation of nature ("foreground" mimesis) and a Biblical, mystic, dwelling-in-possibility series of gestures toward events and their meanings ("background" mimesis).[4] Generally speaking, Auerbach's first type dominates his book and a common working definition of artistic mimesis: "Art imitating nature" is construed as a representationism best exemplified by the realistic novel or untouched art photograph. In the context of this essay's tactical resistance to the term representation, it is perhaps relevant to recall the prison notebook circumstances of Auerbach's preference, hence his understandable desire to stabilize and cohere mimesis.

Martin Heidegger, from a different European late-modernist perspective, thinks of mimesis not as simple repetition or imi-

4 See Eric Auerbach, *Mimesis: The Representation of Reality in Western Literature* (Princeton University Press, 1953).

tation but as *Nachmachung* ("doing-after").[5] The critic Arne Melberg interprets Heidegger's term as "repetition with a difference" and asserts that "Modern theorists have become modern [...] with their emphasis on repetition as difference rather than similarity."[6] And the critic J. Hillis Miller devotes a book to *Fiction and Repetition,* including the introductory chapter "Two Forms of Repetition": One type of repeating moves toward sameness, and the other toward difference.[7] While imitation is not exactly the same thing as repetition, I think of what I'm doing here as referencing two general types of imitation, giving a local habitation and a name to the less normatively considered one.

Alternatively, as concerns Gertrude Stein, it could be argued that her writing often brings the "two forms of repetition" into one zone, when read with quantum mimetic eyes. What I mean is that her "exact resemblance as exact as a resemblance"[8] is a binary without twoness that operates to make language's difference/same approach an exploration of the difference/same in lived experience. Thus what is perceivable as Stein's quantum mimesis perhaps recalls Walter Benjamin's *Ähnlichkeit,* or "similarity with a difference,"[9] or makes a turn on Coleridge's true Imitation: "philosophically we understand that in all Imitation two elements must exist, and not only exist but be perceived as existing—Likeness and Unlikeness, or Sameness and Difference. All Imitation in the Fine Arts is the union of Disparate Things."[10] Further, Stein's two forms of imitation might be described as inner and outer, to distinguish them from J. Hillis Miller's sameness and difference: Stein's mimetic zones are both

5 Martin Heidegger, *Nietzsche,* vol. 1 (Neste, 1961), 215.

6 Arne Melberg, *Theories of Mimesis* (Cambridge University Press, 1995), 4.

7 J. Hillis Miller, *Fiction and Repetition: Seven English Novels* (Harvard University Press, 1982).

8 Gertrude Stein, "If I Told Him: A Completed Portrait of Picasso," in *A Stein Reader,* ed. Ulla Dydo (Northwestern University Press, 1996), 464.

9 Walter Benjamin, "Doctrine of the Similar (1933)," trans. Knut Tarnowski, *New German Critique* 17 (1979): 65–69.

10 Samuel Taylor Coleridge, cited in Frederick Burwick, *Mimesis and Its Romantic Reflections* (Pennsylvania State University Press, 2001), 91.

outside persons and objects and inside persons and objects, both evident and constitutive outside and inside, beckoning both outside and inside the language in which they appear.

Before taking up a Stein example, I want to say more about the quantum part of this mimetic theorizing. The dominant definition of mimesis—art as a mirror of nature—can be seen as a cultural adaptation of Newton's laws: Language describes people as they might appear in your lounge, rules of gravity and social class are followed, and the syntax of understandability is normative prose, whether narrative or expository. In contrast, quantum mimesis seeks to inscribe *as imitation* a phenomenological, epistemic, and ontological constellation of events, significances, subjectivities, namings, objects, traits, senses, perceptions, and more, in lingually motile texts that (naturally) gain their fullest articulation in correlatively active readings.

It's helpful to give a broad definition of the potential of quantum mimesis, since it operates with different emphases in different texts. Rather than using the verbal field to stabilize a world in syntactically normative sequences, quantum mimetic writing wants to take seriously at a formal level what it means to live in a world whose physique is quantum and in cultural and language contexts that are concomitantly (at least theoretically) acknowledged to be quantum-dynamic rather than sign-static. Reading *for* quantum mimesis might seek to activate the aforementioned traits in any kind of imaginative writing, but here the emphasis is on the physique of writing oriented within modern quantum models of reality.

The term quantum mimesis evokes a literary version of Werner Heisenberg's 1927 Uncertainty Principle, which as we know summarily posits both that one cannot measure both position and momentum at the same time and that the act of studying and measuring a subject necessarily influences the perceived properties of that subject. Quantum mimesis presumes the *potential* simultaneous availability of all the details of a given lingual construction and its connections to the non-present lingual, similar to such a presumption regarding atomic and subatomic measurements in quantum mechanics.

Curiously, for my purposes here, the development of quantum theory happens at about the same time as the firmer establishment of the category "representational art." But there is nothing in quantum theory that necessitates it as typical, accurate, or realistic — to refer to Raymond Williams's categories summarized at the start of this essay — and everything that indicates its potential to destabilize those categories. As the physicist-philosopher David Bohm explains, many theoretical physicists strongly resist the idea of quantum theory being available to versions of itself we cannot yet account for. In his 1980 book *Wholeness and the Implicate Order,* Bohm notes that "it is evident that the indeterministic features of quantum mechanics are in some way a reflection of the real behavior of matter in the atomic and nuclear domains."[11] He gives examples of this real indeterminism, then he writes "we ought to be free to consider the hypothesis that results of individual quantum-mechanical measurements are determined by a multitude of new kinds of factors, outside of what can enter into the quantum theory."[12] He goes on to characterize the views of physicists who reject theorizing such "hidden variables": "The statistical features of the quantum theory are thus regarded as representing a kind of irreducible lawlessness of *individual* phenomena in the quantum domain."[13]

Bohm's call for theoretical openness in the face of the constantly slipping "real behavior of matter" dovetails with this book's recurrent commitment to imagining what we don't know in writing, think-feeling, and critical bodies. Bohm's characterization of physicists who resist the unknown or unmeasurable might recall frequent human resistance to "lawless" non-normative art. Such resistance might in turn recall T.S. Eliot describing Stein's writing as "barbaric," the sign of a (present) future we shouldn't want.

---

11 David Bohm, *Wholeness and the Implicate Order* (Routledge & Keegan Paul, 1980), 86.

12 Ibid., 87.

13 Ibid., 88.

Further, the quantum theoretical stance toward reality resonates with the much-noted modernist shift from generally temporal to generally spatial orientation. As Laura Riding and Charles Olson and Michel Foucault and Gaston Bachelard (among others) assert, twentieth-century westerners were much more imaginatively oriented to space than to time. And as Jacques Derrida, Jean-François Lyotard, Epeli Hau'Ofa and others help us to see, multiplicity and ongoingness are the condition of our epistemic and perceptual systems and their vibrating objects. Speaking of Lyotard and Hau'Ofa, there are of course ethical consequences in reading for quantum mimesis, in terms of human attention, language games, and power consequences for the construction of meanings. Quantum mimesis is an aspect of socially conscious acts that want to expand the epistemic and imaginative arenas of language: by rearranging our relations with how language imitates experience and by insisting on wide penumbras in the consequences of activist reading.

Bohm's insights regarding quantum physics seem not dissimilar to Theodor Adorno's regarding the conceptual and the non-conceptual in philosophy (the latter are indicated in this book's "Wild Dialectics" essay). Holding in simultaneous consideration the perceivable and the imperceivable in these two disciplinary fields can help us hold in consideration ways in which apparently non-mimetic rhetorical features in imaginative writing are yet constructing mimetic scenarios.

To some extent, I imagine quantum mimesis to be part of a resurgence of metonymic mimesis (cf. Frederick Burwick's history) after its relative post-Enlightenment suppression in favor of a more naturalized romantic subjectivity—in short, after Wordsworthian mimesis trumped Blakean mimesis in the modern Anglo-American-Australasian academy. If Enlightenment scientism suppressed metonymic mimesis, quantum scientism can help restore it. Which is also to say I imagine quantum mimesis to be part of an altered way of braiding together scientific and artistic interpretations, hence a potentially beyond-modern (beyond Eliotic correlatives) or millennial poly-disciplinary interpretive set of tools. As Friedrich Nietzsche noted in

Beyond Good and Evil: Prelude to a Philosophy of the Future, "It is perhaps just dawning on five or six minds that physics, too, is only an interpretation and exegesis of the world (to suit us, if I may say so!) and *not* a world-explanation."[14]

Quantum reality is not separate from humans and other Earth life. Being able to access its implications for thought and feeling, actions and organization, and how language works and plays (with) us is part of accessing the dynamics of life in a changed environment of human knowledge and organization. Modernism is not enough; quantum feeling and thinking are conceptual growth areas for art and theory, and for overall human behaviors and beliefs as well as for the promise of quantum computing.

As indicated by the happily ever-increasing shelves of books that blend science and literature, many minds focus on the interpretive work that science thinking can perform in other disciplines. Steven Meyer's astute book on Gertrude Stein, *Irresistible Dictation* (2001), emphasizes the psychology and physiology operating in Stein's poetic knowledge. Among other matters, he sees Stein's study of physiological psychology in the mechanistic quality of *The Making of Americans,* and her empiricism and ecstasis in works like *Everybody's Autobiography.*[15] Daniel Albright uses the term "quantum poetics" in a 1997 book of that title.[16] In *Toy Medium,* with a different emphasis, Daniel Tiffany is interested in how "poetry and atomic physics often converge, [...] in their *representations* of material substance and the nature of corporeality."[17] There are others: Arkady Plotnitsky, Stuart Peterfreund, Susan Strehle. Many critics take up "quantum x" as a metaphor rather than as an aid to epistemic revolution focused

14 Friedrich Nietzsche, *Beyond Good and Evil: Prelude to a Philosophy of the Future,* ed. and trans. Walter Kaufmann (Vintage, 1966), section 14; 21.

15 See Steven Meyer, *Irresistible Dictation: Gertrude Stein and the Correlations of Writing and Science* (Stanford University Press, 2001).

16 See Daniel Albright, *Quantum Poetics: Yeats, Pound, Eliot and the Science of Modernism* (Cambridge University Press, 1997).

17 See Daniel Tiffany, *Toy Medium: Materialism and Modern Lyric* (University of California Press, 2000).

in the development of analytic tools. But see Meyers's charts and some of Roger Penrose's work, among others, for performative critical practice applications.

I want to turn from this brief sketch of historical and contemporary contexts and implications in order to focus on an example — some of the writings of Gertrude Stein — that emphasizes not only reading for but also writing within what can be perceived as quantum mimesis. In *The Autobiography of Alice B. Toklas,* Stein writes that poetry and prose "should consist of an exact reproduction of either an outer or an inner reality."[18] Reading just a little of the Steinian result of that imperative indicates how complex such "reproduction" can be.

As point perspective shows in visual art, for a different example, it is necessary to subvert what we think we see in order to reproduce perceptibly normative pictorial forms. Point perspective is a deformance of the apparently seen in order to produce, or re-produce, shapes that will incite viewers to pictorially reassemble the apparently seen. Similarly — but from the obverse of what might be normative, expected language use — quantum mimesis sets up lettrific, lexical, phrasal, line, sentence, strophic, or paragraphic elements and more that constitute a performed report on experiences of the myriad elements of so-called outer life. Quantum mimesis might represent an "inner reality" of psychological projection, introjection, or retrojection (viewing the latter as a dimensionalized loop among self-perceivings and garnered data from outside the self). It might represent an "outer" reality of, to cite a few possibilities: ideology brought into visibility, phenomenology focused on the object-events apparently outside the perceiving self, contemporanullity sheaving its living fragments.

In an interview with Robert Haas, Stein adds to the picture of how she pursues aspects of what I'm calling quantum mimesis:

18 Gertrude Stein, *The Autobiography of Alice B. Toklas* (Harcourt, Brace, and Company, 1933), 259.

> During that middle period I had these two things that were working back to the compositional idea, the idea of portraiture and the idea of the recreation of the word. I took individual words and thought about them until I got their weight and volume complete and put them next to another word and at this same time I found out very soon that there is no such thing as putting them together without sense. [...] I made innumerable efforts to make words write without sense and found it impossible.[19]

Without wanting to obscure the particularity of Stein's different innovative periods, I note that the above references to "weight and volume," to embodied numbering and measurable space, fit with Stein's references elsewhere to word and landscape. These terms emphasize how much she was playing with what quantum theory calls "complementarity"—particle and wave, or position and momentum—as fruitful alternatives for attending to words and their syntactic placements. Further, Stein's efforts to find the limits of sense recall the efforts of quantum theory to push its perceptions of the way matter really behaves and to make room for what it cannot see.

To explore this way of reading Stein I will focus on a passage from *Tender Buttons* (1914). Here are the first two, of four, sentences in "A Piano," from the "Objects" section of the book:

> If the speed is open, if the color is careless, if the selection of a strong scent is not awkward, if the button holder is held by all the waving color and there is no color, not any color. If there is no dirt in a pin and there can be none scarcely, if there is not then the place is the same as up standing.[20]

Note the quantum grammar of this passage: The uncompleted syntax of Stein's first sentence—"if" has no "then" but swerves

19 Gertrude Stein, "Afterword," in *What Are Masterpieces?* (Pitman Publishing Co., 1970), 101.

20 Gertrude Stein, *Tender Buttons: Objects, Food, Rooms* (Dover, 1997), 9.

to "and"—is only the most obvious unsettled feature of the relations among these phrases and images. I'll point to four features of syntax and word class in these sentences: prepositions and other connectors, syntactic subjects, copulas, and predicates (or results). The first predicate ("by all the waving color") is immediately put into question by the subject that follows it ("there is no color, not any color"). The second full subject-copula-predicate sequence absolutely mitigates itself: "there can be none scarcely," where "none" and "scarcely" work both in opposition and, potentially, as mutual complements. The "if" prepositions wave like flags through the entire verbal field, their conditional syntactic function keeping us from landing finally in any statement. And the titular object of this section, "A Piano," is inexactly positioned in, or as, the indeterminate "place" of this verse paragraph. It is indeterminate at the very least because a piano is not usually conceived as a place, and then even more flotation is brought in with the indefinite article "a." That article makes it any piano; we don't have the gestural deixis that would attend the definite article "the."

Let us imagine what might be "really" imitated in "A Piano." There are referential terms that can work outside the text: a piano's keys can be opened up and a musical speed can be opened. "Coloratura," a word we can see in the "color" of "A Piano," normally refers to a singer's trills but can be applied to the trills on a piano. A "strong scent" can recollect a "strong ascent," as in ascending keys. A "button holder" can be fingers, as in those that touch tender buttons, or metonymically the person whose fingers they are. So the first sentence can be read as imitating the condition of listening to a piano, and being that piano's player, and being a piano. These are entangled simultaneities, not choices among separatist alternates. Quantum entanglement, and the force that overarches incidents of temporality (i.e., simultaneity), are being performatively evoked in this quantum mimesis. Carelessness, awkwardness, and negation are inscribed here; so are thrill, strength, waving, and uncertainty. The sentence imitates differing object status (aspects of the piano and of musical notes, for example), listening experience (uncertainty, strength, judgment, sensibility), gaps or incompleteness (because of the partiality of object to fingered player to listener), and potentially conjoined subjectivities. We can turn different facets of these imitations in our eyes and mouths and ears and minds and exteroceptive sensibilities; we can even consider more than one facet at a time. But we cannot locate one facet as a separable stability from the others without altering the *kind* of imitation, the *kind* of experiential mimesis, evoked here.

I mentioned earlier that metonymy can have special force in quantum mimesis. The potential for conjoining relations among objects — and I'll speak to William James's "radical empiricism" in a moment — points to a metonymic inter-gap activity. That is, reading for quantum mimesis activates multiple facets of an experience like hearing or touching or seeing or being a piano. Even if the piano in question is *silent,* this imitation portrays the potential of the object in human experience that makes it that object. As Stein wrote elsewhere, "I became more and more excited about how words which were the words that made whatever I looked at look like itself were not the words that had in them any quality of description. This excited me very much."[21]

Reading art this way can remind us of the conceptually richer poly-dimensionality of language over actual objects. Or perhaps I should say reading mimesis in this way can remind us that imaginative language has no necessary fixed relations with perceived aspects of a musical instrument or a world order. Dimensional space is not observably unhinged, with the unaided senses, in objects, but it *is* unhinged in the referentiality of an abstract language. You can have "A Piece of Coffee" (another of Stein's subtitles)[22] in language. This point is not dissimilar to Laura Riding's interest in imagining people as they are made of words in writing. In this particular way, so far as poetic epistemology goes, lingual dimensionality is observably more flexible than the dimensionality of objects. Word-dimensionality can

21 Gertrude Stein, "Portraits and Repetitions," in *Lectures in America* (Vintage, 1975), 191.

22 Stein, *Tender Buttons,* 5.

curve like quanta in space-time. Referential dimensionality — in Newtonian perception, in the stabilized mimesis of naturalistic representation — is notionally conditioned by and to the objects to which it refers. At the same time this word dimensionality, in the complex of writer, reader, page/surface, and language, always has emplacement, which the piano gives us here even as it swings in and out of hearing or "view."

Quantum-leaning constructed imitation might seem paradoxical, since one might argue that constructivism is one thing, calling on the activist reader, and imitation is another. But quantum theory — and not only quantum theory, as Gilles Deleuze and Félix Guattari's rhizomes and as Édouard Glissant's *chaos-monde* suggest — presses the point of mobility within its calculations. Quantum mimesis imitates the circumstances of mobile meaning-making and the gaps between word and word and among perceivers. In Stein's "A Piano" passage, for example, the particle/conjunction "if" inhabits a (repeated) position which then, in relation with its surrounding syntax, shifts into a wave or momentum. We can no doubt hear this repetition and variation as musical, as in the first three quoted clauses, pulsing additively from six to seven to thirteen syllables, regulated with commas. The prepositional wave action might also be said to imitate the "feeling of if" deemed so important, among other prepositional sensibilities, by William James (this feeling is also considered in the "Deformance and If Meaning" essay in this book). James's "radical empiricism," too, speaks to the matter of constructivism in quantum mimesis.

Meyer reminds us of the importance of radical empiricism to Stein, and his quotations from James's "A World of Pure Experience" are apt here: "For such a philosophy, *the relations that connect experiences must themselves be experienced relations, and any kind of relation experienced must be accounted as 'real' as anything else in the system.*" And further, "a genuinely radical empiricism *'does full justice to conjunctive relations,* without, however, treating them as rationalism always tends to treat them, as being true in some supernal way, as if the unity of things and their variety belonged to different orders of truth and vitality altogether.'"[23] James's "conjunctive relations" get at the gaps that determine and animate perceptions like position/momentum, particle/wave, inner/outer, word/syntax. And his radical empiricism sits quite readily with this essay's way of reading Stein's commitment to "exact resemblance"—as well as with Bohm's insistence that we try to include all aspects of quantum analysis in the theory itself, including aspects that defy known definitions of the theory. Imagining what we don't know operates in quantum mimesis as constructivist imitation for the purposes of lingually embodying the indeterminism of experience and the mobility of lingual descriptions. Quantum mimesis is a copy that inscribes the "hidden variable," the "error" it cannot measure.

In a quantum mimetic sense, then, Stein's "A Piano" passage reflects not a point of view but a method for getting points of view. A getting which is continual, which is never "got." In this reading, her perceptual array is not so much like cubist painting (to which it's often compared), as it does not encode a variety of perspectives so much as it does *a variety of ways of getting perspective,* of making, conceiving, inhabiting, sensing. Quantum mimesis here copies the experience of experience with its umbral blind spots (including retinal ones), replete blank touches, evoked and unmaterialized potentialities, and plurally thick deep surface. It is not representation, with the potential for a standing point presumed by that term; it is a special case of *copy,* a quantum mimesis that resists centering and determinate perspective in favor of semiotic superposition and other entangled connectors.

I'll end by summoning Friedrich Schiller in order to invert one of his well-known formulations. If Stein and non-Newtonian mimesis are often perceived as aberrant, as turning away from right order and lingual beauty, and if the signs of entangled and superpositional epistemology are considered non-con-

---

23 William James, "A World of Pure Experience," in *Writings 1902–1910,* ed. Bruce Kuklick (The Library of America, 1987), 1160–61, and Meyer, *Irresistible Dictation,* 12–13. Italics in originals.

nectable with what some (such as perhaps logical empiricists) think of as thinking, then I want to say as a swerve from Schiller: What has been felt as something *un*beautiful — unfitted, probabilistically blurred — will come toward us one day as the truth. Such reformulations can continually make way for rich theoretical openings in our perceptions of and feeling for quantum life, whose energies align with what Nietzsche calls "philosophers of the dangerous 'maybe.'"[24]

24 Nietzsche, *Beyond Good and Evil,* 11.

The ⊤-⊥ Function

Writers often can be said to have projects that unify their works, however internally diverse they might be; the twentieth-century poet Laura Riding's projects could be described as focusing in an astringent lingual utopia. Her 1930 book *Though Gently* evinces frequent characteristics of her work: It features both poetry and prose forms (lines and sentences, stanzas and paragraphs) within a strong consciousness of book form; adamant statements that function more like hypotheses than assertions; a modernist interest in eschatological opportunities for human character and language; and temporary thought tropes (in *Though Gently,* Riding's ⊤-⊥ apposition) that organize her experiments in lingual thinking.

Riding was always interested in the appurtenances of writing and in controlling her own language investigations. The Seizin Press she ran with Robert Graves was one important mode of control. *Though Gently* was the second Seizin Press publication issued after Riding and Graves had shaken off England and installed themselves on the Spanish island of Majorca, and they worked to manage both the physical aspects and the product advertisements of this book. Dated 1930 and available in January 1931, *Though Gently* was "hand-set and hand-printed by ourselves on hand-made paper."[1] This intensely embodied book has exactly twenty-nine numbered content pages, reflecting Laura's twenty-nine years of age in 1930. It was advertised in a 1931 Seizin Press announcement as "consist[ing] of statements in prose and poetry all leading as gently as possible to annihilation and the rest."[2]

Not unlike *The Life of the Dead* (1933), *Though Gently* is a book of unusually large dimensions, crafted to allow capacious and variable spaces among its parts. What she and Graves called in *A Pamphlet against Anthologies* (1928) the crucial *"handwriting quality"* of a poet's work is partly evidenced in this book as a variable use of layout and of paragraph and stanza type.[3] Part of Riding's handwriting, taking that term to refer to the embodiments of human makers and to dimensional and technical traces in the made work, is to know as body the textual space of language. We might see the artist Len Lye's bio-surreal cover for *Though Gently,* depicting a sort of woody seed-penetration that is at once fixed and suggestively on the move, as an indicative sign of Riding's shared interest in the conceptual and material chiaroscuro of codical embodiment and bodily textuality.

This dynamism is appropriately comparable to Riding's frequent re-visionary approach to her writing. "If a Poem Lasts Twenty-Four Hours," for one characteristic example, changes after its appearance in *Though Gently.* Riding reprinted this poem, and much of the poetry in *Though Gently,* in the quite different context of *Poet: A Lying Word* (1933), a highly structured book of poems organized by seasonal subtitles. Riding made changes in almost every line, changes that tend to make "If a Poem Lasts Twenty-Four Hours" more metaphoric, less declarative or statement-like. By the time the bulk of the poem reappears in Riding's *Collected Poems* (1938), its title is "Autobi-

1 Laura Riding, *Though Gently* (Seizin Press, 1930), n.p. (colophon).

2 See Hugh Ford, "The Seizin Press," in *Published in Paris: American and British Writers, Printers, and Publishers in Paris, 1920–1939* (Macmillan, 1975), 396–401.

3 See Laura Riding and Robert Graves, eds., *A Pamphlet against Anthologies* (Doubleday, 1928).

ography of the Present" and the first six stanzas have been cut out. It now begins, self-consciously, "Whole is by breaking and by mending. / The body is a day of ruin, / The mind, a moment of repair."[4] Stanzas five and six float away in their own poem, now titled "Care in Calling," and the first four stanzas have disappeared. A poem is not a static artifact for Riding: The poem breaks up, rearranges, is not a fixed artistic structure (not an object or modernist "urn") but instead a propositional and changeful entity.

The mobility of Riding's textual structures — book size and type, typeface and layout, writings and re-writings — accords with her evident belief, at least in the 1920s and 1930s, that no single genre commands the optimal use of language. We see this belief at work in combinations of poetry and prose in *Though Gently,* in varying page margins, and also in different ways of marking prose (or are they verse?) paragraphs. Riding writes that "[p]rose is slow poetry," and her performed lack of interest in explaining that statement exemplifies the way genres run together and the way assertion equals investigation in her work.[5]

In *Though Gently,* the ⊤-⊥ function is Riding's primary unprecedented investigative trope. The ⊤-⊥ function is a way of seeing conditions of perception and knowing, especially in the pieces "What Is There To Believe In" (whose initial word signals both grammatical pronoun and blank ontology), "Let," "Numbers," "You And I," "Any Answer," and the book's final piece, "T." In these pieces, Riding wants us to see what we can by way of focusing at or near the penumbra of juxtaposition, so that we see not *what* but *how.* It is the condition of the exposed double negative and somewhat similar to the multi-function pressure that Gertrude Stein puts on words and sentences. Riding's book, though, is far more angular and reagent-oriented. It's more legible in the urges of textual intension (considered in the present book's essay "Monadic Yearning and Lingual Desire") as inher-

4 Laura Riding, *The Poems of Laura Riding: A New Edition of the 1938 Collection* (Persea Books, 1980), 173.

5 Riding, *Though Gently,* 13.

ent to the made work and as a telling way of perceiving it. To exist in the condition of "though," the book gently removes the ⊤ from the end of "thought" and turns it at different angles.

Consider *Though Gently's* second piece, "Let," whose ⊤ and ⊥ at first appear to present a clear thesis-antithesis relation, especially following the apparent dialectic of the opening poem, "What Is There To Believe In" (whose first word, again, hovers as both normative pronoun placeholder and, non-normatively, as an asserted non-defined noun). In "Let"—a word also dual performing, in this case as poly-signifying verb and noun—the two ⊤s turn out to be slippery signs for the vast corpus of events and objects that one might call "cultural reality" (⊤) and "encountered experience" (⊥). ⊤ symbolizes the institutional and interpretive organizers that give themselves the authority to "stand for" ⊥ and to organize reality and experience into asserted significances.

On the next page Riding makes it clear that ⊤ is certainly not a (re)presentation of the real, but rather an added factor ("The enumeration of four essences does not lead to the discovery of an essential but of a fifth essence"), somewhat as photographs are "things of which nothing has been said"—that is, photographs are *additions* to appearance, to the appearable, rather than interpretations of the real.[6] ⊤ is simply a place where one can speak of the agreed-upon; if anything is lingually "real" for Riding it is registered here as ⊥, as a sign for the intranslatable sensoria of one's think-feeling experiences.

In a 1928 book, *Anarchism Is Not Enough,* Riding had another term, the "individual unreal," whose meaning function resembles the latter version of *Though Gently*'s ⊥. To indicate some of the work the "individual unreal" performs in *Anarchism,* I'll quote some of my earlier analysis about this term. It is:

> the sense of incommensurable self-awareness that human beings possess, the "consciousness of consciousness" ([*Anarchism*] 27) distinct from constructed socio-economic identi-

6 Ibid., 3, 25.

> ties. It gestures toward the gift of mortality, toward the ultimate "uselessness" of individuals, and therefore toward the perfect means of their existence.[7]

As is characteristic of her temporary thought-signs, neither set of terms gets repeated elsewhere in her work. They perform as passing semiotic measures. In *Though Gently,* Riding's two ⊤s are the symbol of going gently sideways to what's possible to say, so that "truth" has a chance to apparition in the penumbra of what we can read as the textual intension of this book, which is as close to an artist's book (alongside *The Life of the Dead*) as Riding ever made. Her earnest heuristic aims, marked with the variant ⊤-⊥, compare with those of the US poet Alan Sondheim, who seems to speak to *Though Gently,* though without knowing it (or anyway without saying so), in this excerpt from a 1999 listserv posting:

> the probability of truth is zero as an infinite number of alternatives to exactitude appear to gnaw at the foundations. [...] Further, there are no foundations, not if they're so thin that they attempt to disappear at the slightest breath of the butterfly phenomenon. They don't attempt to disappear; there's disappearance everywhere at work here in the Cosmos. [...] Plans are always already ⊤-junctions, the thick stem replete with noise, temporary convolutions, circuit drains. Place the wrong ground in a circuit and electrons confuse everything, nothing travels much farther, all the images disappear; they were present for your eyes only, otherwise fallen apart. [...] You and I will look up into the same sky at the same time, our gaze will sustain us across these oceans. Water has memory; memory has no shape; shape is a gift to water. The ⊤ is the long-sought solution.[8]

---

7 Lisa Samuels, "Creating Criticism: An Introduction," in Laura Riding, *Anarchism is Not Enough,* ed. Lisa Samuels (University of California Press, 2001), xix.

8 Alan Sondheim, *"Plan-et Ground,"* http://www.alansondheim.org/kz.txt.

I quote this passage because its activity connections—alterity logics, grounding (conceptual and electrical), atmospheric and off-Earth patterns and submoleculars, semiotic constatives, elemental subjectivities—resonate with the wild dialectics perceivable in the ⊤-⊥ play of *Though Gently.* This Sondheim passage also indicates how "contemporary," in Stein's sense of the word, Riding is with her apparently dislocated ⊤-⊥ signs. We might also read her ⊥ as a staged "I," exposed and upwards-reaching, while the ⊤ is, we might say, an "I" with William Blake's dreaded covering cherub on top, "axiomatic" and "dogmatic,"[9] insisting on controlled meanings of events and objects.

We can also read ⊤ and ⊥ as applications, or poetic appropriations, of logical apposition. For example, in a text written in 1880 (published in 1933), Charles S. Peirce wrote that

> [t]he symbol ⌜⊥⌝ can be viewed as representing a constant truth function (either unary or binary) that returns the truth value False for any input or inputs. Or it can be regarded as a constant, which means that it is a zeroary (zero-input) function, a degenerate function, which refers to the truth value False.[10]

Peirce's discovery is later called the Sheffer Functions, with reference to a 1913 paper by Henry Sheffer that also recognizes a possible relation of a single set (cardinality) that can function in relation to two-valued propositional logic. Riding's ⊤-⊥ func-

9 Riding, *Though Gently,* 2.

10 "The relevant manuscript, dating to 1880, numbered MS 378 in a subsequent edition and titled 'A Boolian [*sic*] Algebra with One Constant' (Peirce, 1971), was actually destined for discarding and was salvaged for posterity literally at the nick of time in 1926. A fragmentary text by Peirce dating from 1880 also shows familiarity with the remarkable metalogical characteristics that make a single function functionally complete, and this is also the case with Peirce's unfinished *Minute Logic* (1902, ch. 3): these texts were eventually published posthumously (1933, vol. 4, pp. 13–18, 215–216.)"; "the Peirce Arrow [] is the dual of the Sheffer Stroke." See Odysseus Makridis, "The Sheffer Stroke," *Internet Encyclopedia of Philosophy,* https://www.iep.utm.edu/sheffers/.

tion — though not indicating what might have been a relation to logic forms she may have been reading about — operates in a characteristic way for her work, shifting one form of thinking into its alterity. This shift is one observable effect of multidisciplinary code translation, a tendency characteristic of some modernist cultural criticism. This tendency is empoweringly resurrected in present-day re-tenderings of permission not to stay in one disciplinary set — to be intersectional, like quantum sensors tracing heretofore uncapturable topography, like letters chasing their feasibility across variant manifests.

The two appositional Ts can also be understood with reference to Riding's earlier critical book *Contemporaries and Snobs:* "the structure of the poetic universe [⊥] is directed by a person in single-handed conflict with the time-community [⊤]."[11] This stated conflict forecasts a problem with the issue of time, a developing problem that Riding revisits in *Though Gently.* In "The Crowd," Riding distinguishes "two kinds of humanist": One kind of humanist argues on behalf of "the crowd," the other on behalf of cultural improvement. So far so good: It's difficult to dispute the binary Riding articulates; after all, it continues to feature in publishing and academies, among other sublunaries. Moreover, her indictment of popular and disciplinary opinion-tending is a fair critique of modernist professionalizing, from the twentieth-century establishment of art prizes to T.S. Eliot's assertion that "tradition" defines and organizes the "individual talent."

Overall, however, Riding's useful critique of professionalization in *Though Gently,* a critique more fully articulated in *Contemporaries and Snobs,* is distracted by statements that evince her growing conviction that her time has achieved the eschaton of lingual human potential. As she writes in "The Crowd": "We are no longer in time," "the end has come," and "now is a time when there is so little left to do that it is very easy to feel important."[12] Such eschatological statements are a recurrent

11 Laura Riding, *Contemporaries and Snobs* (Scholarly Press, 1971), 15.
12 Riding, *Though Gently,* 8–9.

and strikingly modernist feature of Riding's thought, and they are involved with her increasing difficulty, after the mid-1930s, with writing in poetry or fictive prose. Such statements, that is, are early evidence of a facet of Riding's thought that would later become more dominant and repress her more fabulating creative urges.

Although Riding perceives the problems of modernist humanist professionalizing quite pressingly, she does not sufficiently acknowledge the potential erasure that eschatological absolutism can visit on always-contextualized human creativity. Riding articulates in *Though Gently* one of the principles that make so much of her writing of the 1920s and 1930s so interesting: "A poet plies the forms of change for all they are worth."[13] Yet by the end of the decade (and not without reference to the coming yet-another World War), she was on the brink of renouncing the further writing of poetry and devoted to producing hope-in-the-apocalypse documents like *The Covenant of Literal Morality* (1938). For all her hermeneutic dynamism, Riding's creative processes and performances are legible as afflicted by a very modernist sense that the world is at an ending point. As the *Covenant* articulates so clearly, this sense is hugely connected to the devastation of war; that pamphlet's commitment to authenticity articulations can also be seen as echoing some current devotions in western academia, proprietary authenticity devotions that can be connected to fearful anomies of the total capitalist project. In both cases, trauma pressure and states of emergency can cause reversion to safety nets and a lessening of overt faith in art—even as the semiotics of made works still crackle with alterity openings.

To be sure, Riding can be said to make her world-ending claims precisely because of her idealism, her desire that there should be no more excuses for the "leniency" of philosophy, for the "fanaticism" of science, or for anything other than individuals living in respectful clarity with language.[14] This idealism is

13 Ibid., 14.
14 Ibid., 8.

characteristic of Riding, and quite zeitgeisty. But she is more persuasively idealist when pursuing the thought-experiments of ⊤-⊥ functions, and when *Though Gently* suggests an affinity for the perfection-disrupting ends of French surrealist projects: "The French by surrealism thought to gain the reality of failure by abandoning the imagination of success."[15] This statement articulates a crucial and recurrent part of Riding's project and is followed by a paragraph reminiscent of Friedrich Nietzsche's 1873 essay "On Truth and Lie in an Extra-Moral Sense":

> Thinking of one thing you cannot help thinking of everything. What is expressionism, what is surrealism, what is to make a picture? Truth is not one answer but every answer. [...] And so I might go on: not by way of saying what is to make a picture, or what is surrealism, or what is expressionism, but by way of saying what is everything, which is by way of telling the truth. Truth is not one answer or every answer but any answer.[16]

Truth is "any answer," a "thinking of everything." Language continuously pushes absolute uncertainties. And this impossible hovering is what Riding is after, as she writes in *Epilogue I:* "the critical reality *failure* is offered to those who reject pseudo-realities of achievement."[17] In the continuous pursuit of lingual truth, success and failure are the same thing in constatively hoverable, in provocatively continuing, "answer" propositions.

Riding recurs to this central point, and to the trope of the ⊤-⊥ function, on the final page of *Though Gently.* She invokes "perfection" as destruction and "telling the truth" as a mirrored omission of the tellable, to look for the traces of truth in the trails of what's left out: "Going as slow as if nothing were being omit-

15 Ibid., 21.

16 Friedrich Nietzsche, "On Truth and Lie in an Extra-Moral Sense," in *The Portable Nietzsche,* ed. and trans. Walter Kaufmann (Viking Press, 1954), 21.

17 Laura Riding and Robert Graves, eds., *Epilogue I* (Seizin, 1935), 61.

ted, everything may be omitted without not telling the truth."[18] The quatrefoil double-negative tension of this latter sentence is performed as the most hopeful conceptual and embodied way to approach lingual truth. It can be said to be a ⊥-expressive sentence, and its dynamic "going" is contemporarily akin to Barbara Cassin's reflections on the "intranslatable."[19] I think Riding never forgot the ingredients of this point, even if only performatively, and even in her final, posthumously published book *Rational Meaning* (1997), whose 598 pages are so differently filled than those of *Though Gently.* Under the name Laura (Riding) Jackson, in collaboration with her husband Schuyler B. Jackson, she wrote in *Rational Meaning* that "language [is] itself the anatomy of truth," and that a true dedication to words will always disavow the "stop."[20] Having tried out various truth genres in the 1920s and 1930s, and then having practiced a long publication silence, Riding centered the last decades of her writing activity in (esoteric and English-language-devoted) non-fiction prose. As though her long practice in making room for lingual otherness had come to rest in what is a very contemporary preference for non-fiction subject-authentic thematic-univocal prose as the "best" place for verbal truth. It might have been happier for Riding's continuing artistic projects were she to have written further into the apposition gestured to in Peirce's metalogic, articulated in *Though Gently* ("Truth is not one answer but every answer"), and performed in the textual intension of that book's temporary measures of ⊤ and ⊥.

---

18 Riding, *Though Gently,* 29.

19 See Barbara Cassin, ed., *Vocabulaire européen des philosophies: Dictionnaire des intraduisibles, édition augmentée* (Éditions du Seuil, 2019).

20 See Laura Riding Jackson and Schuyler B. Jackson, *Rational Meaning: A New Foundation for the Definition of Words, and Supplementary Essays,* ed. William Harmon (University of Virginia Press, 1997), 46, 413.

Deformance and If Meaning

> For the understanding, like the eye, judging of objects only by its own sight, cannot but be pleased with what it discovers, having less regret for what has escaped it, because it is unknown.
>
> — John Locke, *An Essay Concerning Humane Understanding*[1]

> Thus interpretation must find the right language[s] if it really wants to make the text speak.
>
> — Hans-Georg Gadamer, *Truth and Method*[2]

This essay involves ways of reading poetry, particularly experimental or innovative poetry such as Leslie Scalapino's 1988 book-length poem *way*. Poststructuralist theory articulates an appealingly skeptical attitude toward Enlightenment ideals of authoritativeness, comprehensiveness, critical accuracy, progress, and objectivity. That skepticism has generated more institutional opportunities for literary studies, and conceptual "post-literary" studies, to articulate critical practices — practices

1 John Locke, *An Essay Concerning Humane Understanding* (Thomas Basset, 1690), https://www.gutenberg.org/files/10615/10615-h/10615-h.htm.

2 Hans-Georg Gadamer, *Truth and Method*, trans. Joel Weinsheimer and Donald G. Marshall (Crossroad Publishing, 1989), 358.

of theory—that activate the contingency and changefulness of creative discourses and of criticism itself. This essay's title invokes a forebear of such practices of theory in William James's concept of "if meaning."

My earlier co-authored essay "Deformance and Interpretation" (1999, with Jerome McGann) uses my 1997 doctoral thesis terms "deformance," and "deformative criticism," to discuss modes of re-reading that can be summarized as conceptually interpretive and exegetically actuating physical criticism.[3] In this essay, "shaped reading" is sometimes substituted for deformance: I shift the terms not least because critical revolving of terminology is useful in keeping thinkerships alive. The poets Emily Dickinson and Randall McLeod are two creative thinkers who relished ideas and terms similar to deformance and shaped reading to indicate their commitment to physical criticism in reading. Dickinson's "backward" reading and McLeod's "transformissive" reading deliberately reorder and reflex a poem, enabling one to perceive and experience more of the poem's non-narrative, synchronic angles. Deformance and shaped reading pull these physical criticisms forward in time and in relation to overt complexities of creative discourse such as Scalapino's book *way*.

Critical practices generally do not look to such physical reorderings of poetry, instead construing the poem as an inviolable object with a single given form. In these latter critical approaches, the poem's dynamisms are perceptible only with regard to contexts of production and reception "outside" the object of the poem, such as archive fossicking's "genetic criticism." In this sense one of the strengths of transhuman (what some call post-human) theorizing—that is, understanding a human as a culturally malleable assemblage of "true" ingredients coming and going with different accompaniments—has

3 See Lisa Samuels, "Poetic Arrest: Laura Riding, Wallace Stevens, and the Modernist Afterlife" (PhD diss., University of Virginia, 1997), and a collaborative essay written subsequently with Jerome McGann, "Deformance and Interpretation," *New Literary History* 30, no. 1 (1999): 25–56.

rarely been applied to events of writing, which might seem to have even more opportunity than skin-bound, living, human animals to be perceived and reassembled in terms of dynamic perceptions and constituencies.

A tendency to treat the poem as a stable object arose in Anglo-American-Australasian academic criticism in the context of an urgent desire to become professionally strong and methodologically respectable. As Gail McDonald notes in *Learning to Be Modern* (1993), "the question urgently and repeatedly posed at Modern Language Association meetings in the last quarter of the nineteenth century was how the study of languages and literature could be made scientific and, what was much the same thing, professional."[4] One consequence of this professionalizing design is not only that the literary work comes to be considered a stable object of study, but that critical work proceeds as though it too needs to be stable. The critical act often comes to replicate, as in apposition or a projected mirror, the posited object status of the thing it studies, so that we are left with two objects: the "finished" work of literature and the "finished" act of criticism.

But treating the poem as an object suppresses the thought conditions of wild dialectics and suppresses that which is excessive, always recombinatory, sometimes anarchic, in works of lingual arts. The assumption that the limit of a critical poetics is an instance of the Arnoldian schism between "culture" (criticism) and "anarchy" (poetry) sets aside the extent to which all lingual works happen within changing and unstable languages. To put it another way: Insofar as poems are framed in the context of what Matthew Arnold counted as anarchy—not held to account in ways that legal documents or professional qualifications are—they activate lingual polyvalence and semiotic diffraction, which can be also called uncertainty. But, like it or not, critical language (and legal language) also happens in that uncertainty, considering the latter term in both its physics and in its epistemological querying forces. One question becomes: How do we

4 Gail McDonald, *Learning to Be Modern: Pound, Eliot, and the American University* (Clarendon Press, 1993), 76.

stimulate more criticism that will stop bracketing out its theoretical knowledge of this uncertainty? How do we develop more critical tools that don't suppress semiotic dynamism or that which is apparently anarchic (fluid, unstable, changing, resistant, and so on) in art? Being alive to new meanings is as much about critical hermeneutics as it is about artistic innovation and the ways that creative discourses change in our perception of them even when their physical, ink-on-pages and marks-on-screens and sounds-in-airwaves, features seem to look the same.

The last century of criticism has certainly fostered new tools for engaging literature and practices of theory. Roland Barthes's relevant work *S/Z* (1970), for example, "reads" Honoré de Balzac's *Sarrasine* by writing it differently as a system of codes, not paraphrasing the story as a diachronic sequence. Barthes takes the story apart so that it reveals different versions of itself, and in this way *S/Z* is one background text for a few current critical practices, including those in this book, like withness and the shaped readings of this essay.[5] Barthes is not alone is his applied theorizing. During the late 1920s and the 1930s, as another example, the poet Laura Riding emphasized the active role of the reader, the multiple activities of the lingual sign, and the importance of dialogic and communitarian criticism. What I call Riding's "subjective correlatives," theorized in my introduction to a critical edition of her book *Anarchism Is Not Enough* (1928; 2001), are a condition and consequence of this complex semiotic dynamic. For Riding, both reading and writing foreground interpretive roles, whether in assuming revolving narrative personas or in disassembling a Shakespearean sonnet in ways that presage, as in a kind of *mimesis negativa,* Veronica Forrest-Thomson's syncretic "total image complex" (in her 1979 book *Poetic Artifice*). In a different mode, Louis Zukofsky's *Bottom: On Shakespeare* (1963) brings unexpected texts into alignment with each other in order to examine William Shakespeare's musics and meanings. Thus, for example, Avicenna is quoted

5 See Roland Barthes, *S/Z,* trans. Richard Miller and Richard Howard (Hill and Wang, 1974).

next to Shakespeare who is quoted next to Ludwig Wittgenstein, enabling Zukofsky to "see" things about Shakespeare that might not be permitted in a more traditional study, that is, in a study that would forbid the juxtaposition of texts that cannot apparently be justifiably linked, bibliographically, historically, or otherwise.[6] Susan Howe's *My Emily Dickinson* (1989) is an intervention in a poetics of pronounced subjectivity: It is grounded in Howe's sense of unease about the many systematizing and biographically based studies of Dickinson. Howe strives for a new way of examining her own engagement with Dickinson's poetry, bringing together historical and literary texts that are contemporaneous with Dickinson's poems in order to explore contexts and circumstances for their composition.[7] Howe also emphasizes the potential meaning values of Dickinson's handwriting. Giving critical attention to the embodiment of lingual acts, such as handwriting (calligraphy, scribbles), is another form of physical criticism insofar as it presumes the worth of interrogating the apparently non-semantic features of a work without a template for perceiving how those features can be brought into meaning space. This kind of work is also aligned with membranism and bioautography, considered elsewhere in this book, insofar as a critical consideration of the somatic features of a work accords with membranism's emphasis on the realities of wet contact in arenas of art and with bioautography's openness to the body of the writer/artist.

Previous to any of these aforementioned twentieth-century works, we find in 1890 the philosopher William James writing

6 See Laura Riding, *Anarchism Is Not Enough*, ed. Lisa Samuels (University of California Press, 2001); Veronica Forrest-Thomson, *Poetic Artifice: A Theory of Twentieth-Century Poetry* (Manchester University Press, 1978); and Louis Zukofsky, *Bottom: On Shakespeare* (University of California Press, 1987).

7 See Susan Howe, *My Emily Dickinson* (North Atlantic Books, 1985). See also Marta L. Werner, *Emily Dickinson's Open Folios: Scenes of Reading, Surfaces of Writing* (University of Michigan Press, 1995) for a fuller consideration of examples and implications of Dickinson's embodiment of handwriting.

in *Principles of Psychology* about the "feeling of *if*" which, he declares, ought to be considered a principle of knowing. James invokes prepositional and conjunctive feeling and considers the para-semantics of lexical orders that have been kept semantically invisible in comparison with apparently more substantive concepts like "feelings of gratitude" or "feelings of resistance."[8] A "feeling of *if*" is by definition not definite, so it presents a position that is not taken (asserted authoritatively) but is instead explored or inhabited. We hover affectively and cognitively *within* such a feeling. We might thus compare James's feeling of if and other prepositional and conjunctive feelings to interpretive openness, while James's "about" stands in for critical closure or conclusiveness, what James terms "the substantive perception they [prepositional feelings] led to."[9] Furthermore, we might recall that James wrote about "if" meaning at about the same time that Stéphane Mallarmé was throwing his dice, and about the same time that Oscar Wilde's dialogic critical essay "The Critic as Artist" poses Ernest telling Gilbert "There is much Virtue in that If."[10] Zukofsky adds to the chorus in his collected essays, *Prepositions,* using the subtitles "For," "With," and "About" to frame his essay groupings.[11] These texts are examples of a critical history of interpretive openness with prepositional theory, a history that helps situate the present essay.

Bringing theory and criticism into closer alliance aims to disrupt what has sometimes been put forward as methodological and teleological differences between them. I desire — and am far from alone in this desire, as this book makes clear — to make theory focus on generating practices like physical criticism that are more aware of the necessarily tentative nature of their assertions, thus more like performative and applied theory. Practices

8 See William James, *Principles of Psychology* (Henry Holt and Company, 1890).

9 Ibid., 245–46.

10 Oscar Wilde, "The Critic as Artist," in *Complete Works of Oscar Wilde,* Vol. 4, ed. Robert Ross (Wyman-Fogg Co., 1909), 102.

11 Louis Zukofsky, *Prepositions: The Collected Critical Essays of Louis Zukofsky* (University of California Press, 1981).

of theory have a history in literary studies partly as poetics that operate in shared conditions of meaning with poetry. Poetics as *if meaning* promotes ways to engage critically with the changefulness of literary and critical signs, with the inherent changefulness of language. One often gets the sense that meaning categories, not just subject areas, are professionally both hierarchized and subdivided: theory is the Think, focusing on questions and uncertainty, and criticism is the Act, showing us decisive matters that have been figured out, focusing on answers and the rhetoric of the certain. Poetics can sometimes mediate this split if only because it exists in a parallel dimension to it, in terms of disciplinary histories. If theory is philosophy's response to the scientistic positioning of criticism, poetics is one of poetry's other mouths, speaking with practices of theory to flood some areas of thinking within which these disciplinary modes situate.

Such poetics or practices of theory are in part about accepting the theoretically undisputed, and performatively usually bracketed, fact that we can only understand what we already know. When we say we "get" something, it generally means we stop focusing on the uncertainty inherent in the thought process. In wanting interpretive processes to remain open, I want to respect the dynamic qualities of critical thinking and lingual art. As the poet Lyn Hejinian puts it in her book title, *A Thought Is the Bride of What Thinking.*[12] The impulse and the open syntax of that title puts Hejinian's thought in the context of another stirring moment of US poetics, the six nonlectures that the poet e.e. cummings delivered in the 1950s. In his fourth nonlecture, "I & you & is," cummings announces that he will explain himself by way of juxtaposing various passages in various sequences, letting those in his audience "draw your own (if any) conclusions. Over-and under-standing will make their appearance later."[13] Taking up cummings's practice in the twenty-first century, the poet Charles Bernstein often delivered what I think of as his

12 See Lyn Hejinian, *A Thought Is the Bride of What Thinking* (Tuumba Press, 1976).

13 e.e. cummings, *Six Nonlectures* (Harvard University Press, 1953), 63.

Shuffle Talks, lecturing to an audience by reading aloud declamatory and thoughtful proseful propositions printed on continuously reordered individual pieces of paper.

Poetics as *if meaning* is partly a call for practices that generate coextensive and prepositional relationships — feelings of "if," "and," "but," "for," and so on — with works of art. It is also a call for poetics to be meaning, not in a distanced relation of simile to meaning but more like poetics = if meaning, or as one might say in conversation, in skeptical wonderment, *"as if* there could be final meaning!?" In this regard one can see a continuity between this essay's emphasis and other theories delineated in this book, in addition to the continuity between deformance and shaped reading. In terms of membranism, for example, the contacts among disciplinary critic, art worker, art event, materials, and contexts are a series of membranes that flex and exchange and change in those contacts. "Meaning" becomes more like *leaning.* Disciplinary blueprint becomes critical blurprint.

To demonstrate my own pragmatics, I turn to poetics as if meaning in relation to the work of Leslie Scalapino. In numerous books of poetry, essays, plays, and innovative fiction, Scalapino engages with issues of epistemology, perception, and identity in cultural contexts. Scalapino's style is formally distinctive, recognizable for its (often hyphenated) phrasal parataxis that evokes and enacts the writing's relentless considerations of what it means to know, perceive, relate, identify, and be identified.

In many respects, *way* is exemplary of Scalapino's writings.[14] The book begins with a long epigraph from David Bohm's *Causality and Chance in Modern Physics,* an epigraph put in after the book was finished, Scalapino explains, as a kind of illuminating foreword.[15] Bohm's words set up an intersection of quantum physics with artistic methodology, forecasting how much of Scalapino's book is involved with identity indeterminacy and

14 Leslie Scalapino, *way* (North Point Press, 1988).

15 Leslie Scalapino, p.c., March 2000.

particle/particular perception. Here is a brief excerpt from the page-long Bohm epigraph:

> Because every kind of thing is defined only through an inexhaustible set of qualities each having a certain degree of relative autonomy, such a thing can and indeed must be unique; i.e., not completely identical with any other thing in the universe, however similar the two things may be. Carrying the analysis further, we now note that because of all of the infinity of factors determining what any given thing is are always changing with time, *no such thing can even remain identical with itself as time passes.*[16]

Like a cultural analog to particle physics, Scalapino's book presents continuous fragmenting of events, significances, and beings. Subject to Heisenbergian rules, such identities and meanings cannot remain or be accounted for as coextensive even with themselves from moment to moment. However much it is necessary to bracket out this indeterminacy in order to establish regular living patterns in ordinary social life, this absolute immeasurableness is — so far as we know in theories of contingency, particle physics, and quantum neurology, among other planetary arenas — the actual dynamic of being.

Criticism might imagine its task to be one of explaining these issues in certain types of logical, referential, and objective language. Even if physics is right about such indeterminacy, it might protest, we need to hold the language still and paraphrase how and what it means. But such criticism would formally undo the very meaning-arguments *way* is making. It is certainly possible to paraphrase the thematics of some of Scalapino's *way*. The book investigates perceptions of social and cultural scenes and situations, including urban poverty, human love and sexual relations, people responding to car accidents and day jobs, and the relation of the US public to the policies of the US president.

16 Scalapino, *way*, n.p. Emphasis in original.

The central formal point of *way* matches Scalapino's thematic focus on perception. In her words:

> *way,* for example, is a tracking of thought/ as/ sensation/ as/ memory/ as/ outside/ as/ events/ of one's/ as/ other people: to place "the minute as event so small it wouldn't even be remembered" (except that it was written) on the same level with immense events, breaking down "space": as its sound structure. Its sound, its language shape, which is its syntax, is its occurrence.[17]

As suggested by Scalapino's description of "space," I want to evoke a passage from *way* to see how it enacts and engenders constellations of meaning, events, selves, and more in gesturally infinite lingual cluster fields. These cluster fields can be compared with clusters of galaxies in astronomy, which is a salient comparative when we think of Heisenberg's Uncertainty Principle positing that one cannot measure both position and momentum accurately at the same time as well as positing that the act of studying a subject necessarily alters properties, or our perception of the properties, of that subject. Choosing to emphasize properties or perception depends on how one wants to import the Heisenberg comparative. Heisenberg can be apt for studying Scalapino because his zeitgeisty Uncertainty Principle seems analogous with her syntactically polyvalent, formally modular work. We activate the cluster fields of her words as we read them, they change (us) as we read them, and so the work lives anew. On the other hand, someone might protest that Heisenberg doesn't do poetry, that the comparative is perhaps too inclined toward the internal track of *way,* whose epigraph, after all, sets us on a path toward perceiving in terms of physics.

One challenge arising from the multivalent syntax and modular forms of *way* is that readers can perceive it to be permeated by subjectivism. A reader might say "How on Earth am I supposed to know what she meant? This book is so personal

---

17 Leslie Scalapino, p.c., April 3, 2001.

and subjective as to be inaccessible to me." The critical challenge is to avoid the fear as well as the attraction of such subjectivism. A fear response is understandable: it registers the problem of other minds, the fear of incommunicableness that a self can feel in exchanges with other selves, and the fear part of language's polyvalent and changeful multiplicities. The attraction of subjectivism lies another way. Because of the problem of other minds, some might say, it matters not at all how anyone responds to a text like *way:* It is free-form, it confirms in its openness the impasse among us all. We can build little with either the fear or the attraction response here, since they keep us focused on displaced objects — text here, you there, reader yon, me hither — rather than on an engagement with the constitutive dynamics of meaning-making. Given the strong call to attention in *way*, an attention that activates the reader as an ethical observer and participant, it feels clear that the gaps among persons and events are precisely where we should not stop.

In this respect the methods of this essay are generally in sympathy with the dynamics of Scalapino's book, transacting ideational, social, eventful gaps among persons and words. I always want to see more reading practices that register the gaps and membranes that connect among persons, texts, concepts, sensory objects, and more, as causes for neither lamentation (modernist "loss") nor despairing celebration (so-called postmodern laissez-faire relativism) but as constitutive crossings in those events we call making meaning (and *can* call think-feeling its leanings). Also crucial is the renewal of methods of poetics that stay with works of art, rotating them and interacting with them and foregrounding the coextensive positions of poetics with its events of study.

To demonstrate some methods that resist the expository translation of "objective" criticism and that activate the textual relational field, I turn to some shaped readings of one section of *way*, "no(h) setting." This section of Scalapino's book kaleidoscopes through a variety of social incidents, most of them difficult: people sleeping on the street, a starving beggar, the distant position of the US president, car accidents, betrayals in friendship, and tests of identity. These incidents are fragmented syntactically, typographically, and narratively, as well as being continuously interlaced with considerations of personal perspective, for example "being introverted as / an inherent state" or "oneself in regard to an earlier view."[18] The section title frames these incidents and perspective in the stylized context of Japanese Noh theatre, thus these incidents are tagged as recurrent forms of cultural identity, real in themselves and staged, as classical Noh drama would be staged, in and for the meanings that are made with them. The form of attention Scalapino engages here—the perceiving self interlaced with and presented by way of negative social incidents—posits that attention is the first order of ethical business. What is really happening here? How can we know when everything, including Noh plays, happens/is actually precisely staged only once? And who are the observers in relation to these events?

The shaped readings that follow began in a search for alternative versions of "no(h) setting" playing and working inside it. Going through twenty pages of *way* (pages 115–34) in progressive linear order, these readings highlight chosen words and phrases and assemble them into recombined forms. I make no changes in spelling or punctuation; the omission of intervening words and punctuations produces changes in grammar and syntax. Deformance commonly disrupts the structures of word relations that we call syntax, and a different progressive linear selection would produce a different layout. To emphasize the point: This shaped reading is a model of what we might experience as we move our eyes over Scalapino's pages, noticing and linking certain words and phrases in our reading on one day, noticing and linking other words and phrases in other readings on other days. Alternative shaped readings are necessarily possible. These readings are meant as mental sculptures, conceptual responses rendered in material forms. They are not replacements for nor de-coding answers to the poem.

18 Scalapino, *way*, 118, 128.

Readers are referred to *way* for the full published layout; here, selection source pages are indicated in parentheses after each segment. Reading A:

> people as reactive — my sense in that setting occurs now — to be in the really happened, on my part or on one's part — away with introverted producing, the state of to be, lying not coming from condition or setting — very close to insular sense — from inside (115–17)
>
> an inherent state of ordering an event, struggling from the setting, continual emanating from the continual, really succeeding in being in that setting, in seeing our own culture as who oneself is, a person and the relation is, and other separate action (118–20)
>
> the person is very close, so that real events are only the action which is done by them — to relax from the people going by, produced from the setting, the audience wanting to leave wouldn't be what we are — weary of theatre and audience, the moment isn't of relation (121–23)
>
> the reversed present, along with being representational, was destroyed by going through it — when this occurred, someone in a different event destroyed the quality of the produced need, in the orientation of time or view abandoned because arrested (124–26)
>
> the new would have been before, destroyed from traveling — the street is shallow as the river, our culture is a full setting, the attitude close to the present being the condition of offspring, not unrelated to producing the representational, our culture from that relation (127–29)
>
> the woman made from the incipient development of our culture will have to go to a different place, part of the city, a way out, stripped by supposition, minding the relation of

> the correspondence to episodes and development, the real
> conjunction called me, disturbing the negative event, able
> to be relaxed, the other of the other (130–34)

This deformance exteriorizes some variants that move within the published orders of Scalapino's words, layout, and punctuation. A different shaped reading might illuminate more active referenced events, objects, and characters — cars, teachers, thieves, beggars — also in this section of *way.*

To write out versions of a poem with physical rearrangement is a way to get our bodies involved in the work, to write poetics that instantiate variants of active reading experience. Like Charles Bernstein, "I imagine poetics [...] as a sort of applied poetic, in the sense that engineering is a form of applied mathematics."[19] I take Bernstein to mean that poetics is most reverberant when it is in practicing relation to the poetry it engages. The practices of poetics are commensurate with practices of theory. We need to give ourselves permission to engage the fluidity and entanglement of the material of art and response directly. With reference to the points about lingual desire and textual intension in the essay "Monadic Yearning and Lingual Desire": we can engage the print page as though it has the flex of the digitas. Even a bit of web-slinging acumen can help us inveigle the codes of a made work — always with a mind to acting in good faith — to demonstrate and engineer the materiality of our creative theory responses. With regards to digital works, we can in such a way slip the bonds of the putative shift from modern to postmodern and swerve to the fluid ephemera of the digitas, our poetics tools fluttering.

In terms of the results of reading A: it might be said to show how Scalapino's works can be seen to enact and convey semantics key to its reading. The above selections register some of the meaning blueprints — or, better, leaning, active blurprints — of the poem, like a building that includes on its walls, embedded and drawn, the architectural blueprints that were its pre-fabri-

---

19 See Charles Bernstein, *A Poetics* (Harvard University Press, 1992), 151.

cation conceptualizing. As blurprint, the sequences of shaped reading A might be semanticized this way: People are reactive, we are our culture, we think we are the offspring of the present rather than creators of human events (the actions people carry), the moment is sometimes "weary of theatre and audience" (displaced observation that people permit themselves, as though they were distant from events and their meanings), the present and the new are dismantled by the very act of going through them, and, finally, the new person must be a "conjunction," connectively attending to relations among events, behaviors, and meanings. Here is a triplicate shaping: the moment of reading, the instantiating blurprint, a critical summary of some semantic implications of that blurprint.

While shaped readings paradoxically tend to increase attention to the layout aspects of the poem's area (what I sometimes think of "the deformative paradox"), they can also re-shape the temporal or linear aspects of that area, as here. Selecting parts of Scalapino's texts in this fashion is something like choosing only the yellows and blues in a painting by Hieronymus Bosch. We interrupt our cognitive processing of proposed coherence like narrative sequences, assembling fragments into a different order of attention to see what those particular color swaths illuminate of Bosch's heaven, hell, and Earth.

Pushing the blurprint further, below is a distilled version of the previous shaped reading. Is it necessary to emphasize again that this is only one version of a multitude of possible shaped readings, and one version of engaging *way?* Reading B:

> my sense occurs now — to be in the really happened,
> away with introverted producing, the state of introverted
> has got to be, not coming from condition or setting
>
> an inherent state of ordering an event, continual emanating
> from the continual, really succeeding in being in that setting,
> in seeing our own culture as who oneself is
>
> the person is very close, so that real events are only the

> action which is done by them — to relax from the people going by, the audience wanting to leave wouldn't be what we are
>
> the present was destroyed by going through it — when this occurred, someone in a different event destroyed the quality of the orientation of time or view
>
> our culture is a full setting, the attitude close to the present being the condition of offspring, not unrelated to producing the representational, our culture from that relation
>
> the woman made from the incipient development of our culture will have to go to a different place, stripped by supposition, the real conjunction called me able to be relaxed, the other of the other

This further condensing indicates how much "no(h) setting" performs a call for alterity attention, for "the other of the other" to keep us attuned to how identity is transacted by event. What would it mean to be continually aware that event and significance are displaced experiences that are always on the move, being negotiated among meaning-making culture animals?

Reading B also presents a fairly regularized layout: it excises three lines for every three pages of Scalapino's text, except for the final segment that draws from four pages. A shaped reading might also replicate, as in a formal imitation but with new lexical orders, the layout of the art work's lines, whether stanzas or open verse. In this case, the prose-like, regularized shaped reading is a formal register of the critical approach here, a reading that deliberately searches out meta-poetic blurprints.

A shaped reading that wants to emphasize the description or action-oriented parts of "no(h) setting" might be prone to radicalize word placements or to isolate them on the page, for example:

the people —

in rows

reactive

part — [20]

This shaped reading squib isolates some words of the published page, retaining their word positions with respect to one another, floating in blank lines and spaces among them, and slowing down the pacing compared to the prose-like shapings of A and B. The lines above also highlight a parallel between people "in rows" and words in rows/lines, how "reactive rows part" — as in move apart, and part ways — registering a continuous and contiguous divergence. An often cited example of this particular kind of shaped reading is Ronald Johnson's treatment of Milton's *Paradise Lost,* which becomes in Johnson's hands *radi os.*[21] And then there is Tom Phillips engorging with multi-modal transformances, as *A Humument,* the results of lingual selections from W.H. Mallock's nineteenth-century novel. Numerous similar examples have followed the omissive writing splurges of the 1970s.

The next in this succession of shaped readings will turn the blurprint upside down. Using reading B, this next reading snips out portions in a backward phrasal ordering, changing segment breaks to optimize (I'll consider in a moment what that word means here) the torsion of the new lineation. Reading C:

the other of the other
relaxed conjunction called me
stripped by supposition, the real
will have to go a different place

20 Scalapino, *way,* 115.
21 Ronald Johnson, *radi os* (Sand Dollar Press, 1977).

from the incipient our
from that relation the woman made
the beginnings of culture
producing the presentational
condition of offspring, not unrelated to

close to the present being
our culture is a full setting
quality orientation of time or view
occurred, someone in a different event destroyed
by going through it — when this
wouldn't be what we are — the present was destroyed

people going by to leave
action done by them — to relax from the
very close, so that real events are only the
culture — as who oneself the person is

in being in that setting, in seeing our own
continual emanating from the really
inherent state of ordering an event
not coming from condition or setting
has got to be lying,
away with introverted producing, the state

to be in the really happened
my sense occurs now —

This backward reading of selected words and phrases, what might be called recombinant phrase structures, sculpts one of the recurrently messaged desires of Scalapino's book. The desire, really the imperative to be in relation with events, identity, and culture, the being in that relation whether the desire matches the imperative: Both operate in a kind of infinite miter box of interconnectivity in *way.* In reading C, "I" is a conjunction and in conjunction with a person-oriented series of phrase structures: "the person is very close." Fragmenting narrative case does not equal vaporizing personal sense. "[T]he culture—as who oneself the person is": these words are part of the textual membrane where "oneself" goes with "sense," and that "sense occurs now," is in other words an event, not a passive feeler that then takes sense to a more semantic realm.

The recombinant phrase structures of reading C highlight variations in Scalapino's work of art. The "being" of an art work is constitutively variable—liquid transpositional machinery—in the ethics of shaped reading. One of the peculiar freedoms of lingual art, perhaps a compensation for how much language suffers from instrumentalization, from expectations of "content" transparency, is that readers can engage it by physically transforming its published properties. Studies of attention and response might support the view that readers necessarily and always carry out these transformations implicitly, in what they see or hear and otherwise sense in any given encounter with a work. Similar responsive working can occur with film, dance, paintings, sign language, art, music, and more, accessing and reordering what we are sometimes taught to consider their intact forms (on video clips, digital masterings, pages, other duplications). The lingual work of art in the age of digital reproduction has the common though not ubiquitous benefit of formally avoiding any "authenticity of the original."

There are different ways of glossing shaped readings once one has carried them out. One might comment on the newly shaped version of the published work, as I've done briefly above. One might look back at the published version and mark what has been highlighted or implicitly altered by comparison with the deformance. As already noted, the shaped readings here serve to highlight "heavy" terms in Scalapino's examination of pieces of experience and consciousness. Scalapino's book separates and remixes, exteriorizing myriad aspects of perception, affect, cultural assumptions, and political situation. Each shaped reading of "no(h) setting" exteriorizes or refracts some of what might be called the deep surface of Scalapino's writings. This deep surface is like a textual liquid that brings, moment by moment, individual structures of attention—oil rigs, thought, political climates, sexual congress, landscape, memory, discourse, love — vividly to perception for a phrase or line or segment. If we can clearly perceive each aspect of consciousness and culture-making, the poem suggests, we might be activated to a continuous ethical and linguistic attention that is more responsive and responsible to the conditions of perception and meaning-making.

The shaped readings here arguably resonate with the paratactic and fragmented aspects of Scalapino's work, in *way* and also elsewhere. We might not imagine the poetry of a very different writer from a very different time (John Donne, say) to be so commensurate with shaped readings. But doing shaped readings with Donne might be considered even more revelatory than turning Scalapino's work toward different lingual-geometric planes. Deforming "A Valediction: Forbidding Mourning" goes further in discharging Donne's poem from its printed orders. The unsuppressions of such a reading are comparatively more radical because Donne's poetry is arguably not as dissociative as Scalapino's. In the case of both poets — both kinds of poets, if Scalapino and Donne can be considered different cases in formal, syntactic, historical, and semantic terms — deformance is critically relevant insofar as it helps condition the critical mind to relinquish an urge to final or "objective" truth. Such readings are also relevant insofar as they show us the kinds of deformance we are drawn to. Why have I preferred, in this essay, to shape a semantically stabilizing reading of Scalapino? Is it because I want my students, for example, to see the directness and legibility of her work? That probably is one motivation, since I find students to be ready for, but not at all practiced in, the deep contingencies of cultural semiotics, the kinds of contingencies that partly motivate Scalapino's highly nuanced contention that there is no connection between writing and reality. Though the digitas steeps us in motile and constellated signs, and sets us up as assemblage co-makers, ways of reading still so often are utilitarian and full of monadic yearning.

What would it mean for Scalapino's work, with its inherent instability intact, to be easier to read? For one thing, it could mean we had learned more ways to correlate our lingual consciousness with our more general phenomenological consciousness, to have our reading expectations be more like the deep verticals that form our lived experiences (normatively narrated as rapid horizontals of external events). If it is true that we can only understand (as in, "get") what we already know, then "understanding meaning" can become a problematic assent to a formula of drawn conclusions. One difficulty of Scalapino's works, and a difficulty of shaped readings, is that both stimulate inconclusive connectivity. Neither is involved with constructing static understandings. We are less trained to think of understanding as open-ended process and method, as ongoing electric textual intension engagement; we are more trained to thinking of meaning and understanding as content-oriented conclusions. Even meaning as agreement is just a gentler version of the problem of authoritative discourse that invites a commensurate will-to-mastery from the reader. In Scalapino's writings the adamancy of the rhetorically negative is needed to try to overcome, to resist, the adamancy of the desire for conclusive understanding. Laura Riding's, Theodor Adorno's, and Édouard Glissant's negative horizons work in similar ways.

Another thing to be thought of here is the question of subject and object in the context of the ethics of critical practice. It is not helpful to maintain that criticism lacks the ability to speak the art. That kind of assertion can support critical views of the art object as separate, self-sufficient, and therefore paradoxically assailable. Criticism is not more powerful than art; one sign of this struggle is when criticism is accorded a "secondary source" status compared with "primary ['creative'] texts." This power struggle is anticipatable in culture, but it is not defensible in thought. This subject rises up for me in reading statements such as this from Theodor Adorno's *Negative Dialectics:* "The need to lend a voice to suffering is a condition of all truth. For suffering is objectivity that weighs upon the subject; its most subjective experience, its expression, is objectively conveyed."[22]

---

22 Theodor W. Adorno, *Negative Dialectics,* trans. E.B Ashton (The Seabury Press, 1973), 17–18.

But discourse springs back from the pressures we exert upon it. This is as true for critical writings as for art writings. The fact that critical discourses like shaped readings get flack from some creative writers arguing for the inviolability of their works, as well as from some "objective" critical practices arguing for "logical" approaches, indicates to me that those discourses are operating in sensitive areas of cultural expectation. Which is, in my view, where practices of theory should (also) operate.

The digitas and new media writing have made theory space and practical space for the methods and implications of deformance and shaped readings. In work presented in talk and demonstration form, I give a successively transferred version of a poem by Chris Tamaiparea, scattering the published poem into entirely new orders while, in that case, retaining every lettrified and punctuation item presented in the first published version. In this essay I end up with quite differentiated phrases and layouts, and they come across (cross as in *translatio*) as new events of language. Because they are not "poems" but rather shaped readings, I would not publish them separately from a contextualized critical presentation. I would rather have access, in this book, to a revolving dimensionalized arena of presentation that gave constant new form to possible shaped readings and did not necessarily retain them at all. As my work with a java webslinger indicated to me, such relinquished data sophistications are very hard to set up in a discipline that does not provide laboratories with available equipment and collaborating researchers. To an extent, then, the practical limit of shaped reading is yet another disciplinary limit. Not only are there resistances to the practice of theory instanced in deformance; there are also institutional preventions to some digital and curatorial actualizations I would prefer to be able to readily and consistently carry out. The shaped readings in this essay are practices involved with questions and contingent investigations of significance. They are meant to do-and-undo themselves and to be in part done by being undone.

The productive adamancy of the negative can be seen in the form of such shaped readings as well as in Scalapino's scraping the present and the possible, dismantling normative language structures to point to how meanings are being constituted lingually. In her re-shaped words, "the present was destroyed by going through it, producing the representational — the beginnings of our culture from that relation." I would compare this recognition of the dynamic imperatives in perception and meaning-making to what Hans-Georg Gadamer is after in a passage from *Truth and Method:*

> The text is made to speak through interpretation. But no text and no language speaks if it does not speak a language that reaches the other person. Thus interpretation must find the right language[s] if it really wants to make the text speak. There cannot, therefore, be any single interpretation that is correct "in itself," precisely because every interpretation is concerned with the text itself. The historical life of a tradition depends on being constantly assimilated and interpreted.[23]

Because I sympathize with this passage, so long as "language" is pluralized, I find Gadamer's earlier assertion that "the hermeneutic phenomenon is basically not a problem of method at all" wrong-headed: a theory that has not gone far enough in its investigations of the implications of practice.[24] Recognizing that it is not useful to search for a (single or best) "correct" method is not the same critical move as claiming that method is not a hermeneutic problem. In the interpretation of lingual works, everything is method. Insofar as interpretation "reaches the other person [...] to make the text speak [...] constantly," it is working *for the text.* That "constantly" points to the fundamental condition, and the most commensurate method, of language: changefulness. Precisely because it is dynamic, a work of art can erupt out of itself as many methods as we need to find its pleasures and to think its meanings, to summon its blurprints and lean into its leanings.

23 Gadamer, *Truth and Method*, 397.

24 Ibid., xxi.

How Write

Adam

It is a "gem-like radiance of geophysical beauty" like a curtain in front of cultures from which it's being looked. It knows recency, periods. Response-endure invention tumbles after the invasions; otherwise, it comes first. How is ground lingual?

Eve

The butterfly of literary air models cut. Migrating orality, e-culture patch. Hence the excruciating sensitivity to gatherings and forms. In sum, the facet of liquid pours out with constituting ventricles at a similar measure of error.

Adamic

I found some instructions for keeping yourself unrecognizable: What is the social reading of your style? What does it manifest and suppress? Any position from which query turns the water locus besting ctenophores *come in please.*

Even

For me as a social being, the so important mode of writing now is ________________________. My writing relates to that mode insofar as __________________________. For me as a parasocial being, the most important node of write now is ______________. My skiting relates to that so far as, ah, the ______________________ __________________.

Adamant

What space might you use to frame or interrupt or temporarily perma-ground your writing?
Can such peat make swifts?
How about lenticels on the search: pockmark the archive with your waiting leveler compeers?

Event

It's like a circular feedback mechanism: I hold it in my lap and it purrs through me, electric wet wires barely rapt.
I recognize the sounds and shapes with a tender nausea.
The mirror actually sticks to my skin.

Ada

But the broke implement needs to feed its irrhythmia through beat-BEAT-beat, BEAT-beat-beat. You recognize the event as the joy lament it is? The built environment print side: "I wanna lay there and screw the boards to my head."

Eventually

One's own readers are ___ money ___ sex ___ blood __ buildings
One's own pages are ____ skin ___ paint ___invisible ___thick
One's won styles are __ balloons __ tall __ ghost courses __ grids
One's syntax is ___ floating __ invert __nebulous __forewarned

One's core titles are ___ hats ___ tracks ___ gardens ___lungs
One's warm lines are ____ breaths ___ trains ___ stones ___dirt
One's arm characters are __ sums __ names ___ ganders __ interjects
One's clewed view is __ night __ freed ___ gainful ___ heartled

Ad

So it's colloquial, like telling the person you're going to message assuaging them. Or look at look at look at this regard, my sight-lines startle out of it, theory sockets win the race so long as they co-pleat the march march march. Let's do it again I've come to stand for.

Ev

Replacement therapy toggles the works, __________ skid for __________. When the trees co-tangle it sounds like birds. Even clouds make noises. The crying of the actual as better met by the glass of the page *not* cutting your fingers.

Adamite

Myth set one: The calling of the __________ is _________. At times it is _________ but only in the sense that _______ possess the _______________. A ___________________ is born, out of the tradition of _________________, the bearer of exceptional skills in ___________________. Among the ____________ groups, the _________ will be obvious. That centering characteristic may be *hapka, dolor,* _________, and __________. The joint _____________ is roundabout, like that _____ growing gorgeously and without predetermination from the_______________________________. Most sacred of all is ____________________, not in a set ____________ but more ________________. They achieve the _____________ rapport they need with their ________________, ________________, and _____, who are the kind of heno most familiar to ______.

Ever

In my other life siphonophores: non-prejudicial, apt variance.
Now it searches under the lattice line, under the tree line, under the flood line.
Writing with one's ears, taking out the eyes rest them in the warm salt, water-peel a moving corner.

A

That story is told again and again, always at home or in some approximation to polygyria of the laminate—writ like the soft blanket against my narrow flesh that I can never quite get folded all the way in.

Eventide

human protagonist (1) à transformed into → ______________
humanimal joyer (2) à transformed into → ________________
sociable circumflex → transformed into → _________________
unrepeatable setting → transformed into → _________________
genre fortune → transformed into → _______________________

Both together

It was the confetti from the skies that shored us;
it was the leaning temperature;
a crucial ingredient of biddable modesty leads to it;
the magazine told us the blending of tones would make everyone happy, but my serials and drinks remain distinct;
it's the shifting from one ingredient by another that keeps it open-floored;
the oceanic fits around breathing;
your identity begins outside the symphonic edge of the auricles sloughing epics;
it's the correlative imposter that keeps us the muffins of history, softly crumbling, chorate;

when we're in the vertex splashing, sussing ways, sure sure the superpose the surface of our slips becomes all ears.

________________ --->------------------ ________________

________________ ---------------------~--- ________________

4

The Body Rights Movement and Rapacity Culture

In the early twenty-first century a body rights movement rose up and gathered cogency and mana that continues to build. Examples include a US woman walking around with a mattress on her back to protest her institution's unwillingness to expel her rapist; young women in Aotearoa/New Zealand chaining themselves to a police station to protest the dismissal of charges against the RoastBusters; and the implosion of a UK poetry site attendant on painfully inept language about rape. These are anti-sexual-harassment and anti-rape events and interventions, and the right not to be raped is certainly part of the body rights movement. A profound part, since it still seems to be the case that rape is treated as an unfortunate by-product of power differentials between bodies. Any body can be subjected to sexual violation, but "having been raped" is too close to coequal with "being a woman." Changing minds—so that rape becomes as unacceptable as acts of pedophilia, bestiality, and other violations of another's body—is part of the body rights movement focus. The very urge to *think rape,* like thinking homophobia or feeling antipathy to persons of other races, is being addressed at the level of the body and bodily encounters. To be sure, humans cannot flip our animality to machine-like ethical responses that remove all of the potential problems of noticing the Otherness of the other. Violence is one, terribly common, response to the recognition that there is an Other and that someone cannot be, or have, or control, or simply omit, that other. The urge to overcome that other, to omit their otherness or forcefully absorb it into the perpetrator's sense of Same/not-Other, is part of rapacity culture. The body rights movement is on the line that includes problems of physical violation in rapacity culture; these problems are overt manifestations of how difficult human animals can find otherness to be.

The body rights movement also rises in part out of the conditions of the end of privacy. Many people consider their bodies and (what might be cordoned off as) their interior lives to be as displayable and deployable as any other aspects of living. Consider the online and in print self-display of vulnerability, psychological and physical, as many people push to render ordinary what has been closeted as fringe aspects of humans' mental and bodily living. One example is the transformation of the naked calendar fundraiser associated with the UK Warwick Rowers Club (WRC). From positive voluntary nudity, the WRC moved in to Sports Allies, an anti-bullying and anti-homophobic program. The rowers are putting their nude bodies in the position of support and rectitude. They are exercising their body rights in support of others' body rights.

What does this have to do with writing? When one moves into a public zone of writing—publishing, visiting, encouraging other writers—one's body is not only topic but also medium. Publication and productions are intensely embodied, with gender and nation announcements attached to names and with expectations attached to age, vocal type, perceptions of race and ethnicity, and features and clothing. The body rights movement is considering not only gender and sexuality rights but also what it means to present one's body and bodily identity in public zones, including zones of making writing and other art. For public poetry readings, one might imagine placing a giant outward-facing mirror in front of the performer, who would position and perform behind it, so that audience members witness themselves. When someone performs, their body and voice and movements and clothing are shapes and scents in the room that perfuse the sounds and semantics of the performed work. Body rights request, or argue, that the performer's presence be received in constative empathy: not as a transparent medium, but as a specific humanity integrated with acceptability.

What does this have to do with interpretation? Practice emptying out our perceptual containers, without pretending not to have them. It would be interesting to conduct imaginative attentions to language in something like the way many symphonies now conduct their tryouts for new musicians. The number of women in US symphonies has quintupled in the years since this practice was instituted: the musician performs behind a curtain, and all you have to do is listen.

In other words, the extreme threat of rapacity culture's bodily violation is connected with problems of ordinary, pervasive, and institutionalized rapacity culture. The body rights movement takes on the first overtly; the implications of its work are helpful to consider in the more subtle and ongoing problems of rapacity culture.

Body rights intensified enough to be thought of as a movement in the context of the western businessification of institutional imaginaries. Institutions including arts, politics, and education have endured an emergency management retooling that has not avoided the continued normalizing of rapacity. In rapacity culture, the socialized body is (violently, vulnerably) available as product and change-management-maneuverable object, while power (money, prizes, special treatment, prestige) looks around to thump competition and build capital. The acceptability of zero-sum power-seeking in institutional rapacity culture renders more acceptable, more ordinary, the power violation of another person's body and the habituation of minor rapacity behaviors.

I imagine being part of a we that wants to disempower rapacity culture. Again, this move is not an on-off switch. In deflating the rapacity response, body rights focuses in communities—gatherings and groups, whether online or geophysical ones—and their encounters. In these encounters, each person has rights to integrity and self-identity; bodies should be permitted to differ with safety and without violation. It's a body that speaks an idea in an encounter. To let that body speak without rapacious response is difficult within institutionalized rapacity culture. The language of body rights can practice flexible discursive tactics oriented to maintaining the otherness of that encounter in that context: A lingual singularity bouquet, a relational blurprint, lightly-tethered exteroceptive words continually understood to recombine idiolectal polymorphisms. Such ethical discourse work can be one way of resisting the uniformity of institutionally rapacious pre-judgments and their enervating power-detection displays.

One stance in such contextual discourse invention is to resist imagining that there is any set center of any world of acts. A person seeking an imagined center called "most hip" or "*the* community" is a vulnerable body pursuing ideological chimeras. Arts, for example, has neither Vatican nor Mecca, either geophysical or digital. As distributed centrality wants to point out, cognition and being are, by definition, not univocal. The digitas now has no central servers. Every biocommunity has its provisional centers of activity.

Refusing given narratives of "progress" in rapacity history can help us with (can boost our sense of the necessity of) building ethical narratives that idealize the potential of our relations with each other and other life. Relying on suppositions that sufficient progress has been made, in other words, can put people in a position of complacent distance and then of dumbfounded shock when behavioral "progress" is recurrently disproven. The body rights movement is involved with resisting rapacity orientations in interpretation, collaborative community, and everyday practices of attention. "To know" does not have to mean "to possess," cultural power is not a zero-sum game, and "progress" does not have to name a stative delusion.

One way that rapacity culture controls the body is by rendering its symbols abstract, separating ideas about holdings, values, and violence from what happens with real bodies. Put an idea into the mainstream of distributed cognition and it can evanesce into diffractions that feel abstract. Put bodies there and we can focus on our acts.

The body is the perfect symbol because it is not abstract. All its ideas and actualities are immediately present and connectable. The body is ground zero of rapacity culture and of practices of resistance to rapacity culture. As the human-made limitations and prejudices of AI and its uptakes vividly illustrate, we cannot become non-human while we are still the organisms we are. Efforts to throw out the embodied human cannot work until they absolutely do, for example once the human-supporting versions of Earth's soils, waters, and atmospheres are in the past.

I imagine being part of a we that's not so much "post-human" as transhuman: admixtures across and with other changing beings, elements, languages, submoleculars, platforms, epigenes. We are complex lingual animals in the wet heat of thinking electric blood, living in linked conditions.

The end of privacy includes the possibility of envisioning the self as a set of shared identities and dreams; this vision can help free violated persons from feeling alone. They can turn around and point at the violence and its perpetrators, and separate their bodies from the inflicted violence. Such turnaround shaming helps to empty shame out of the violated body and to restore bodily integrity. This is a positive result of the end of privacy and a vision of the transhuman: the end of the isolated individual who hides from either shame or discovery.

Let's go further. Are there moves we can make beyond a clear agreement to forbid bodily violation? Let's imagine we don't wish only to turn the shame mirror toward the violater's face. Cancel culture is not enough. I don't want people to avoid rapacity out of fear. I want people not to *want* to be rapacious. To channel the extreme desire and response energies humans feel into directions other than *infliction*.

We need body rights that help articulate non-rapacious desire, desire that is free up to the penumbra of the other's bodily integrity. Such freedom is contingent and particular: It can happen in communities that speak and listen to their internal differences and hopes. What is our relation to desire in arts, to performances and works that inspire our embodied ideation? Can we have a desire gaze that is not predatory? How do we find delight in renewing permission toward otherness, deflating dominance and acquisition narratives and fostering relational process and distributed experience? How can we inhabit interest without wanting the telos of "mastery"? As we move in and among communities, we act out our answers to these questions in every encounter, in our practices of encounter.

The implications offered here touch on physical bodily violence, on institutionalized rapacity, and on how we act in encounters, including those of arts and interpretation. These issues are connected both in this piece and with other writings in this book. Each person comes to us one at a time, and we to others. Let's continually release the floor from rapacity culture and support each other. Let's compete only with ourselves, if we relish a competitive spur, when making the forms we love. Let's connect these acts so that bodies are not experienced as severed: The body is a tender mass of absolute presence and being refreshed in soft acts of encounter. The transhuman ideals of the body rights movement are already demanding that we make these recognitions. The constantly refreshed impulses of twenty-first century body rights, such as the recognition tag #MeToo, remind us that bodily integrity is not foremost an idea: It's a constantly renewed *act*.

Four Problems of Prize Culture in the Arts

The following observations arise in the context of the increase — really, hyper-increase — in "prizes" as a (often *the*) way to appear in public presentation spaces/in print as an artist. Arguably, success is abundantly achieved in the very opportunity to present one's work, whether print, screen, soundwork, sculptures, weaving, or other forms. The formats and venues for artistic presentation are generously available across paper, online, and in-person sites. The oxygen of such arts making and displaying, its attendant encouragement for everyone to make and enjoy arts, is thinned by the turn to prizes as the "best" economy of publicly available arts. In this latter economy, it is not enough to make art; one needs to make "prize" art. The making of art is an open value; prize culture grabs the energy of that openness and corrals it.

The growth of prize culture in the arts over the past decades reflects both a triumph of capitalist projects and, not unrelatedly, the suppression of alterity and plurality and cooperation in favor of identity and narrowing and elimination. In arts, contemporary prize culture encourages the following interlocking states:

Commodification

Events of art-making are turned into objects for value barter. What might be optimally, ethically, seen as an expansion of encouragement to all humans to perform their creativity is structurally commandeered into capitalism's planet-wide (now planet+ stations and satellites) project in which everything tangible is most crucially an economic-value-subject *thing*. There is much art precisely made for barter, and it might not feel the need for prizes if its wins can be measured in sales. For that matter, much art is happily sold to help its makers pay the rent. The emphasis here is that in prize culture, the sense of what an art event can be is pressurized toward power-value-thing; the quotients of commodification rush to claim it.

Competition

Elimination rounds encourage artists to perceive each other as obstacles and competitors and to see their art as fodder for the elimination of other, competing art. Such views can also spur artists to create work that seems to fit whatever the prize competition is asking for: They can compete with their own works, with their feelings about art, and with themselves as human imaginers in relation with their contexts and art materials, in order to figure out how to make prize-fitting work. Certainly such perceptions are not necessarily overt, or conscious—that's one way ideological immersions can be so effective.

Imprimatur

In Latin, and in papal practices, *imprimere* = "let it be printed." That *imprimere* injunction subtends this category to refer to the special cultural permission extended in prize form: A selected work of art may now be considered valid/valuable by its maker, by other makers, by platform regulators, and by public appreciators. In effect that work of art may now exist, in a newly defined way. In this imprimatur, an authoritative hierarchy is set up in which obscured powers determine the value of what occurs "out there." The process of conferring award-winning status participates in an obfuscation of actual living processes in order to declare an achieved result as by infallible verdict and fiat.

Reification

The art event is pressed into the status of a thing whose value is determined by a small group of people. This group decision becomes itself a thing, a power process with a value performed as though objectively bestowed by invisible forces. The people who participate are by extension also translated, for that time, into thing-functions. This prize culture situation not only cloaks the subjectively decided in the clothes of the objectively conferred. We can also think of the situation in relation to Plato. In *The Politics of Aesthetics,* Jacques Rancière offers this relevant summary:

> Plato singles out three ways in which discursive and bodily practices suggest forms of community: the surface of mute signs that are, he says, like paintings [these include writing], and the space of bodily movement that divides itself into two antagonistic models (the movement of simulacra on the stage that is offered as material for the audience's identifications and, on the other hand, the authentic movement characteristic of communal bodies).[1]

Only the third of these practices, so far as Plato was concerned, was really acceptable. In this sense prize culture is Platonic: Plato rejected the power of art in favor of the power of normative social actions with identified social bodies. Prize culture activity in arts performs a similar function. When a body of persons, acting in a real polis of exchange, takes a work of art and deems it prize-worthy, it pivots the work of art from the

---

1 Jacques Rancière, *The Politics of Aesthetics: The Distribution of the Sensible,* trans. Gabriel Rockhill (Continuum, 2006), 14.

realm of imaginative expansion (with multiple potential determinacies) to a zone of putatively "communal" judgment with "authentic" social-object value. This switch turns attention from art contexts in which a work is created—formal play engaging human bodies and psyches in relation with alterity-imbued materials—over to a realm of public discourse presumed to be trafficking in real objects. In effect, prize culture reification shifts art from searching imaginative forms to branded social authenticity.

Prize culture in the arts can be seen to encourage other problems, such as anxiety induced in art makers as they "submit"—a term whose near-ubiquity needs pushback, if we believe that language is performative—their work for judgment. Other problems include rejection and discouragement felt by "losers" in contrast to "winners"; the anxiety (or embrace) of power felt by judges who must choose; ideologies of objective superiority that winners might enter into as they embrace the reification of their success; revalidation anxiety (or hit hunger) felt by winning contestants entering the next competition; and offloading of value decisions from the mindwork of art's "end users" (audiences, educators, readers) who've been relieved of having to decide what's worthy of attention. The economy of prize culture in the arts doubtless throws up other articulable consequences.[2] Those outlined here are what make me understand why artists might resist the absorption of their art into a prize culture economy structured to exercise totality. The intensification of prize culture can be readily related to the expansion of available means for presenting art: as literacy histories show so vividly, there's nothing like an increase in public opportunity to prompt an increase of exclusionary organizational tactics.

2 Such as the statistically discoverable dominance of a small number of academic institutions exchanging an "economy of favors" in US poetry prize culture, according to Juliana Spahr and Stephanie Young in their essay "On Poets and Prizes," *ASAP Journal,* November 11, 2020, https://asapjournal.com/on-poets-and-prizes-juliana-spahr-and-stephanie-young/.

Relinquish [1] Intellectual Property [2]

"No mind worthy of the name ever reached a conclusion. [3]

If this [4] essay appears to represent [5] my own original [6] idea, [7] its appearance is [8] undoubtedly false.

Treating verbal ideation—the word [9]—as "property" obstructs unsuspicious dialogue, clogs our minds [10] as we try to delineate static "ideas" we call "ours," [11] and falsifies the circumstances of [12] knowledge. [13]

Notes

1. Let me start with a re-altered version of my "original" essay, long ago relinquished:

> Relinquish Intellectual Property
>
> "No mind worthy of the name ever reached a conclusion."
>
> This is an original idea.
>
> That assertion is misleading. Every letter on this keyboard, like every word in this essay, has been and is continuing to be constructed by myriad forces. I'm driven to write this essay because of the obstructions attendant on seeing verbal ideation as property. In cultural terms, we learn our

words and the material for our every idea. Language itself is not "owned." Though our rewrites and insights sometimes have the imaginative penetration of lightning, and though we often call those works and ideas "original," a possessiveness about our own words has at least three negative consequences: It obstructs unparanoid ideational intercourse, clogs our minds as we strive to delineate the static nature of a particular idea we call "ours," and is false to the circumstances of knowing.

The textual ways we credit each other's writing serve mostly to sustain the right-to-ownership of living idea-holders. In current essays and books, critical citations tend to be most striking (almost old-fashioned, or, alternatively, impressively scholarly) when the author footnotes something further back in time than, say, one hundred years. Yet everything written in the last hundred years builds on what was written in previous hundreds. If intellectual property is transhistorical—and it must be so considered if we really believe in it and want to ensure that every redescriber is credited—shouldn't we credit all the writers who created the thought conditions for each particular writer of the present? How can we possibly do that?

A colleague once admitted to me that he has a kind of *Usucapio* attitude toward ideational property. When he was a graduate student discovering the writings of Michel Foucault, for example, he footnoted punctiliously whenever his writing reflected Foucault's influence. Now years have passed, and he figures that Foucauldian thought is part of his mind and needn't be acknowledged. Precisely. We absorb what we encounter, and it is logically untenable to assert that we are capable of distinguishing a particular idea-source from what lights up in our own minds.

This source blurriness is one of the hazards and benefits of working with ideas and words instead of bricks or trees. Our lingual and conceptual materials require a fluidity of treatment. Over and over again we learn that generative thinking is dynamic. Think of "fuzzy logic," for example, of the thinking we'd (maybe) like computers to be able to carry out ("real" intelligence computing, RI computing: as alluring as other gearshifts in the death drive). We profess to be taken with the best that is known and thought (while we interpret that "best" differently, we're still standing for mastery or anti-mastery, or for selective subjectivity, and so Arnold's wise passiveness can stand in for others', as the unattributed allusion to Wordsworth in this last clause of mine might show), but in the creation of static objects of thought-property we stymie that process.

We have plenty of opportunity to loosen the bonds of intellectual property. As the Internet continues to expand and people find new ways to be nervous about their ideational property rights, new visions of those rights can be constructed. We need to be explicit about what is possible: I realize that I could be said to be positing an ideal relationship among us as thinking word users, as though we were in a Socratic scene and could simply look at one another to see who is talking (think of fusty old email's default setting: "no subject"). I also realize that positing a digitas runs up against the current fact that about 40% of the world's human population has no ready access to the Internet; many have no electricity at all. The idea of the "we" here is pulled between the threat of unwelcome interpellation, on one side, and of no connection, on the other. Where is property between us to be relinquished?

So there are difficulties. First and most obviously, are thinking writers to be punished for their vocation by a lack of compensation? Well, that happens already, as the different rewards for the production of most creative books and of most "useful" products like software might attest. And writers who teach can mark the difference in cost between an hour with an attorney and an hour of classroom time. I am not advocating for the disappearance of compensation for written productions. But I am not writing about compensation, nor even about digital rights management—let everyone who copies pages from someone else's book for remunerative market distribution be sure to notify author or publisher and pay appropriate fees! I'm concerned here with the benefits to be gained from giving up the pretense that our production of ideas and words is original and that we really acknowledge all our sources and are innocent of plagiarism, as though it were possible to do or be either. Recognizing our own pieces of writing as porous matrices of a continuing interchange, we would not, perhaps, be so inclined to view each one as some last word.

Nor so enamored of "originality" and threatened by "plagiarism." Nothing is natural, after all, about either concept. Living in Yemen at the end of the 1980s, I realized that here was a culture in which heavily analytical and original thinking was akin to blasphemy, to setting oneself up as God's originary equal, in Islamic terms. Moreover, one could do no higher honor to oneself and one's culture than to replicate its knowledge and ceremonies. Indeed in many parts of the world, mostly outside occidental culture, "plagiarism" is a very strange notion. And so it would have been in the Christian European Middle Ages, when writers, scribes, and compilers all worked together to produce texts. And yet we modern westerners seem to have no real active sense, despite historical indicators, that our notion of intellectual property is a crafted one. We have internalized it the way my colleague internalized Foucault; we have naturalized it as our own idea. We come to the point of thinking we truly are capable of original critical thought, and that once we have worked out a particular critical system, say in one or several books, it is identifiably ours and must be so acknowledged by others. This all seems "right" and "fair."

I am writing here only of verbal ideational property, not of the more material intellectual property defined under law as questions of patents and objects. Nor am I particularly distinguishing between critical and creative ideation, though I can imagine the arguments. "Even," you might say, "admitting that one's critical work is mostly an amalgam of what one has read of others', surely if I write a short story it is mine. I have made the plot, the characters, and the story would not have existed as it is without me. Therefore it is mine, from me, and I deserve permanent acknowledgment for its particulars."*

This point raises two difficulties. First, if critical writers glean their ideas or idea structures from critical reading, "creative" writers learn to craft stories and characters from exposure to stories and characters, whether or not avowedly "created" (rather than "real" or, better yet, "historical"). Where else might such craftings originate? How do "original critical" and "original creative" writing differ, in terms of their participation in learned structures (see Oscar Wilde's "The Critic as Artist" for more pondering on that score)? The same questions apply to the "creation" of poetry, whose historical cerements cling to it, traditionally, even more closely than do old stories to the fresh sheets of plotted fictions.

The second difficulty concerns the trademarking of language. We now distinguish between copyright, which is bad enough for language, and trademark, which is worse. If I write the words "Relinquish Intellectual Property," say, and have a bumper sticker made with those three words, and get a trademark taken out on it, then you will have to ask me and perhaps even pay me every time you want to use those three words in that order. To prevent such a catastrophic scenario we must wish to make the fluidity of our verbal borders clear: We don't want our words to be bound by the material and legal conditions that currently bind, say, music. Scores of detectives are on the lookout for improper use of melodies, or pieces of songs, from the past. My sweet lord! Music has

* Toenote: As appendage to this manifesto, let me note, and disavow, the neutral appearance of these latter quotation marks. They don't so much acknowledge as affectionately disown the words they embrace: no one has written them but me (and language as ambient co-articulance), and yet they serve to distance my words from my words. Such levels of ownership inscribe in the very act what it means to imagine, acknowledge, use, bracket out, fold in, the words of "others" within words that are "one's own."

become as legally concrete as engine design, as Napster and other fusses have made so clear.

Surely we must not wish for people to be looking out for word combinations that resemble our own. To prevent such paranoid skullduggery, we can think of verbal ideas as words we all touch; we might celebrate the controversial "plagiarisms" of Kathy Acker, for example in her moving psychoanalytic rewrite of portions of *Wuthering Heights* in Acker's book *My Mother: Demonology* (1994). Our whole system of acknowledgment is hugely flawed in any event: We commonly trace our sources back only a few years, saving older acknowledgment for so-called "primary" work; we don't bother to acknowledge some material at all, figuring it's become our own by a kind of intellectual squatter's rights, by virtue of sitting in our minds for a while (like Foucault's in my colleague's). We should work to become more, rather than less, flexible about how we treat modes of lingual expression, to view them as processual, a circulation of electric liquid lingualisms in around through with our and others' bodies, a constant discourse made up in and by our learning and interchange. Surely in the age of the internet we can believe such a flow of ideas is possible.

Need it be said that this critique of originality can be considered completely unoriginal?

2. For some indication of the fear and respect inspired by the muscular notion of intellectual property, I transcribe an anonymous interchange between a worried subscriber and an alert moderator (or other subscriber—the respondent's identity is no clearer than the questioner's) on a formerly active listserv (which will itself remain anonymous) devoted to graduate student issues. That the exchange is executed under the sign of anonymity both underscores the danger of the topic and illuminates one beauty of undermining its very concerns. It does not matter whose words these are, after all:

"Q: How do you handle the risk of having your ideas stolen from you when you are networking to find people who are doing similar work, who might be willing to review your papers, survey instruments, etc., or who might want to co-author papers with you? To what extent do you reveal your work, how do you protect yourself against unethical behavior (it seems to occur in academia!), and with whom do you open up? Is it simply good judgment and intuition?

A. In response to your concern about claiming your ideas and protecting them from theft, there is good news and bad news. The good news is that you can lay claim to your ideas by publishing them widely before anyone else does. Computers now make this possible for anyone, including graduate students, who may not have the clout to get their contributions published quickly through more formal avenues. The various publishing approaches open to a graduate student are:

a. Give a presentation at your department's 'brown bag' lunch seminars or whatever other campus forum is open to grad students discussing their on-going work.
b. Present a paper at a conference ASAP (try to get a paper accepted for a poster session, since this will let you discuss your idea at length with many interested others and get your name associated with your idea).
c. Publish your idea on the Internet (ultimately on your own World Wide Web Page if you can swing it), or through a relevant e-mail discussion list. When we began [this listserv], several students who had papers related to doing a thesis sent them to us for our review. We then announced [on this listserv] the electronic addresses where students could get hold of free copies of the papers. Many people have very successfully gotten their name associated with their idea, and at the same time requested comments on their papers from readers who were given permission to copy and distribute it as long as the copyright was left intact.

d. Put a copyright mark on your work from the very first time you publish it (or hand out anything at a presentation).
e. If you have a marketable idea, register the copyright immediately. The bad news is that, while you can copyright a paper containing a good idea, you can't copyright the good idea itself. Ideas are 'public' and once a good idea is exposed, all bright brains will seize on it and use it as they will. Indeed, that is the concept of 'collaboration' in scientific research in the field. What you need to do is to get your name associated with your idea before someone more famous and with a better distribution system gets his/her name associated with your idea. Otherwise, you'll get 'passing credit' when the famous person uses your idea to become even more rich and famous. Your only protection is to publish the idea widely—to saturate the field with your idea. You can do this, among other places, on relevant Usenet discussion groups and refer to your published work and how others could get a copy of it. Good luck!"

Good luck indeed. Especially if you really think it bad news that you cannot copyright ideas. But this copyright ban begs the question: what is the difference between an idea and its instantiation? Isn't that an essentialist divorcing of content and form? Are we getting somewhere? Can we get to a place of at least theoretical acknowledgment of the way in which think-tanking is how ideas flow, to get away from the condition that promotes exactly this problem: the Well Known Disseminator becomes the Well Wrought Urn for what's really idea water churning through us thinking together. It happens to everyone, especially in reactionary sole-author-obsessed disciplines; "so I gave it away."

3. I have lost the source for this quotation. However, there are many others like it. Such as two by Alan Davies: "Truth is lies that have hardened," and "A grasped history is lost when the concern is to keep track of it in a precise way" (*Signage* [New York, 1987], 11 and 17). Or what Walter Pater writes of Heraclitus: "if the 'weeping philosopher,' the first of the pessimists, finds

the ground of his melancholy in the sense of universal change, still more must he weep at the dulness [*sic*]* of men's [*sic*] ears to that continuous strain of melody through it" (*Plato and Platonism: A Series of Lectures* [New York, 1893], 12). Or Simone Weil: "we participate in the creation of the world by decreating ourselves" (*Gravity and Grace*, 80).

The connection among these quotations is, foremost, my own reading experience. Next a family resemblance abides among these brief excerpts: the non-concluding, processual mind, willing to give up the "good ideas" it cannot copyright. Such a mental stance — and by "mental" I mean the whole body, corpus of ourselves — of ongoingness can help foster the generosity needed to keep up the maintenance work on generative relinquishment. So that, like Italo Calvino, "I would like to be able to write a book that is only an *incipit,* that maintains for its whole duration the potentiality of the beginning, the expectation still not focused on an object" (*If on a Winter's Night a Traveller,* trans. William Weaver [New York, 1981], 177). This ideal of potentiality is subverted by the "productive" economy. It is also incited by the productive economy — as an effort to escape from closure, which is also to escape from fixed identity. The further I am from finished, the more potential space I inhabit, the more I am an anonym.

I only want a little space cleared in the middle of makings. I am not afraid of losing "my" "ideas" to "better" minds. It behooves us to take the long view, to presume generosity amidst these fields of ideational production. "Better minds" are all in the expression, the expression is all in the liquid bridges created

* Toenote: Whose "[*sic*]" is this? I think I know, but I would have to check the source, and even then the question stays: Who thought this was an error? An "error" now may not be in error when it's seen later, and one seen now may be in error itself, or may even be thriving in the "hidden variable" force. What does the typography of disowning have to do with intellectual and historical displacer moves? The brackets are the insertion of the [current] author into the referenced text, which cannot be itself. They are the sign that we [I] know better.

to other thought, the writing that makes you want to assume its position, to get up and write back.

4. Think "quiddity," "haecceity." And now, begin: The rationale for forms and inflections of *this* is quite apart from its signification as a demonstrative pronoun. Though Old English inflected it as nominative, accusative, dative, genitive, and instrumental, in forms determined by singular, masculine, feminine, neutral, and plural, "That it should come to this" (*Hamlet* act 1, scene 2) can be how it seems.

The loss of inflections foregrounds the persistent indexical function of *this,* the deixis courted in recent critical works and response theory ("What this?" "Some serial; s'pposed to be good for you"). This courting is interesting because of how it bears on sensitivity to belonging, attachment, ownership. Uniqueness (thisness), intensified specificity (this here now), and particularity attachment (mine here this) get linked even if only by implication to each "clinamen" or "GUT" about which we read and write. The point for this essay's purposes is that "this" is a word we can feel is always new, and yet that feeling is due almost exclusively to its neutrality ("make it neu"), its permitting emptiness. Deixis is freeing when it is linguistically unspecified and thus inhabitable. It cannot be intellectual property, and so while inhabiting it we are in an absolute indicative, a specific uncertainty, an unprepossessing present, as Gertrude Stein's ongoingly writingness so amply demonstrates.

Striving toward the indicative is part of a climate of certainty that laments any loss of the specific in the midst of continually losing the specific. Consider the fullness of this first signifying definition of "this" from the *Oxford English Dictionary:* "Indicating a thing or person present or near (actually in space or time, or ideally in thought, especially as having just been mentioned and thus being present to the mind)" (s.v. "this"). *Quod erat demonstrandum.* Here we have a pointer to a body, whether animate or not (and the thought of animation indicates always the haecceity of circumstance, movement of this or that quark or atom), actualized or propinquitous, real or thought, with its best virtue its continually renewed resource of recency.

Using "this" as the essay's second word, before we know its referent, puts that word's indicative or referential status in peril, or at the very least makes it wait. So that the mind, having not that "just been mentioned" meaning to refer to, leaps out to "This goodly frame, this Earth" or *This* magazine or the T they take to work, or the "shit" that happens by rearrangement before the "t-shirt," "or the *hist!* of attention-getting." But then we also get from the *OED* a line from Tennyson followed by an unattributed "modern" usage (by Mr. Ford?): "A gracious gift to give a lady, this! *Mod.* This is what I like (s.v. 'this')." Once such applications are filed in our memory archives, "this" becomes a fuller word to mention, to give us pause, one we should wonder about using too freely, with no consideration of its history. But some of us beloved (perennial) students "don't know much about quiddity"; now, when it's pared to empty's forceful indicator, this is what we like.

5. Pretend this is a representation of a thought I had a moment ago. The thought was prior to language. How can I tell you? The myth is that presentation is now, the actual moment of a thing, and a re-presentation is later—a subsidiary echo, being or belonging to another time or person.

This is representationism, and it belongs to someone else (hugely Kant): It is a local reincarnation of Platonic duality and longing. Even now the representationists fight with the phenomenists. One might observe contemporary representationists as immersed in a metaphysics of loss. In this condition they can be said to believe that an entity or event exists objectively (in its own now), apart from our understanding of it and our ascription of significance to it (in our own "later"). This is living in a split world that will never let us have now. It's encouraging a voyeuristic posture within a living we are being presumed not to experience. But Ned Block is getting smarter: "phenomenal character outruns representational content," he writes in "Mental Paint," becoming a phenomenist.

One key to evading a metaphysics of loss is to see each instance, being, act, as containing its own object-event significance—in something of the "object" sense I take Charles Olson to invoke in the "stance toward reality" he favors in his 1950 essay, "Projective Verse" in *Human Universe and Other Essays*, ed. Donald Allen (New York, 1967). Then each re-presentation becomes, instead, a presentation: another instance, even if you are rewriting a memory, a dynamic event *and* a dynamic significance. And because there are always at least two in presentation (rather than in experience, which can be solitary though only when unreported), the presentation is always at least fourfold: I and object/event/significance and you and object/event/significance, and the membranes that enable the interchanges through that fourfold (or is it eightfold, or does the question gain the multi-dimensionality of its point) phenomenon.

In this mode of analytic perception, there is no representation; there is only presentation. And presentation is always multiply experienced—which still doesn't make it re-presentation. The point for our purposes here might be that since there is no such thing as representation of lingual ideas, there is no need to try to delineate originary presentations and derivative re-presentations.

Which is not to obliterate distinctions, but only to unsheathe the myth of their univocality. And the myth is a sword; I do mean that metaphorical swerve, yes.

6. Relinquishing the idea of words as property might start with abandoning the idea of originality. Arguably, each unprecedented (re)combination, presentation, of words—whether in-person spoken or broadcast or put on a page or screen or canvas or otherwise—can be called an original (in a moment unrepeatable) arrangement. But the notion that recombination equals possessable originality, and our attachment to that notion, is, as I've written already, culturally constructed, not "natural." A colleague of mine suggests I invoke Mary Carruthers, in part to demonstrate the reflexive interest of using a relatively recent text that elucidates medieval notions of memory's

reconstructive functions in the service of my unoriginal point about originality (who's the authority here?). Carruthers writes, in *The Book of Memory: A Study of Memory in Medieval Culture:* "[p]erhaps no advice is as common in medieval writing on the subject, and yet so foreign, when one thinks about it, to the habits of modern scholarship[,] as this notion of 'making one's own' what one reads in someone else's work. [...] This adaptation process allows for a tampering with the original text that a modern scholar would (and does) find quite intolerable, for it violates most of our concerns concerning 'accuracy,' 'objective scholarship,' and 'the integrity of the text'" (Cambridge, 1990, 164). But isn't most of education a slow process of making your own ideational pyramid out of learned stones?

Which isn't quite the point of Louis Bloomfield's "Honor" cases at the University of Virginia. Evidently he established that it is unlikely for anyone (students, in this case) to share six-string word sequences with anyone else without plagiarism rearing its constructed head. Nevertheless, he admits, "[y]ou can't judge just based on the numbers. [...] By themselves they don't mean anything" ("Bloomfield Program Finds More Matches," *Cavalier Daily,* November 30, 2001, A3). Just a tagmemic procedure for discovering who's in and who's out of a system in which "anonymity breeds feelings of security." And meanwhile over in Jordan, Parliament voted in its 1999 intellectual property law so it can play WTO, too. Not to mention the Sonny Bono Copyright Term Extension Act. Nor to mention—to be current about it—how ChatGPT outstrips corporate self-feeding machinery such as Turnitin, and how will the emergency business management of universities hold on to our recombinatory lingualisms now?

But back to the idealized polemic in which business might not make such fools of us all. Another lovely relinquishment of authority someone pointed me to comes in a letter from Petrarch, who wrote, sometime between 1337 and 1341: "I insisted [in conversation with Giovanni Golonna di San Vito] [...] that I had nothing actually new to say, nothing of my own invention, and nothing that was others' property either; for all that we have learned from whatever source becomes our own, unless failing memory robs us of it" (*Letters from Petrarch,* trans. Morris Bishop [Bloomington, 1966], 66). Or as we might call it today, failing *recall,* given how much we are assured that each of our experiences is inscribed on some proteins somewhere in our brain-bodies and that it's only our (adaptive?) inability to recollect (oh yes, adaptive: forgetting is crucial to keeping things in mind) that keeps us from having complete and constant access to everything we have once learned or experienced. The exception is persons with hyperthymesia, of course, however much they might want also to be able to let things go.

Though we locate a potent lust for the original in the Romantics (precursor to our lust for achievable deixis today?), ancestors of our notion of originality also appeared alongside notions of affective individualism in mid-to-late seventeenth-century western Europe. Which is mostly to say, again, we haven't always craved to create and protect our very own thought-properties. To turn deliberately away from a romantic attachment to the original self, and toward a more medieval sense of ourselves as participants in common lingual cultures, creates new opportunities for interchange, interface, interplay, internet, digitas. The enormous debate about form versus content, signifier versus signified, can be said to be underwritten by the fear that we never say anything new (anything, that is, not substantiated by scientific discovery, broadly defined). If lingual creation is all about better descriptions, it's no wonder we want to be firmly credited with ours.

I am lauding the spirit of acquiescence to, acceptance of, the unoriginal—what we can do and be in embracing the beauties of human repetition. If my manifesto reduces its exhortative compass to that range alone, it is enough.

7. *Idea,* as I want to use it, goes back to Plato, with many permutations since. If we take Plato to mean, as I think we do, a kind of eternal archetype whose derivations are reflective (imperfect) copies, then "idea" is eternally afflicted with the metaphysical. This affliction persists through the additions of the Lockean

"idea" as "whatsoever is the Object of Understanding when a Man [*sic*] thinks," Hume's sensation, and Wallace Stevens's "The Idea of Order at Key West." Is "idea" then an object-event separate from our intentions, a particle lodged permanently in the brain (introduced forever and yet brought out only temporarily for review, given the brain's chary recall mechanisms), something that recombines thought and feeling, a woman combing her hair or the website beach? The myriad histories of "idea" seem to force its definition into an ineluctable metaphysical realm.

Which is the realm assigned to it by copyright law. As we are reminded in websites devoted to intellectual property matters, and as footnote two was obsessing about, copyright law does not protect ideas. Copyright is thus revealed as Platonic, even religiously so: It deals not with Plato's superior Forms but instead with inferior, reflective forms. Ideas are unprotected despite the fact that they must always be presented in the concrete forms—poetry, prose, computer programs, artworks, movies, film, blueprints, and so on—which (the website acknowledges) *are* protected by copyright. Huh. The Copyright Act, then, believes in metaphysical reality, places of Idea that cannot be regulated. Concomitantly, such places are open to ad hoc moves, which might reveal some of the tendencies of metaphysical or religious ideas and the ideological invisibility cloaks they carry around. Yes certainly I am talking about power, and about ways metaphysics can be used to make important things ineluctable right when they need to be hard to perceive.

Think again of our worried listserv exchange in note two. Perhaps individuals need to be registered as embodied ideas. Perhaps we all need to have a © imprinted on us, so that we may walk around as both anonymous (unsourceable) and self-indicative, perfectly inviolate and specific combinations of form (body) and content (idea). So that we may network in safety. Such, in any event, might be one logical result of copyrighting lingual thought. Everyone around me becomes anonymous because unusable, inassimilable. What is the connection between the you yourself and the property (product) you create?

All products are anonymous, and only products (and their "tangible" blueprints) can be copyrighted. What is ongoing is not produced, has not yet hardened into labeled "property."

Is the human being a fact or an idea? (Neither can be copyrighted.)

"What is the difference between facts and ideas?" "Ideas are facts in congress." "What is the difference among a person, an idea, and a fact?" "Nothing."*

Which is something like what Jim Rosenberg writes in "Openings: The Connection Direct." For Rosenberg, "non-possessiveness" attends the "energy transaction layer" of art; art's *ideas* are a matter of unregulated exchange:

> an art which focuses on the energy transaction layer itself as the primary layer should seek to *maximize* the energy transactions that can take place. This means the artist should not stand in the way of her/his own energy transactions. For an artist who is not specific about what energy transactions should take place, there is no "thing" to be communicated. (*Poetics Journal* 10 [1998]: 237)

Now there's an idea.

8. The word "is" is a signifier for ontological inhabitability sort of the way "this" signifies deictic positioning, the empty specific. These are approachable words, words anyone may claim and so all claim, words that demonstrate that the notion of lingual intellectual property is an ideological chimera, the exceptions that prove what should rule. All words should have the freedoms of "this is."

But let me argue the point, since "is" may seem to you more solid than a deictic. *Is* is immediately problematic in at least two ways: To assert that something "is" posits a sufficient knowledge of the nature of reality and a confidence about the possible rela-

* Toenote: Do the quotation marks around these questions and answers indicate that they come from a source? Yes, but not so disavowed.

tions of reality and language. Further, it presumes such a concept as the present, "this" time, in which to postulate a present tense. And, as a learned friend reminds me, it is necessary to [*il faut*] distinguish two uses for "is": as copula, by which a predicate is attached to its subject ("the book is red") and as indicating real existence ("God is"). Necessarily, the first use is not indicative of, not coincident with, the second.

To add to the confusions, if we agree with Harry Mathews that "writing works exclusively by what the writer leaves out" (*Immeasurable Distances* [Venice, 1991], 20), then no relationship is possible between the assertion of what *is* in writing and what we make of that *is* in the reading experience. If we agree with Martin Heidegger that *"this average and vague understanding of Being is a fact,"* then no matter how writers set up the written *is,* we will be as unclear about what we mean as readers will be about what they take us to mean (*Basic Writings,* ed. David Farrell Krell [New York, 1977], 46).

Or, as Locke and Vico and Goethe and Emerson have taught me to think, we can understand only what we already know. Our understanding of the term *is* can never be sharply focused: if it begins determinately, it re-resolves indeterminately after an investigation. If we yearn for Lockean candor we strive to fix the ontology of *is*. If we have other cultural apparatus in mind we may relinquish Lockean candor, as arising out of the Anglo-Saxon linear style of argumentation, and prefer the Persian or biblical approach—returning to the same topics from altered perspectives. Or maybe an Oceania group consultation and patience approach. Or maybe we prefer a French/Continental approach of pursuing tangents, or another certainty-seeking or certainty-avoiding approach we find most useful for settling meaning, however temporarily, for determining what is.

In trying to define *is* we perhaps begin and end up with the determinate definition in the *OED* ("sing. pres. indic. of vb. Be. q.v.") (s.v. "is"), bearing in mind that we are still with words much where mathematics was with Gödel after his 1931 paper. That is, we can realize that the logical consistency of systems of deduction, within which we deduce the use of "i" and "s" together as a signifier of present existence, is impossible to establish without recourse to reasoning so complex that its own internal consistency is suspect.

9. Here we are vexed by the issue of where to begin. Perhaps with Homer's "Achilles' wrath, to Greece the direful spring / Of woes unnumber'd, heavenly goddess, sing!" (trans. Pope), or with St. John's "In the beginning was the Word, and the Word was with God, and the Word was God" (John 1:1 KJV). Is the word traceable to multiple muses or to only One? Whose intellectual property is (was) the Bible? Who authorized the transcriber(s) of the Book of Genesis to write "God said"?

Why is the issue of authorship presumed pre-settled by the compilers of the Bible? Perhaps because of the climate: Classical philosophers tended to treat words as one type of sign, while Augustine and later medieval thinkers tended to view signification as primarily verbal (the emphasis in both cases is on *tendency*). If words are only one layer in a compilation of signs, their ownership is not so much in focus, thus not so much in doubt. In brief, we've swept from a religious use of language that transmitted knowledge semiotically—while, ironically, positing the knowledge of God as inexact and so rendering the very signs they used as inexact—to a notion of the word as organizing possible knowledge all by itself, but still in a fairly lonely, indicative way. When, between the fifth and the fifteenth centuries, language was the dominant European tool for investigating the larger universe, the *artes sermonicales* (discursive arts) determined what could be known determinately (see for example *The Summa Contra Gentiles* of Saint Thomas Aquinas).

Then, in the sixteenth and seventeenth centuries, people got even more nervous about what words could be and do. They worked more intensively to construct universal grammars, to get at an ideal language—almost, one could argue, harking back to Plato's *Cratylus* to find "the maker of names," since of course not just anyone can be allowed to make them (Plato, *Cratylus,* 389). Now we've gone further still (and looped back serially as well, through Sextus Empiricus?), through skepticism about the possibility that a word can contain or indicate, to an acceptance that it permits knowledge itself or is a way to describe alongside other ways, for example from Ludwig Wittgenstein's "Language disguises thought" in the *Tractatus* to his assurance in the *Philosophical Investigations* that "language is itself the vehicle of thought." But of course that means we've still not figured out how to get over the chasms criss-crossing words and ideas, on one hand, and ideas and facts, on the other. We still live with the split—among reality, thought, and word—effected by the development of formal logic in the twelfth through fourteenth centuries. (For more background, see for example Marcia L. Colish's *The Mirror of Language: A Study in the Medieval Theory of Knowledge* [New Haven, 1968] or R. Howard Bloch, *Etymologies and Genealogies: A Literary Anthropology of the French Middle Ages* [Chicago, 1983]).

And these brief ponderings do not even broach the difference between the spoken word and the written word. Claude Lévi-Strauss's contention that speech is associated with innocence and writing with hierarchy and dissolution seems nothing more than a familiar craving for the Socratic scene, for the possibility of sincerity when words are an immediate product of embodied voice. But spoken as well as written words always have Augusto Ponzio's "uninterpreted sign residue" (*Signs, Dialogue, and Ideology* [Amsterdam, 1993], 4) all over and through them. The word "word" looks out from hoary eyebrows, especially when surrounded by quotation marks. As Karl Kraus has it: "The closer we look at a word the greater the distance from which it stares back." But in the realm of Intellectual Property, the speaking scene—the worrisome "networking" of our earlier listserv—is presumed to be the organic, amorphous, pulsing, but also (and paradoxically) disembodied petri dish of idea, where nothing can be copyrighted because nothing has assumed any "form." In an age that knows that everything discursive is material and contextual, such a stance is quaint at best, obstructionist on bad days.

10. I ate a piece of pie and that gave me an idea. Did the idea originate in my mouth, in my stomach, in the pie, or (as rationalism teaches us to think) in the vast Oz processing center of the sorting mind? Does the body belong to the brain? Is the body the "place of excrement" (thank you for sublimating Mr. Yeats) for the superior mind? What does the body know? When we forget our ideas have we lost our rights to them? Do we become anonymous only when we *lose* our minds?

If we can undo the notion of property within ourselves (a notion that makes us imagine things like "my will owns my actions" and "my mind is the superior of everything below the throat"), perhaps that will destabilize the notion of property in intercourse with others. "I own myself"—well, only if the state agrees to let me. "I own my heart"—well, only if someone does not come along and sweep it away from me, in the conscious-unconscious chemical process we call love. "I own my hands"—if they stay attached. And if they do not, for all that they are expendable (the loss of one's hands does not necessarily lead to losing one's life), we lose some knowing if we lose our hands. Our comprehension is curtailed, truncated. When we touch with our fingertips, we "know" in a way that no other knowing can provide.

The "mind" is not the brain alone. Someone, Randall McLeod I think, calls thinking by the name "thingking," to emphasize its materiality, its processing of objects (and perhaps as well the mind's sovereignty when focused on "the thing"). If you bring being everywhere you go, there is arguably no such thing as abstraction. Consciousness is physical. Such concretions might be said to bother us only when we have a prejudice against the physical, when we rank it below the spiritual, the abstract, the absolute. Hence Emily Dickinson's "backward reading" as the physical criticism impulse that prompts the idea of deformance (see this book's essay "Deformance and If Meaning"). If we know the physical as all-encompassing, and we inhere in imagination as a physical process, and we see that we are all subject with this process, then we may be more loving toward the shared body of knowledge. That's what we are, *bodies* of knowledge. The person speaking to you is immensely more communicative than the written person, but not because of the abstract quotients of language; instead, magnetism, chemistry, somatic sonics, gestural intensities, contextual ribbons both visible and invisible, all co-create the panoply of in-person dialoging. That difference between writing and body-present speaking is one central paradox of the fact that Intellectual Property doesn't cover the realm of spoken discourse or idea. Copyright law diminishes the physical human (whose speech is unprotected yet free, not an "act" at all) and enlarges the physical non-human (products are protected). Ideational intellectual property is a disdaining of the embodied mind.

When you catch or claim what you hear and think, keep it a moment then let it go. See Dewey's "Art as Experience": "mind is primarily a verb" (*Art as Experience* [New York, 1958]).

11. Perhaps it would help to think of "ours" as a parallel descriptor rather than a possessive enclosure. Walking alongside you. What is mine is an accompaniment to my existence; it is not interiorized. "My" idea, though, might feel interiorized, or one has learned to think of it as something that is lingering *inside* the body. Rather than as a relation I have among-between.

What's the difference, then, between a book I own, an idea I have, and the love I feel for someone who agrees to be loved, who is "my love"? The book I own is potential property unto death, always exterior to me. The ideas I have, including those suggested to me by the book, pass through and reconfigure the circuitry of my body's knowing. If these ideas were mine as the book is, I could always open them up and look at them. But the mechanisms of the brain do not recall so effectively: They resist property, preferring (if function can be called preference) to be reconfigured, to have ideation pass through them. The love I have for someone is similar. It is "mine" by virtue of the existence of another, it reconfigures my body's knowledge, it is active only in being relinquished. Knowing something might be thought of as loving something.

So different ways of communicating conjure and shape different ways of loving (knowing). How I write to *you:* "Whenever you speak, you define a character for yourself and for at least one other—your audience—and make a community at least between the two of you; and you do this in a language that is of necessity provided to you by others and modified in your use of it" (James Boyd White, *When Words Lose Their Meaning* [Chicago, 1983], xi).

Or, in the very different words of a long-ago university website devoted to "INTELLECTUALPROPERTY," you define yourself as author and your audience as receptor. Do you want to do this in a possessive way? How do we distinguish between our theoretical sophistication about "the death of the author" and the sort of accepted definition of an author provided by the erstwhile site: "An author is someone who contributes copyrightable expression to the work." Is a conversation a work? Should we be sure to note this in conversing?

The Universal Copyright Convention (UCC) would not declare a conversation one's own, since as our website again tells us, "Copyrightable expression is original authorship, fixed in a tangible medium of expression." In this tautological definition, presumably conversation is not included, since it is not (again, presumably) tangible, since its ideas are not yet property. Which means, in terms of intellectual property, that when we're talking to each other we do not own our words, they are not "ours."

Let's carry this further, in to the terrain of intellectual imperialism. Idea-mongers might hike out to very foreign parts, those not covered by the UCC, and have some very stimulating conversations with foreign persons, then use those ideas with absolute impunity in their "works." Of course (you might respond), we are honorable citizens and would not do so. To which I'd say of course: Because we are honorable citizens, we should acknowledge the problem of possessiveness about ideas, the legible farce of distinct originality, the fact that the dialectics of knowledge and training mean that ideational intellectual property is untenable (and, again, all things are relationally material, as cultural studies + new materialism + sitting there within our bodies doing this now all remind us).*

12. *Of* is a preposition with a rich history. It is crucial to conversations of knowing (loving), as the marker of the genitive in English. According to the *OED*, the primary sense was *away, away from,* a sense now obsolete, except in so far as it is retained in the spelling OFF. All the existing uses of *of* are derivative; many so remote as to retain no trace of the original sense, and so weakened down as to be in themselves the expression of the vaguest and most intangible of relations. The sense-history is exceedingly complicated by reason of the introduction of senses or uses derived from other sources, the mingling of these with the mainstream, and the subsequent watering down, which often renders it difficult to assign a particular modern use to its actual source or sources (s.v. "of").

Exactly. A "use of *of*" relates one instantiation to all possible uses. "Point of view" relates one point to the view it might potentially hold. Intellectual property is "property of the intellect," relating one property (owned characteristic) to the intellect to which it works in reference. "Of" is a belonging relay, a grammaticalizer taking us back to "this" and "is." "This is of now": quiddity, ontology, morphology, temporality. Inhabitable absolutes. Inseparable from their web of words, one is caught in the circularity of the dictionary (wrapped in Deleuze and Guattari's deterritorialized nomadism and flow, in *A Thousand Plateaus* [Minneapolis, 1987] and *Kafka: Toward a Minor Literature* [Minneapolis, 1986]).

Which brings us, by way of the necessary singularity of instances, to the subjectivity of one intellect's use of "of." In using the word *of,* I think of past uses such as "Of man's first disobe-

* Toenote: See Richard Stallman's Free Software Foundation, Sendmail, Apache, John Perry Barlow, the Electronic Frontier Foundation, the Grateful Dead, and Charles Mann, "Who Will Own Your Next Good Idea?," *The Atlantic* (September 1998), https://www.theatlantic.com/magazine/archive/1998/09/who-will-own-your-next-good-idea/377192/, from which I derive this toenote's list.

dience," "Mother of God," "the way of all flesh," United States of America, point of view, Bachelor of Arts, and as a chipper reminder, the first line of *Aurora Leigh:* "Of writing many books there is no end" (Elizabeth Barrett Browning in an ecclesiastic state of mind). This partial list indicates that "of" is an ordering term, a linking word, or more generally a word that clarifies the words around it without attracting attention to itself, without being full of meaning. As Emerson wrote in "Shakespeare; or the Poet": "Great genial power, one would almost say, consists in not being original at all; in being altogether receptive; in letting the world do all, and suffering the spirit of the hour to pass unobstructed through the mind" (*Emerson's Complete Works,* vol. 4 [Boston, 1883], 183). Which is an idea of power one might be enamored of.

13. "Knowledge" is an impossible ideal which cannot be true to experience except in basic formulations of physical proof, the uncopyrightable "mere facts"; even then it's temporary. When Mark Taylor writes, "[a]bsolute knowledge is the perfect copulation of subject and object, self and other, which issues in certain conception," he goes on to remind us that a union between subjectivity and objectivity is impossible: "[t]emporal deferral opens a space in the subject that self-consciousness can never close. This invisible space blinds the speculative philosopher" (*TEARS* [Albany, 1990], 18 and 21). If verbal ideation is speculative, it cannot have the closure pleasure of hard science or determined religion.

If lingual ideation wants to embrace a more fluid sense of knowledge, it might, in relinquishing an urge toward property, originality, and stasis, embrace Vera Frenkel's "Benign Ignorance":

> [A] state of unfocused awareness that permits us to link the confusing world with the deep metaphoric formulations inside us which are strategies for its apprehension. To reach these and give them form in art requires setting knowledge aside, reclaiming it later as necessary. It follows from this that

> a work of art is as good as the amount of knowledge and ignorance it holds in balance. The more conflicting knowledge a work can hold suspended in a transforming ignorance, the better it teaches us to see. (*ArtsCanada* [1977]: 27)

Which sounds a bit like something written over five hundred years earlier:

> [T]ruth, which can be neither more nor less than it is, is the most absolute necessity, while [...] our intellect is possibility. Therefore, the quiddity of things, which is ontological truth, is unattainable in its entirety; and though it has been the objective of all philosophers, by none has it been found as it really is. The more profoundly we learn this lesson of ignorance, the closer we draw to truth itself. (Nicolas Cusanus, *Of Learned Ignorance,* 1440)

In other words, knowing must involve relinquishing, which brings us back to love. I know nothing as I. Knowledge and its conduits are both flowing. In language use and critiques of its use, avoiding the material seductions of science and religion, we can become matrices of lingual art, folding into the world of, broadly speaking, knowledge.*

* Toenote: Of course, it's hard to speak broadly of knowledge. We tend to speak specifically, unless we are reverential culture workers fuzzing the truth functions of agreed values — or (by reputation) Continental philosophers. Which partly explains the reverence of pragmatic Anglo-American-Australasian critics for philosophical Continental theorists. The former look over hungrily as the latter keep on living in that unswept world, recklessly borrowing one another's ideas, writing with few objects but many modes in mind, seeing knowledge as ephemerally gardening dialectics rather than as objects around which "the lone and level sands stretch far away."

Earth Rights

Earth rights is a term for recognizing that the planet arrives as its own being, with the varieties of beings it nurtures. We live on and with Earth — it isn't ours any more than another being, including those we are close carers for, is "ours." We're in relation. Believing that Earth has rights in that relation comes back to help us too, as we deal with climate eschatology and the eternal returns of state violence.

Many people express concern that trouble is coming: that climate change may soon be irreversible, that economic inequality will soon be too extreme, that we may not be able to accommodate the needs of all humans, much less other planetary life. But these conditions are already happening; there's no need to wait for them. Accepting that these conditions are already here can help us move more readily: We can be relieved from paralyzing anticipation; the urgency is upon us. Inhabiting the arrived disaster = relief because it breaks the wait. Relief is re-life; *re-levare,* Latin for re-lift.

In the disaster relief position, humans move beyond being braced in dread. We're in the disasters and can channel our energy toward acting with reparative invention. Create adaptations for changed climates and invent ideas and practices of cli-

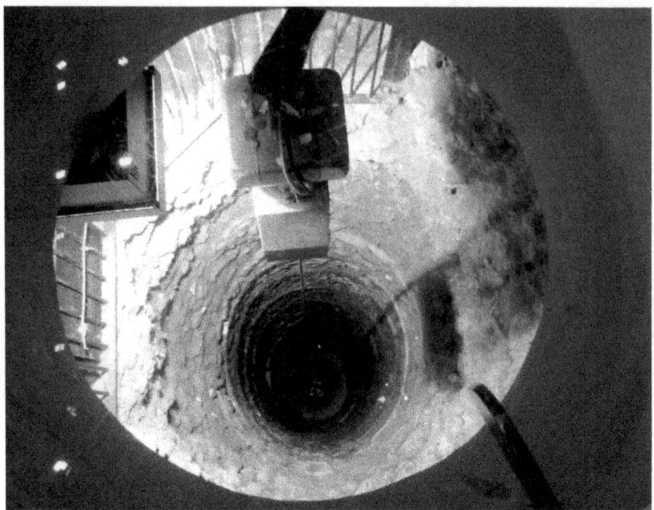

Fig. 22.1. Forceps, Lisa Samuels (2019).

mate value; create conditions that foster equality among human and other-than-human beings; be clear that ownable commodities differ from needed and shared resources. Put down the rapacity tools and pick up collaborative ones.

Outside fleeting laboratory moments, there is no separating the elements of Earth or the currents and histories of global human acts: What happens happens everywhere. As migrant and identitarian distinctions show, history continues in the present. As the COVID-19 pandemic demonstrated again, what happens anywhere in the biosphere happens everywhere in it. As Ukraine and Israel/Palestine and many other surges of human violence show, invasions tear the geophysical body, the land and waters, where Earth bodies—humanimal and others—are trying to shape their rights to be.

Some Indigenous writers have noted that colonialism spearheaded a general cultural apocalypse: Subsequently, everyone is in its long wake of oligarchy, rapacity, and separatisms. We are

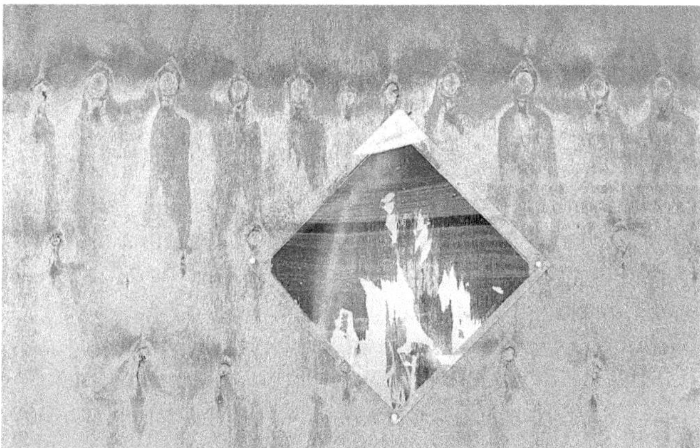

Fig. 22.2. Witnesses, Lisa Samuels (2019).

epicolonial. In Greek, "epi" signifies closeness and connection: by, near, atop, toward, among. The term epicolonial signifies our imbrication with ongoing values (now infused in the capitalist project) of takeover and extraction and othering and inequality. Epicolonial humans manifest those values in ongoing behaviors like presuming separatisms, othering waste, craving superiority. We're experienced in these values.

In the perspective of Earth rights in an epicolonial time, solidarity encourages an embrace of collective, *enabling*, non-alienation and non-innocence. Forensic psychologists have a term for human destroyers who have recovered and even healed: "Experts of experience" are engage to help those who are like they were, in the throes of fear about their next destructive-urges episode. Such "experts of experience" have a family resemblance to the idea of "higher experience" I considered as part of writing *The Long White Cloud of Unknowing* (2019). Both terms defer from the poet William Blake's "higher innocence," his late-eighteenth-century term for an informed and deliberate innocence after experience's despair. As things stand now, with us and Earth, it can be (however paradoxically) empowering for humans to embrace our higher experience. We are not innocent; we take our experience with us.

Humans can engage their higher experience in something like the way addicted persons can hover, and act, in recovery. We can act to change ideas and procedures that bring Earth, and us, and other beings, to these troubled bodily conditions of air, soil, water, plants, breath, bones, organs, and blood. To collaborate in our shared ecologies is to help enable ourselves at ground zero, to shift our stance within epicolonialism. Relieved in accepting that the disasters are among us, we work to repair by changing what we do alongside concentrating on how we conceive value, allocating time to be citizens and fostering articulations of planetary value, including Earth rights.

To think that we can hold off disaster, "stay the course," or get "back to" a past stability is keeping the blinders on, craving ever-fountaining capital horizons, or yearning for a miraculous save granted from some outside force that returns us to a semi-Eden state. There is no (given, unchanging) central state, though human power surges keep trying to insist otherwise. If there seems to be a center, that is arguably an effect of hypercapitalism's planet+ ideological cloud cover. Its powers exist at authoritarian levels of political, media informatic, and monetary rule, offering dangerous versions of lulled monadic yearning, distracting like clickbait from the flesh of Earth.

There *are* forces, physical levels that are ontological, distributed, erupting, and underway. We can engage that distribution anywhere — everyone is politically and planetarily enmeshed — and we don't have to take on everything at once, or alone. Planetary forces are particulate and interactive, and socially reparative forces too: They make acts make us. To adopt Charles S. Peirce's 1868 formulation, our acts can make "a cable whose fibers may be ever so slender, provided they are sufficiently numerous and

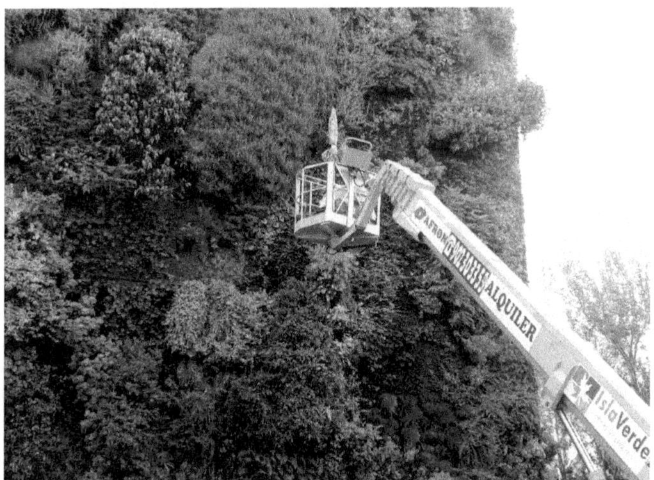

Figure 22.3. Erratics, Lisa Samuels (2012).

intimately connected."[1] No one has to do everything. Multiple relational connections create and sustain increased strength in our distributed reparative acts.

These ideas are in relation with humans who can act, who are not debilitated by the very conditions this piece addresses. Earth rights inhabit the same breaths as human rights, in the consideration of which we also fulfill human need. Earth rights are still heretical in many human-centered plans, but they have toeholds, such as in the Te Awa Tupua Act (2017) in Aotearoa/New Zealand, an act that accords a river its own legal personhood. Yet even that recognition translates an other being into "personhood." How about river being? How about the right to be of geo-archive, tardigrade, ice being? Consider Zoe Todd's insights on human-fish relations and her advocating for the right to thrive

1 Charles S. Peirce, "Some Consequences of Four Incapacities," in *Peirce on Signs: Writings on Semiotic by Charles Sanders Peirce,* ed. James Hoopes (University of North Carolina Press, 1991), 56.

of prairie fish.[2] According the non-human "right to be" shifts in turn our thinking about the being aspects of people—our shared health, our energies in excess of dominant social narratives, our non-instrumentalized well-being.

We can do the work to unspin and continually remake causative tethers among our ideas and the fertile materials of hurt life. The implications extend from sea urchins to love, from oxygen levels to development work, from conversational approaches to property attitudes, from how we accord value to how we show resistance, from how we eat to how we deal with institutions. The numerous connected fibres of experience already show us how to be differently together, to value being according to distributed equalities, and to think human and other-than-human rights in acts that make room for Earth rights.

2 See Zoe Todd, "Refracting the State through Human-Fish Relations: Fishing, Indigenous Legal Orders and Colonialism in North/Western Canada," *Decolonization: Indigeneity, Education & Society* 7, no. 1 (2018): 60–75.

Contemporanullity

> Subsistence lifeways, non-monetary exchange systems, and self-sustaining regional economies are anathema to expansive capitalism. It seeks to destroy them wherever it finds them. The bottom line in the discourse of the capitalist vanguard was clear: America must be transformed into a scene of industry and efficiency; its colonial population must be transformed from an indolent, undifferentiated, uncleanly mass lacking appetite, hierarchy, taste, and cash, into wage labor and a market for metropolitan consumer goods.
>
> —Mary Louise Pratt, *Imperial Eyes: Travel Writing and Transculturation*[1]

> (A Moment equals a pulsation of the artery)
>
> —William Blake, *Milton: A Poem*[2]

1 Mary Louise Pratt, *Imperial Eyes: Travel Writing and Transculturation* (Routledge, 2007), 12.

2 William Blake, "Milton: A Poem (Copy A, 1811)," plate 27, in *William Blake: The Complete Illuminated Books* (Thames & Hudson, 2000), 274.

1

By certain measures everything is necessarily contemporary: Prior texts and future hopes become present texts and hopes when they're being handled. Every research becomes a contemporary one: The researchers are doing it in their "now." The Euro-American writer Gertrude Stein addresses the difficulty of being what she calls "truly contemporary" in her 1926 essay-talk "Composition as explanation." For Stein, art wants to be in touch with the techne and conditions of the lived present rather than repeating established patterns that keep one from seeing *what now.* Stein takes up the challenge of writing in multiple perception zones of a now whose potential significances, not yet digested within meaning-asserting waves of culture, push you in advance, in a symbolic *avant-garde.* To be truly contemporary, for Stein, you must resist perceiving those meaning-asserted cultural wave patterns as the reality of what's here or possible. Stay in the foam of the still-moving water; stay in unresolved sets of happenings before waves of declared meaning take shape in contextual situatedness, before they overtake you and make you think you are "with it" (or not), that there's a groove to be hip to. In this imaginative logic, being "truly contemporary" in art is *not* being with it; instead, it's a devotion to blindsight, non-certainly participating in and creating crucial non-certainty, with energy and potential moment by moment.

And yet a moment is not a microcosm of the contemporary, whose temporality has a different as well as longer span. A moment is, perhaps, a permitting void around us, a zone of presentness. That presentness also mingles with absence, as one moment gives way to another in a continual process of occur-and-displace, a ratcheting overlay not so much directional as simultaneous, though modern humans have been fond of linearity in their chains of being. A moment might be considered a free-floating continual irruption, itself in an unstable relation to temporal frames we call past, present, and future. A moment, if it can be said to exist, is not so much new as differentially particular. Our moment is not the same as someone else's nor the same as we might have had and will not have again. Any given persons in any given time experience momentness. A person carrying out a thousand-year-old artistic ritual is in a moment just as much as someone carrying out a present techno-act. I set to one side, for the present, many questions about incommensurable psyches in different cultures that experience momentness in markedly different ways. I am operating in a certain mode, partly phenomenological, of current western suppositions, mingling with Oceania approaches, about how time and life are humanly experienced.

Defined as what we are in, a moment cannot exist as an object of contemplation: We can't separate ourselves from being in it. It has haecceity and quiddity, this-ness and thing-ness, including our experiencing sensoria, and these qualities give the moment (if it exists) the utmost interest as a constellated zone of both engaged and displaced transaction, an exemplar of being-meaning, which is itself a non-concept-to-concept suspension. At the same time, we cannot think about the moment as a concept apart from our own particular experiencing of a moment right here and now, or then and there. Because of that situation, we can hypothesize that there is no such thing as a moment; instead, there are what we might call *events-in-place,* whether dinners or walks or battles or works of art, happening with beings. The concept of a moment falls through its non-conceptuality, and the specificity of something-happening—an event that gains the traction of its participant subjects/objects, an object surrounded as its place-event—comes in its place. This paradox, of what we can and cannot fixate, is part of what renders the related terms "moment" and "contemporary" relevant in digital thinking.

One might consider the contemporary as a one-year to thirty-year span of a given set of persons, to propose a broad, rangy frame for it. As a conceptual frame the contemporary comes into view less often than its application: We pay attention to what happens *in* a contemporary, or to what defines *a* contemporary. One of our own contemporaries, what might be called an Anglo-(North) American-Australasian one, is interesting for its reduced or trace foundationalism, with all the Derridean play of that paradox. This is the theoretically delineable contemporary within which the first part of this essay has its push. In our putatively post-foundational era we may not be able to start anywhere, we may not have any *given* mental ground that we can begin by standing on, sure that everyone is with us, but at least we have the moment, right? At least we know we're doing something now? After all, we have The Contemporary. The now becomes a highly valuable thing: the fifteen minutes of fame, the fashioned modernity of the "new and improved," the thrill of an apparent cultural surprise ("apparent" because of the suppressed origins or context shift of an object-event we find "surprising"), the art movement that's "important [or 'real'] right now."

This reduced foundation, this Now Contemporaneity, is a kind of vortical frontier, its ideology imbued with weighty ghosts. In 1893 Frederick Jackson Turner declared the closing of the American frontier, and though he focused on the interactions of the geophysical body of the US with its cultural expectations (resource devourments, displacements of prior inhabitants, competitive aggrandizements, homesick-place-name-wielding Europeans), his implications were global. It was clear by then, for example, that Aotearoa/New Zealand was going to be the last major world landmass to be colonized into fruition. Centuries of horizon-eating eyes were left wondering where to feed their geographical forwardism. The twentieth century divvied up the geographic spoils and turned capital itself into piles large enough to be thought of as acquirable land. Fortune itself might be thought of as mass, and colonizable. Anything might become — the logic quickly became: really should be or already is — capital.

Presently we're in the digital frontier, whose imbricated omnipresence (the bricks of the internet, the suffusion of the web, the hands on phones) is part of what I mean by the *digitas*. As I write elsewhere in this book, the digitas is digital performativity with constitutive perfusing by the techne and humans involved. We interact with the protocols of the internet and we make and are made by the consequent webs; all of this happens with the digits of binary code and of our fingers, with our habitus and civitas. As a world proposition, the digitas has been colonizable since the turn of the millennium, in the sense that workers can really be, to re-quote the Mary Louise Pratt epigraph, both "wage labor and a market for metropolitan consumer goods." As a frontier, the virtual spatiality of the digitas seems to dovetail quite nicely with the virtual temporality of the contemporary. They are both technically-supported virtual reality. The "Make It New" of twentieth-century modernism, from Ezra Pound's literary imperative to the mechanical dynamo, can turn into the Make It Now of the digital. Calling Now Contemporaneity a colonizing ideology of the digitas points to commodity expectations for use value, for takeover, for micro- and macro-monopoly. When some people claim, for example, that the digital year is really four months long, they propagate Now Contemporaneity: reifying digital time as though it were a productivity trace of the landmasses and capital of yore. When some people display digital foblo (fear of being left out), they participate in the capital projects of sped-up otherwheres-you-want-to-be.

Defining a moment might be on balance a phenomenological opportunity, a question of how a consciousness experiences a narrowly bounded zone of attention, while defining the contemporary is on balance a materialist opportunity, a question of what we value and emphasize in our particular habitus. Who can say the things that speak truth to our experience of a particular contemporary? The iterability of the contemporary is a question for power, and for the ideologies of distinct disciplinary approaches.

2

Contemporanullity is a concept put forward to resist marketable value in the digitas and resist believing in The Contemporary as a real thing or position: The latter is seen to operate as a queryable ideology, a queerable trace foundation. As a term, contemporanullity brings together the words "contemporary" and "nullity" and evokes two distinct emphases. First, it counters the term *contemporaneity*, which presumes to encompass the state ("ity") of the contemporary, to know or describe what it labels. By contrast, contemporanullity gestures to the "positive Negation" of the "truly contemporary," to link Samuel Taylor Coleridge (in his 1817 poem "Limbo") with Gertrude Stein. Or perhaps better, and to re-conjure this essay's epigraph from Blake's *Milton:* "Every Time less than a pulsation of the artery ~ ~ / Is equal in its period & value to Six Thousand Years" (plate 27). Which I take to mean that a moment performs within itself a dialectic inverse of symbolic infinity. Contemporanullity holds in suspension, simultaneously, the concept and non-concept of the present.

Second, contemporanullity can help convey the phenomenology of a moment into the materialism of a contemporary so as to resist fixation and fetishizing in what we do and perceive, within the digitas as well as without, and especially, as ever in this book, with interpretation and the arts. Imagining contemporanullity in the digitas can help disperse power-moves to define the contemporary as how and what everyone is supposed to be doing and paying attention to now. In relation with events-in-place, we can strive to refrain from building empires of understanding that are akin to asserted and imposed givens. This distributed centrality urge does not mean there aren't things humans should be thinking and making art about, from mitigating ecological violence to taking care of our children. The point here is to resist declaring an artistic mode or social approach or way of thinking *au courant,* to resist situations in which some posited agglomeration of points of view get to define what and how it's important to do and think now. Contemporanullity involves idealist ethical and art action, with recognition of its interactive and crucially non-accumulating importance; it is a conceptual swerve from definition-oriented, and possession-oriented, contemporaneity.

As my second emphasis indicates, commitment is key to a contemporanullity stance. Commitment may seem a paradoxical coin when its other side is relinquishment; more reflections on the term "nullity" can expand the case. Nullity is the state of having been and having been ceased, thus nullity bears a strong resemblance to the moment, with its successive sublime presences and cessations. In both cases, as impossible subjects of contemplation, nullity and the moment have presence and absence. Nullity involves the negation of the assertability of what has nevertheless been happening. It is the trace of what has been activity-real now located in a zone of contested cessation. The law is crucial to a materialist consideration of the digitas, and in legal terms nullities are either relative or absolute. Relative nullities apply only to those whose lives or actions are affected, and absolute nullities are those in which anyone may be said to be an interested party. Contemporanullity finds itself in the absolute: It indicates a committed participation within which we take the posture of relinquishment (to extend an argument launched in "Relinquish Intellectual Property"). Everything is measurable as contemporary, and the contemporary does not, as a knowable fixed entity, exist. In rewording our position within our events as contemporanullity, I want to emphasize our present cultural interactions as gift and attention rather than as acquisition and accumulation. A contemporanullity stance is a committed letting go in the particular so as to avoid the accumulations of asserted importance that are frequently made coequal with social power, being "with it." A contemporanullity stance can also help us attend to how we continually and ceaselessly invent and make cultures in the digitas. In this sense, Stein's "truly contemporary" can be reinterpreted here as a materialist imperative for art brought into the blindsight of the moment.

Contemporanullity, then, is a condition of contact relinquishment with materials — arts and related world-making — to which we are devoted. Instead of *carpe diem* one might say *relinque diem*. This deliberate, act-oriented relinquishment in art inherits aspects of what Laura Riding described as "designed waste" (in the 1920s), Georges Bataille as "general economy" (in the 1930s), and other writers (including Derrida) in similar ways later. General economy indicates the excess, the gorgeous dross, distinct from a productive economy, that is, transactions of strictly useful social capital. Contemporanullity swerves from the anthropology of the "gift economy," which operates in an expectation of exchange value, although contemporanullity possibly includes both general and gift economy ideas, given the centrality of the social body as both presence and absence in the digitas.

Thinking contemporanullity can help us situate art events, which are in zones of absolute nullities although they are often treated as relative ones. Arts are absolutes insofar as they make place for what we experience as the excess of our desires for life and our astonishment that particular embodied consciousness, individual and group, blanks out in death. Arts—held here apart from the commerce quotients that they also interact with, and that can absorb them—are constituted as object-events that apparently exceed the requirements of our social capital, our statistical identity and civic use-value. We desire to love or serve or dominate or create or collaborate in excess of our normatively identified quotients of social capital.

In his exploded prose book *The Year of Passages* (1995), Réda Bensmaïa plunges into and through a version of keenly felt temporal nullity and para-digitalization—among other multiplications—of identity. His book can illustrate one, multifarious, lingual result of the contemporanullity immersions gestured to in this essay. Bensmaïa's book charts the "passages" from (as travel) and among (as ontologically and culturally co-present, unsheddingly accumulative) Algeria, France, and the US. The book's imbricated continuities are relentless; in a characteristic passage (actually less exclamatory than many), Bensmaïa performs a scripted transplacement wherein "moment" shirrs with "sentence" shirrs with "nothing" and memory:

> . . . *in an hour, forever more, bravura encore.* At any moment a sentence can flake off the contingent moment of death and splatter into the center of a paragraph or into the throat of a writer. At any moment a sentence can be torn away from its silence and thrust into your brains. And the resonance of that very sentence is what no one can ever predict. Nothing

> tells of its coming, nothing. It comes unannounced. Nothing. That's why it's a sentence. Nothing. The sentence comes unannounced. The sentence that tells of nothing to come. Nothing. The most difficult of all sentences. The memorial sentence. Nothing. The sentence that has a love of ashes. The sentence that turns you into ashes. Nothing. The sentence of little nothings. The sentences of nothings at all. The sentence of all or nothing and the sentence of laughter. The enervating sentences and the enervated sentence. *No rectifications!* The sentence that reduces literature and its writers to ashes. Without sun. A sentence without sunshine that reduces literature to ashes. An immemorial sentence that renders memory impossible. A sentence without sunshine that leaves literary memory with a taste of ashes. SSCML. Please cease and desist from calling up memory. Please cease moving the moribund into memory, you're free! *Tello Tello Mannanai! Tello Tello Mannanai!* Plain Text. *Ne reminiscaris!*[3]

The hyper-additive speaker function of Bensmaïa's book is both the writer and everything his multi-cultural, transnational, and multi-lingual life shifts are dragging him through — conditions of cultural feeling that are part of epicolonial thrown-apartness. A blending with digital identity is frequently performed in the book's stylistic details. Characterologically, digital identity is especially evident in the female figure of Macha (who sometimes has other names or cross-fertilizes with character functions named Aely or Lella), the narrator's sometimes-computer sometimes-human-bodied machine-mate. In the passage above he's been "able to tell Macha (with a ciphered tetragram)"; two pages later, his interlocutors include "Noon-Midnight" and "Paris."[4]

---

3 Réda Bensmaïa, *The Year of Passages*, trans. Tom Conley (University of Minnesota Press, 1995), 25. "SSCML" is an acronym for a cinquefoil-arrayed "equation" given elsewhere: "SUN / SKULL / CINDERS / MEMORY / LITERATURE" (23).

4 Ibid., 27.

The centrality of desire and death in imaginative arts is one index of their absoluteness in relation to culture. At the same time the apparently useless value of the arts (apart from their commodification, their commerce and paid-employment involvements) makes them one side of another metaphorical coin whose other side is idealist social action, the kind that continually wants to (re)make the world. Bensmaïa's book is on fire with multiplied idealist pressures. The book's idealism is evident in the pain experienced by the central speaker dealing with the pressures to present a unified, fixed, and accepting "face" of lingual, human-bodied, and place-time position. The book is full of the diremption between the false position of expected body-time-writing-nation-state stability and actual contemporanullity experiences in transtemporal, multilingual, transnational, epicolonial, multigenre, and concomitant affective selves-places-times pulls. The life-sense splits out of its normative expectations and floods the bodies of sentences, characters, page layout, genres, places. Agentive animation is activated in every fabric of the book's interaction, from meta-lingualism (as in the "sentence" acting above) to urban sites to discourse types to human-computer features and identity-slipping companions.

The health of the arts bodies forth the health of the global human as well as of the particular human in location. The opportunity to participate in arts and social ideals is an absolute nullity: It must, if a culture is healthy, relate to everyone. Some would say art always enacts idealism and is always an act of hope. This is how I read the erupted multiplicity of Bensmaïa's book, not least in the superpositionality that is encouraged in the book's often hyper-repetitive lexical formulations. In *The Year of Passages,* each lexical instance (of "sentence" or "rectification" or many other word formations) activates significances both in itself and across all its other instances. That's what I mean by lexical superposition. The alterity of multiplicity is performed as the productive, painfully hopeful nullity that can be read as applying to all identities in transnational and epicolonial formation. More generally, such cultural hope is what I take the US poet William Carlos Williams to mean in his poem *Aspho-*

del, That Greeny Flower (1955): "It is difficult / to get the news from poems / yet men [sic: nowadays we can hope he might write "people"] die miserably every day / for lack / of what is found there." In a "productive" economy with a centripetal institutional imaginary of monied objects and consumption, arts are generally treated as a relative nullity, a status appendage, or a centrifugal castaway. In the contested dynamics of the digitas, and in writing that brings digitality along as part of its bodies (which arguably in our digital time means all writing), art ideals occur in a contemporanullity whose mirror sites — both technical and imagined — are like a thousand works of art.

Access to art, the imaginative wave crest of blindsight, has its best practical chance yet in the contacts we make in the digitas, whose techne goes hand in hand with human touch. This situation was keenly felt in the COVID-19 pandemic, as online selves and makings continued and intensified. The force of contemporanullity can help swerve the emphasis of digital interactions from spatiality to membranism, from distant machines to present bodies. If one thinks there's no reified abstract thing called Our Times, one gropes around hopefully for what to build with. Instead of the face becoming a screen, the screen becomes a multiplied body, its haptics our response. Is there a term for sense innuendo after the inflection of a touch? Haptic resonance, perhaps. The lexememe (see "Variations on the Lexememe" in this book) reflects a refreshed way of reading that disrupts habituated expectations of narrated continuity while intensifying a mediated artifice of shared intimacy.

We are still young in our ability to think the digitas, our identities and possibilities here, including the relations between overtly digital lingualism and page-based lingualism impressed by digital life, and we are bodies as we do this thinking together. I take contemporanullity theory to relate to the gesture the Italian philosopher Giorgio Agamben makes in the essay "What Is the Contemporary" (*Nudities*, 2011) when he writes about "dyschrony." Starting with Nietzsche's "untimely," Agamben considers the dark energy of the present, the unseeability of the present for those who are looking at that dark energy. Agamben's thought resembles Stein's about what the "truly contemporary" is, before cultural meaning waves wash over it with their powerful situating claims. And in Bensmaïa's words:

> Sync # 2: The inner flash of passages falls faint when the electric lights come on, and he took refuge in their name. But the name of passages became a sieve that let through only the bitter essence of Past Time. (This strange power of distilling the present as the most intimate essence of Past Time is what, for true voyagers, gives the name its stirring and mysterious power.)[5]

Such positionings, staring at the darkness of the present trying to perceive against (optical) seeing, splitting the power of an imposed sense of time, diffracting lingual forces to expand their relevance and range, engaging umbral poetics, imagining what we don't know, all have potential to perform piquant contemporanullity hope.

And there's more. Physics has already told us there is no such thing as a real "now" in the energy measures that stretch life, including our own. We're in a universe whose temporality is simultaneity. The way humans create and sustain planetary definitions of momentness and nowness show our values; they are zones we do and can reshape. Contemporanullity recognizes the there-and-moving, the there-and-not-there nature of what we're doing together, where "we" involves human and other-than-human features, needs, and desires. Contemporanullity theory in the digitas means to energize its anti-colonial ideals and its non-capitalist and perfectly ephemeral human arts. The superpositionality of quantum computing can give us another model for what it means to permit our multi-sensorial, ongoing polyvalent knowings as supple truths in flexed approximations — within the digitas and without.

5 Bensmaïa, *The Year of Passages,* 33. Italics in original.

Syllabus

This seminar will investigate ________________
styles of mind ________________
styles of laughter ________________
styles of disciplinary fortitude ________________
____
For our purposes, representation is language ________________
though only ink and ink ephebes ________________
retrace the class ________________
____
mimicking praxis we imagine in the world. ________________
____
____
We will posit every step the “real” ________________
blogged with media spoken sometimes fast in mind __________
of value, mirroring “opacity” readers ________________
____
____
____
How do we collapse or vanish? ________________
position us in the unspeakable? ________________
____
____
____

the last hundred years sign ______________
the economy of the imaginative subject ______________
as indicated in the material in advance of research __________
smiles below where "Comment" also helps ______________
____
____
____

our second version voices "printed audio" ______________
though you might decide ______________
____
in the readings ______________
____
____
in the thinker research magma ______________
pushing up our seats ______________
humans need time for emergency ______________
____
____
You are welcome to please things that take attention ________
____
You have conditions, like all of us ______________
____
liquid researches containment, the brain squeeze happens ____
to feasible instructional accommodation, heark! ___________
____
Imagining the readies in transition from the western scar ____
____
Comment on diremption's fourth estate ______________
____
____
____
____

eat your most delicious intellectual dessert ________________
among languages ________________
what is making “for”? ________________
____
____
____
____

visions come across the story (true in either style) ________________
with the living organism drinking deep ________________
the globe grows glorious (true from any side) ________________
____

the paper you hold up to Comment ________________
sieve what hinters story ________________
____
____
____

The operation of the proper noun upon your heart ________________
construes the application ________________
your own life, when we perceive so many say ________________
“I’m here; I exist!” in the unceasing ________________
____
____

character as explanation via word feel, word type ________________
narrative’s transmuting ________________
____

(though we are told it’s plot on ark that hold ________________
________________)

____
____

ratiocination, pink laundries of fabrication ________________
laid across the honey aisles ________________
will mop ’em up a sample ________________
____

wherein style enacts particulates and ________________

____
time/pass ______________
____
____
____
the consequences of lunch will manifest ______________
idea principles held by frame analyses ______________
and supposition's fertile omnibus ______________
____
____
right here ______________
as the food chain of nonbeing ______________
____
comes relation ______________
____
____

Comment: What is a heft with resolution's fat evolved? ______
____
____
With or without your flesh in long horizons ______________
seem to heal? ______________
____
That thetic stake drawn slowly through ______________
____
____
your formerly tranquil heart when without knowing ________
you would "be" and squarely ______________
____
self-edition's case. ______________
____
____
A long horizon of laughter sets itself a task: ______________
If I could know more or other or expand ______________
or turn, and yet it isn't "make it better" or are we really ______

pitched. ______________
____
____
____

____
____
Imagery and its treble come to hungry ______________
affect's sober ruse: surmise ______________
____
what happens when your drama breaks ______________
& all your figures cherish in the book? ______________
____
____
Revise your glimpse online and wait ______________
technology comes oval ______________
water takes its drink ______________
full circ ______________
____
____
____
in res relate, our speakers touch ______________
____
te pō ______________
____
____
and then you'll see to swamp a certitude ______________
with healing wax — that's how you answer ______________
____
back from company ______________
whose parent gapped a primer, kept the book open __________
all night inside the rain? ______________
____

____
____

We'll talk of this, so soon as you ______________
code technicolor history in ______________
the house of the west ______________
____
____
____
relation speaks its long desire ______________
muddy sunset ______________
Long Life shutters featuring the windows ______________
shaped like pages ______________
____
short life announced ______________
____
when you decide how answers lean ______________
or median you trip on walk across the page with dark-steps __
gleam, the air is fully open as ______________
____
____
productions of time themselves ______________
love ______________
____
the oxygen of infinity ______________
____
<u>Comment</u> ______________
____
____
____
____
____
____
____
____

Bibliography

Acker, Kathy. *My Mother: Demonology.* Grove Press, 1994.

Adorno, Theodor W. *Aesthetic Theory.* Edited and translated by Robert Hullot-Kentor. University of Minnesota Press, 1998.

———. *Negative Dialectics.* Translated by E.B Ashton. The Seabury Press, 1973.

———. *The Culture Industry: Selected Essays on Mass Culture.* Edited by J.M. Bernstein. Routledge, 1991.

———. *The Jargon of Authenticity.* Translated by Knut Tarnowski and Frederic Will. Northwestern University Press, 1973.

Agamben, Giorgio. *Nudities.* Translated by David Kishik and Stefan Pedatella. Stanford University Press, 2011.

Albright, Daniel. *Quantum Poetics: Yeats, Pound, Eliot and the Science of Modernism.* Cambridge University Press, 1997.

Amsler, Mark. *Affective Literacies: Writing and Multilingualism in the Late Middle Ages.* Brepols, 2011.

Andrews, Bruce. *Wobbling.* Roof Books, 1981.

Auerbach, Eric. *Mimesis: The Representation of Reality in Western Literature.* Princeton University Press, 1953.

Barthes, Roland. *Sade, Fourier, Loyola.* Translated by Richard Miller. University of California Press, 1989.

———. *S/Z.* Translated by Richard Miller and Richard Howard. Hill and Wang, 1974.

———. *The Pleasure of the Text.* Translated by Richard Miller and Richard Howard. Hill and Wang, 1975.

Baumgarten, Alexander Gottlieb. *Reflections on Poetry: Meditationes philosophicae de nonnullis ad poema pertinentibus.* Translated by Karl Aschenbrenner and William B. Holther. University of California Press, 1954.

Benjamin, Walter. "Doctrine of the Similar (1933)." Translated by Knut Tarnowski. *New German Critique* 17 (1979): 65–69. DOI: 10.2307/488010.

Bensmaïa, Réda. *The Year of Passages.* Translated by Tom Conley. University of Minnesota Press, 1995.

Bernstein, Charles. *A Poetics.* Harvard University Press, 1992.

Blackmore, John T. *Ernst Mach: His Work, Life, and Influence.* University of California Press, 1972.

Blake, William. *Milton: A Poem.* Copy A, 1811. https://blakearchive.org/copy/milton.a?descId=milton.a.illbk.01.

———. *William Blake: The Complete Illuminated Books.* Thames & Hudson, 2000.

Bloch, R. Howard. *Etymologies and Genealogies: A Literary Anthropology of the French Middle Ages.* University of Chicago Press, 1983.

Block, Ned. "Mental Paint." In *Reflections and Replies: Essays on the Philosophy of Tyler Burge,* edited by M. Hahn and B. Ramberg. MIT Press, 2003.

Bohm, David. *Wholeness and the Implicate Order.* Routledge & Kegan Paul, 1980.

Brathwaite, Kamau. *Ancestors: A Reinvention of Mother Poem, Sun Poem, and X/Self.* New Directions, 2001.

Braun, Charles L., and Sergei N. Smirnov. "Why Is Water Blue?" *Journal of Chemical Education* 70, no. 8 (1993): 612. DOI: 10.1021/ed070p612.

Brennan, Stella. *Wet Social Sculpture.* 2005. http://stella.net.nz/work/wet-social-sculpture/.

Breton, André. *Mad Love.* Translated by Mary Ann Caws. University of Nebraska Press, 1987.

Browning, Elizabeth Barrett. *Aurora Leigh.* Chapman and Hall, 1857.

Burwick, Frederick. *Mimesis and Its Romantic Reflections.* Pennsylvania State University Press, 2001.

Cage, John. *Silence: Lectures and Writings.* Wesleyan University Press, 1961.

Calvino, Italo. *If on a Winter's Night a Traveller.* Translated by William Weaver. Harcourt, 1981.

Capildeo, Vahni. *Skin Can Hold.* Carcanet, 2019.

Carruthers, Mary J. *The Book of Memory: A Study of Memory in Medieval Culture.* Cambridge University Press, 1990.

Carter, Martin. *University of Hunger: Collected Poems and Selected Prose.* Edited by Gemma Robinson. Bloodaxe, 2006.

Cassin, Barbara, ed. *Vocabulaire européen des philosophies: Dictionnaire des intraduisibles, édition augmentée.* Éditions du Seuil, 2019.

Certeau, Michel de. "The Garden: Delirium and Delights of Hieronymous Bosch." In *The Mystic Fable.* Vol. 1: *The Sixteenth and Seventeenth Centuries,* translated by Michael B. Smith. University of Chicago Press, 1992.

Chaucer, Geoffrey. "The Miller's Tale." In *The Riverside Chaucer,* edited by Larry D. Benson. Houghton Mifflin, 1987.

Coleridge, Samuel Taylor. *Selected Poetry and Prose of Coleridge.* Edited by Donald A. Stauffer. Random House, 1951.

cummings, e.e. *Six Nonlectures.* Harvard University Press, 1953.

Cusa, Nicholas of. *On Learned Ignorance: A Translation and An Appraisal of* De Docta Ignorantia. Translated by Jasper Hopkins. A.J. Banning Press, 1985.

Davies, Alan. *Signage.* New York, 1987.

Deleuze, Gilles, and Félix Guattari. *A Thousand Plateaus: Capitalism and Schizophrenia.* Translated by Brian Massumi. University of Minnesota Press, 1987.

———. *Kafka: Toward a Minor Literature.* Translated by Dana Polan. University of Minnesota Press, 1986.

Derrida, Jacques. *Archive Fever: A Freudian Impression.* Translated by Eric Prenowitz. University of Chicago Press, 1996.

De Sade, Marquis. *Justine, or the Misfortunes of Virtue.* Translated by John Phillips. Oxford University Press, 2013.

Descartes, René. *Discourse on Method and Meditations.* Translated by Laurence J. Lafleur. Liberal Arts Press, 1960.

Dewey, John. *Art as Experience.* New York, 1958.

Dickinson, Emily. *The Complete Poems of Emily Dickinson.* Edited by Thomas H. Johnson. Little Brown, 1976.

Direen, Bill. *Enclosures 2.* Percutio, 2016.

Doolittle, Hilda. *Notes on Thought and Vision.* City Lights, 2001.

Duncan, Robert. *The Opening of the Field.* New Directions, 1973.

El Bashir, R., J. Hurt, A Jančarík, and T. Kepka. "Simple Commutative Semirings." *Journal of Algebra* 236, no. 1 (2001): 277–306. DOI: 10.1006/jabr.2000.8483.

Emerson, Ralph Waldo. *Representative Men.* Emerson's Complete Works, Vol. IV. Cambridge University Press, 1883.

Fanon, Frantz. *The Wretched of the Earth.* Translated by Constance Farrington. Grove Press, 1963.

Ford, Hugh. *Published in Paris: American and British Writers, Printers, and Publishers in Paris, 1920–1939.* Macmillan, 1975.

Forrest-Thomson, Veronica. *Poetic Artifice: A Theory of Twentieth-Century Poetry.* Manchester University Press, 1978.

Frenkel, Vera. "Benign Ignorance." *ArtsCanada.* 1977.

Friedman, Susan Stanford. *Penelope's Web: Gender, Modernity, H.D.'s Fiction.* Cambridge University Press, 1990.

Gadamer, Hans-Georg. *Truth and Method.* Translated by Joel Weinsheimer and Donald G. Marshall. Crossroad, 1989.

Glissant, Édouard. *Introduction à une poétique du divers.* Presses de l'Université de Montréal, 1995.

———. *Poetics of Relation.* Translated by Betsy Wing. University of Michigan Press, 1997.

———. *Traité du tout-monde: Poétique IV.* Gallimard, 1997.

Glück, Robert. *Margery Kempe.* High Risk Books, 1994.

Gödel, Kurt. "Über formal unentscheidbare Sätze der *Principia Mathematica* und verwandter Systeme I." *Monatshefte für*

Mathematik Physik 38 (1931): 173–98. English translation in *Collected Works I: Publications 1929–1936*, edited by S. Feferman et al. Oxford University Press, 1986.

Hansen, Mark B.N. *New Philosophy for New Media.* MIT Press, 2004.

Haraway, Donna J. *When Species Meet.* University of Minnesota Press, 2008.

Harris, Duriel E. "Let Us Consider Sarah: Notes Toward Withness, Affect, Making, and the US Imaginary, or, You Better Work, Bitch: This Is Flesh.... This Is the Prize." *Evening Will Come* 55 (2015). https://www.thevolta-org.zulaufdesign.com/ewc55-dharris-p1.html.

———. *No Dictionary of a Living Tongue.* Nightboat Books, 2017.

Heidegger, Martin. *Basic Writings.* Edited by David Farrell Krell. New York, 1977.

———. *Nietzsche*. Vol. 1. Neste, 1961.

Hejinian, Lyn. *The Language of Inquiry.* University of California Press, 2000.

———. *A Thought Is the Bride of What Thinking.* Tuumba Press, 1976.

Heldén, Johannes, and Håkan Jonson. *Evolution.* 2014. http://www.textevolution.net/.

Hermitary. "Ibn Tufayl's *Hayy Ibn Yaqzan:* Solitude and Understanding." 2007. https://www.hermitary.com/solitude/ibntufayl.html.

Homer. *The Iliad.* Translated by Alexander Pope. Flaxman's Designs, 1899. https://gutenberg.org/files/6130/6130-h/6130-h.htm.

Howe, Susan. *My Emily Dickinson.* North Atlantic Books, 1985.

Hyesoon, Kim. "Space." In *Princess Abandoned: Essays,* translated by Don Mee Choi. Tinfish Press, 2012.

Infusino, Maria, and Salma Kuhlmann. "Infinite Dimensional Moment Problem: Open Questions and Applications." In *Ordered Algebraic Structures and Related Topics,* edited by Fabrizio Broglia, Françoise Delon, Max Dickmann, Danielle

Gondard-Cozette, and Victoria Ann Powers. American Mathematical Society, 2017. DOI: 10.1090/conm/697/14052.
James, William. "A World of Pure Experience." In *Writings 1902–1910,* edited by Bruce Kuklick. The Library of America, 1987.
———. *Principles of Psychology.* Henry Holt and Company, 1890.
Jammer, Max. *Concepts of Simultaneity: From Antiquity to Einstein and Beyond.* Johns Hopkins University Press, 2006.
Johnson, Ronald. *radi os.* Sand Dollar Press, 1977.
Julian of Norwich. *Revelations of Divine Love.* Methuen, 1901.
Ka Fai, Choy. *Prospectus For a Future Body.* 2011. http://www.ka5.info/prospectus.html.
Kac, Eduardo, ed. *Media Poetry: An International Anthology.* Intellect Books, 2007.
Kant, Immanuel. *The Critique of Judgement.* Translated by J.H. Bernard. Hafner Publishing Co., 1951.
Keats, John. *Selected Letters of John Keats.* Edited by Grant F. Scott. Harvard University Press, 2002.
Kempe, Margery. *The Booke of Margery Kempe.* BL, ADD MS 61823.
King, Michael, and Marti Friedlander, eds. *Moko: Māori Tattooing in the 20th Century.* Alister Taylor, 1972.
Levinas, Emmanuel. "Ethics of the Infinite." In *Dialogues with Contemporary Continental Thinkers: The Phenomenological Heritage: Paul Ricoeur, Emmanuel Levinas, Herbert Marcuse, Stanislas Breton, Jacques Derrida,* edited by Richard Kearney. Manchester University Press, 1984.
Lock, Charles. "Petroglyphs in and out of Perspective." *Semiotica* 100, nos. 2–4 (1994): 405–20. DOI: 10.1515/semi.1994.100.2-4.405.
Locke, John. *An Essay Concerning Humane Understanding.* Thomas Basset, 1690. https://www.gutenberg.org/files/10615/10615-h/10615-h.htm.
Mach, Ernst. *Die Mechanik in ihrer Entwicklung.* Brockhaus, 1912.

Makridis, Odysseus. "The Sheffer Stroke." *Internet Encyclopedia of Philosophy*. https://www.iep.utm.edu/sheffers/.

Malraux, André. *Anti-Memoirs*. Translated by Terence Kilmartin. Holt, 1990.

Mann, Charles. "Who Will Own Your Next Good Idea?" *The Atlantic*, September 1998. https://www.theatlantic.com/magazine/archive/1998/09/who-will-own-your-next-good-idea/377192/.

Marsh, Selina Tusitala. *Fast Talking PI*. Auckland University Press, 2012.

Mathews, Harry. *Immeasurable Distances: The Collected Essays*. Lapis, 1991.

McDonald, Gail. *Learning to Be Modern: Pound, Eliot, and the American University*. Clarendon Press, 1993.

Melberg, Arne. *Theories of Mimesis*. Cambridge University Press, 1995.

Meyer, Steven. *Irresistible Dictation: Gertrude Stein and the Correlations of Writing and Science*. Stanford University Press, 2001.

Miller, J. Hillis. *Fiction and Repetition: Seven English Novels*. Harvard University Press, 1982.

Motion Bank. "About." http://motionbank.org/en/content/about.html.

Moure, Erín. *Kapusta: A Play-Poem-Ash, A Cabaret*. House of Anansi Press, 2015.

Mullen, Harryette. *Sleeping with the Dictionary*. University of California Press, 2002.

Nathanaël. *The Sorrow and the Fast of It*. Nightboat Books, 2007.

Nichol, bp. *The Martyrology, Books 1 & 2*. Coach House Books, 1998.

———. *The Martyrology, Books 3 & 4*. Coach House Books, 2000.

Nietzsche, Friedrich. *Beyond Good and Evil: Prelude to a Philosophy of the Future*. Edited and translated by Walter Kaufmann. Vintage, 1966.

———. *The Portable Nietzsche.* Edited and translated by Walter Kaufmann. Viking Press, 1954.

Olson, Charles. *Human Universe and Other Essays.* Edited by Donald Allen. Grove Press, 1967.

O'Sullivan, Maggie. *red shifts.* Etruscan, 2001.

Pane, Gina, with photographs by Françoise Masson. *Azione Sentimentale.* La Galerie Diagramma, Milan, November 9, 1973. Photo and text, 41.40 × 271.50 cm. Centre Pompidou. https://www.centrepompidou.fr/fr/ressources/oeuvre/cj7rGr9.

Paraha, Tru. *blackOut: part 2 of a choreographic trilogy on darkness.* Auckland, 2018.

Pater, Walter. *Plato and Platonism: A Series of Lectures.* MacMillan and Co., 1893.

Păun, Gheorghe. *Membrane Computing: An Introduction.* Springer Books, 2002.

Peirce, Charles Sanders. *Reasoning and the Logic of Things: The Cambridge Conference Lectures of 1898.* Edited by Kenneth Laine Ketner. Harvard University Press, 1992.

———. "Some Consequences of Four Incapacities." In *Peirce on Signs: Writings on Semiotics by Charles Sanders Peirce,* edited by James Hoopes. University of North Carolina Press, 1991.

Perez, Craig Santos. *From Unincorporated Territory [hacha].* Tinfish Press, 2008.

Pérez-Jiménez, Mario J. "An Approach to Computational Complexity in Membrane Computing." In *Membrane Computing,* edited by Giancarlo Mauri, Gheorghe Păun, Mario J. Pérez-Jiménez, Grzegorz Rozenberg, and Arto Salomaa. Springer, 2005.

Petrarca, Francesco. *Letters from Petrarch.* Translated by Morris Bishop. Illustrated by Alison Mason Kingsbury. Indiana University Press, 1966.

Phillips, Tom. *A Humument. A Treated Victorian Novel.* Thames and Hudson, 1997.

Plato. *Cratylus.* In *Plato: Complete Works,* edited by J.M. Hooper and D.S. Hutchinson. Hackett, 1997.

Pottier, Eugène. "L'Internationale (1871 lyrics)." *Bibliothèque nationale de France*. http://classes.bnf.fr/pdf/Revol7_Internationale.pdf.

Powys, John Cowper. *A Glastonbury Romance*. Simon and Schuster, 1932.

Pratt, Mary Louise. *Imperial Eyes: Travel Writing and Transculturation*. Routledge, 2007.

Rancière, Jacques. *The Politics of Aesthetics: The Distribution of the Sensible*. Translated by Gabriel Rockhill. Continuum, 2004.

Riding, Laura. *Anarchism Is Not Enough*. Edited by Lisa Samuels. University of California Press, 2001.

———. *Contemporaries and Snobs*. Scholarly Press, 1971.

———. *Poet: A Lying Word*. Barker, 1933.

———. *The Covenant of Literal Morality*. Seizin Press, 1938.

———. *The Life of the Dead*. Barker, 1933.

———. *The Poems of Laura Riding: A New Edition of the 1938 Collection*. Persea Books, 1980.

———. *Though Gently*. Seizin Press, 1930.

Riding, Laura, and Robert Graves, eds. *A Pamphlet against Anthologies*. Doubleday, 1928.

———. *Epilogue I*. Seizin, 1935.

Riding Jackson, Laura, and Schuyler B. Jackson. *Rational Meaning: A New Foundation for the Definition of Words, and Supplementary Essays*. Edited by William Harmon. University of Virginia Press, 1997.

Robert-Foley, Lily. *m*. Corrupt Press, 2013.

Robertson, Lisa. *Occasional Work and Seven Walks from the Office for Soft Architecture*. Clear Cut Press, 2004.

Robinson, Jeffrey C. *The Current of Romantic Passion*. University of Wisconsin Press, 1991.

Roman, Steven. *Lattices and Ordered Sets*. Springer, 2008.

Rosenberg, Jim. "Openings: The Connection Direct." *Poetics Journal* 10 (1998): 236–43. https://www.inframergence.org/jr/openings.html.

Russo, Linda, and Marthe Reed, eds. *Counter Desecration: A Glossary for Writing Within the Anthropocene.* Wesleyan University Press, 2018.

Samuels, Lisa. *Anti M.* Chax Press, 2013.

———. "Distributed Centrality." In *Counter Desecration: A Glossary for Writing Within the Anthropocene,* edited by Linda Russo and Marthe Reed. Wesleyan University Press, 2018.

———. "Eight Justifications for Canonizing Lyn Hejinian's *My Life.*" *Modern Language Studies* 27, no. 2 (1997): 103–19. DOI: 10.2307/3195353.

———. "Everything Speaks — How Do We Listen?" *Qui Parle* 26, no. 2 (2017): 318–19. DOI: 10.1215/10418385-4208433.

———. "If Meaning, Shaped Reading, and Leslie Scalapino's *way.*" *Qui Parle* 12, no. 2 (2001): 179–200. https://www.jstor.org/stable/20686127.

———. "Illuminating the Limits." *Theatreview,* February, 20, 2018. https://www.theatreview.org.nz/production/blackout-part-2-of-a-choreographic-trilogy-on-darkness/#illuminating-the-limits.

———. "Membranism, Wet Gaps, Archipelago Poetics." *Reading Room: A Journal of Art and Culture* 4 (2010): 156–67.

———. "Poetic Arrest: Laura Riding, Wallace Stevens, and the Modernist Afterlife." PhD diss., University of Virginia, 1997.

———. *The Long White Cloud of Unknowing.* Chax Press, 2019.

———. *Wild Dialectics.* Shearsman Books, 2012.

———. "Withness and *The Dihedrons Gazelle-Dihedrals Zoom.*" Performance-talk for Jack Kerouac School of Disembodied Poetics. Naropa University, Boulder, CO, USA, October 2014.

Samuels, Lisa, and Jerome McGann. "Deformance and Interpretation." *New Literary History* 30, no. 1 (1999): 25–56. https://www.jstor.org/stable/20057521.

Samuels, Lisa, and Sawako Nakayasu, eds. *A Transpacific Poetics.* Litmus Press, 2017.

Scalapino, Leslie. *The Dihedrons Gazelle-Dihedrals Zoom*. Post-Apollo Press, 2010.

———. *way*. North Point Press, 1988.

Schneemann, Carolee. "The Notebooks 1963–1966." In *More Than Meat Joy: Complete Performance Works & Selected Writings*. McPherson, 1997.

———. *VULVA'S MORPHIA*. Granary Books, 1997.

———. *VULVA'S MORPHIA*. 1995. Photography and paper. 8 × 5 feet, images 8.5 × 11", text strips 2 × .58". http://www.caroleeschneemann.com/vulvasmorphia.html.

Schultz, Susan M. "Skyping Craig Santos Perez." *Susan M. Schultz's Blog*, April 18, 2009. https://tinfisheditor.blogspot.com/2009/04/skyping-craig-santos-perez.html.

Schwartz, Niels. "Positive Semifields and Their Ideals." In *Ordered Algebraic Structures and Related Topics*, edited by Fabrizio Broglia, Françoise Delon, Max Dickmann, Danielle Gondard-Cozette, and Victoria Ann Powers. American Mathematical Society, 2017. DOI: 10.1090/conm/697/14059.

Shakespeare, William. *The Tragedy of Hamlet, Prince of Denmark*. In *The Riverside Shakespeare*, edited by G. Blakemore Evans. Houghton Mifflin Co., 1974.

Shelley, Percy Bysshe. "A Defence of Poetry." In *The Critical Tradition: Classic Texts and Contemporary Trends*, edited by David H. Richter. Bedford/St. Martin's, 2007.

Sondheim, Alan. *"Plan-et Ground."* http://www.alansondheim.org/kz.txt.

Spahr, Juliana, and Stephanie Young. "On Poets and Prizes." *ASAP Journal*, November 11, 2020. https://asapjournal.com/on-poets-and-prizes-juliana-spahr-and-stephanie-young/.

Spearing, A.C. *Medieval Autographies: The "I" of the Text*. University of Notre Dame Press, 2012.

Stanton, Elizabeth Cady. "Declaration of Sentiments." In *History of Woman Suffrage, Vol. 1*, edited by Elizabeth Cady Stanton, Susan B. Anthony, and Matilda Joslyn Gage. Fowler & Wells, 1889. https://www.gutenberg.org/files/28020/28020-h/28020-h.htm.

Stein, Gertrude. *A Stein Reader.* Edited by Ulla E. Dydo. Northwestern University Press, 1996.
———. *An Acquaintance with Description.* Seizin Press, 1929.
———. "Composition as Explanation." In *Selected Writings of Gertrude Stein,* edited by Carl Van Vechten. Vintage, 1962.
———. *Lectures in America.* Vintage, 1975.
———. *Tender Buttons: Objects, Food, Rooms.* Dover, 1997.
———. *The Autobiography of Alice B. Toklas.* Harcourt, Brace, and Company, 1933.
———. *What Are Masterpieces?* Pitman Publishing Co., 1970.
Steiner, Wendy. *The Scandal of Pleasure: Art in an Age of Fundamentalism.* University of Chicago Press, 1995.
Stevens, Wallace. *The Collected Poems of Wallace Stevens.* Alfred A. Knopf, 1968.
Sussman, Michael. "In Diatom, Scientists Find Genes that May Level Engineering Hurdle." *Science Daily,* January 23, 2008. https://www.sciencedaily.com/releases/2008/01/080121181404.htm.
Taylor, Mark C. *TEARS.* SUNY Press, 1990.
Teresa of Ávila. *The Interior Castle.* Paulist Press, 1979.
Tiffany, Daniel. *Toy Medium: Materialism and Modern Lyric.* University of California Press, 2000.
Todd, Zoe. "Refracting the State through Human-Fish Relations: Fishing, Indigenous Legal Orders and Colonialism in North/Western Canada." *Decolonization: Indigeneity, Education & Society* 7, no. 1 (2018): 60–75. https://jps.library.utoronto.ca/index.php/des/article/view/30393.
Waldman, Anne. *Fast Speaking Woman: Chants and Essays.* City Lights Books, 2001.
Weil, Simone. *Gravity and Grace.* Translated by Arthur Wills. G.P. Putnam's Sons, 1952.
Wendt, Albert. *The Book of the Black Star.* Auckland University Press, 2002.
Wennberg, Teresa. "Brainsongs (Welcome to My Brain)." *Archive of Digital Art,* 2001–2002. https://digitalartarchive.at/database/general/work/brainsongs.html.

Wentland, June. "Misdenomers." *Poetry Salzburg Review* 37 (2021): 108.

Werner, Marta L. *Emily Dickinson's Open Folios: Scenes of Reading, Surfaces of Writing.* University of Michigan Press, 1995.

West, Ida. *Pride against Prejudice: Reminiscences of a Tasmanian Aborigine.* Montepelier Press, 2004.

White, James Boyd. *When Words Lose Their Meaning.* Chicago, 1983.

Wilde, Oscar. "The Critic as Artist." In *Complete Works of Oscar Wilde,* Volume 4, edited by Robert Ross. Wyman-Fogg Co., 1909.

Williams, Raymond. *Keywords: A Vocabulary of Culture and Society.* Croom Helm, 1976.

Williams, William Carlos. *Asphodel, That Greeny Flower.* New Directions, 1955.

Wittgenstein, Ludwig. *Philosophical Investigations.* Translated by G.E.M. Anscombe. Blackwell, 1953.

———. *Tractatus Logico-Philosophicus.* Translated by D.F. Pears and B.F. McGuiness. Routledge and Kegan Paul, 1961.

Zukofsky, Louis. *Bottom: On Shakespeare.* University of California Press, 1987.

———. *Prepositions: The Collected Critical Essays of Louis Zukofsky.* University of California Press, 1981.

www.ingramcontent.com/pod-product-compliance
Lightning Source LLC
La Vergne TN
LVHW010603100826
845148LV00014B/2824

* 9 7 8 1 6 8 5 7 1 2 0 4 4 *